THE MEANING OF DISGUST

The Meaning of Disgust

Disgust

COLIN MCGINN

OXFORD
UNIVERSITY PRESS

OXFORD
UNIVERSITY PRESS

Oxford University Press, Inc., publishes works that further
Oxford University's objective of excellence
in research, scholarship, and education.

Oxford   New York
Auckland   Cape Town   Dar es Salaam   Hong Kong   Karachi
Kuala Lumpur   Madrid   Melbourne   Mexico City   Nairobi
New Delhi   Shanghai   Taipei   Toronto

With offices in
Argentina   Austria   Brazil   Chile   Czech Republic   France   Greece
Guatemala   Hungary   Italy   Japan   Poland   Portugal   Singapore
South Korea   Switzerland   Thailand   Turkey   Ukraine   Vietnam

Copyright © 2011 Oxford University Press

Published by Oxford University Press, Inc.
198 Madison Avenue, New York, New York 10016

www.oup.com

Oxford is a registered trademark of Oxford University Press

Library of Congress Cataloging-in-Publication Data
McGinn, Colin, 1950–
The meaning of disgust / Colin McGinn.
p.   cm.
Includes bibliographical references and index.
ISBN 978-0-19-982953-8 (hardcover : alk. paper)
1. Aversion.   I. Title.
BF575.A886M36 2011
128'.37—dc22
2011002230

3 5 7 9 8 6 4 2

Printed in the United States of America
on acid-free paper

CONTENTS

Preface   *vii*

PART ONE: THE ANALYSIS OF DISGUST

1. The Aversive Emotions   3
2. The Elicitors of Disgust   13
3. The Architecture of Disgust   41
4. Theories of Disgust   65
5. Handling the Cases   97
6. The Function of Disgust   123

PART TWO: DISGUST AND THE HUMAN CONDITION

7. Our Dual Nature   135
8. Repression and Disgust   161

9. Thoughts of Death 173
10. Culture and Disgust 183

Bibliography 227
Index 229

PREFACE

This is a syncretistic work, blending the philosophical, the psychological, the biological, and the literary. You might call it "impure philosophy"—and the subject matter warrants the adjective. It is about the things we find repulsive: their essence and significance. I intend the book for a variety of readers, not just the narrowly philosophical—for the subject of disgust has wide relevance. I see the ideas presented as occupying the same territory as existentialism and psychoanalysis, and competing with them (though incorporating some of their insights): what might be called "hermeneutic psychology." It aims to uncover disagreeable truths about what we are, as self-conscious emotional beings with organic bodies. But it tries to do so agreeably (Freud and Sartre were both great writers). The book can be construed as an essay in species self-criticism, and self-pity. It is a sort of lamentation.

I suppose I had been interested in the topic for a long time, in an unsystematic way—possibly since first reading Freud, some forty-odd years ago. But the immediate trigger for working seriously on it came a few years back, when I was scheduled to teach a philosophy of mind seminar with Mark Rowlands in Miami. I found it difficult to face covering the same old material yet again, so I determined that we should include some sessions on emotion. This led me to think about the emotion of disgust, which struck me as interestingly puzzling. I read some texts, notably Aurel Kolnai's *On Disgust* and William Ian Miller's *The Anatomy of Disgust*: these got the juices flowing (so to speak) on the subject, since both are courageous and stimulating. I soon started having my own ideas, delving more deeply into the literature, and producing bits of writing. The result is the book now before you. It has been enjoyable to write, because of the literary challenges and opportunities, but also somewhat disconcerting. I have been compelled to concentrate for long periods on the disgusting, trying to get to the bottom of it—and this is not the usual human attitude (for reasons I discuss in the text). I am not sure it is good for a person to immerse himself so deeply in these filthy waters. The truth is not always welcome. You have been warned.

I would like to thank Mark Rowlands, Jane Casillo, Ronald de Sousa, and Carolyn Korsmeyer for very helpful comments.

Colin McGinn
Miami
November 2010

THE MEANING OF DISGUST

PART ONE

THE ANALYSIS OF DISGUST

1

The Aversive Emotions

DISGUST BELONGS IN THE area of human experience most protected by taboo and hedged with euphemism. It is a difficult thing for us to talk about, practically and theoretically. And there is good reason for that: there are problems of decorum for any detailed and frank investigation of the phenomena of disgust. The realm of the disgusting is by its nature repellent to us—not easily held in view. Dwelling on the topic can lead quickly to the emotion itself. Breaking our natural silence on what disgusts us can elicit alarm. The very question of what vocabulary to use is fraught: what words will be found offensive or ludicrous or unserious? I am well aware of the delicacy of the topic, and the precariousness of my position.[1] In what follows, I shall try to avoid too much coy indirectness and tedious euphemism, but I will also try not to rub the reader's nose too crudely in the subject matter of this study. Laughter is the natural twin of offense, and I shall court that peril too. The subject, however, is of intense interest and significance; it is too good to be left

1. Perhaps I am being too cautious here—my readers may be less squeamish than I suppose (or than I am). There is certainly a big difference between hearing this kind of material spoken about in a class, in a public setting, and reading about it privately. In the former case, the words must be actually said out loud to an identifiable audience, while in the latter their reception is silent and distant. Still, I would not want my readers to think that I fail to recognize the sensitivity of the topic.

decently in the shadows. Moreover, a handful of excellent and intrepid studies have appeared over the years, which deserve to be better known, so I can claim my distinguished precedents for this venture into the vile and repulsive.[2]

The first task is to sketch out a map of the territory, assembling the data and enunciating some distinctive features. Detail and comprehensiveness will pay dividends here, preventing oversimplification and bringing the problematic of disgust vividly before our minds. The ultimate aim is to produce a theory of what unites the class of disgusting things: what all and only disgusting things have in common. This is basically a task of conceptual analysis, though not one that simply takes the word "disgust" and tries to peer into its meaning. Instead, I will survey the class of disgusting *things* and attempt to work out what brings them together in the emotion they provoke: what properties do disgusting things have that make them produce the emotion of disgust in us?[3] As a preliminary, it will be helpful to pin down the emotion we are to be concerned with more precisely, so as not to confuse it with other emotions— because disgust is a very specific kind of emotional reaction.

2. The works in question are Aurel Kolnai's *On Disgust*, Ernest Becker's *The Denial of Death*, Winfried Menninghaus's *Theory and History of a Strong Sensation,* and William Ian Miller's *The Anatomy of Disgust.* I have learned from each of these works and will cite them frequently in what follows. Citations will be by author's name and page or chapter reference.

3. I therefore reject the idea that the class of disgusting things is linked by nothing stronger than family resemblance. I am in general against the Wittgensteinian thesis that a concept may be constituted in this way, for the reasons given in my *Truth by Analysis*, chapter 2; I also recommend Bernard Suits's *The Grasshopper* as an antidote to reflexive invocation of the family resemblance model. In any case, as a methodological precept, we should seek necessary and sufficient conditions first, abandoning that project only if we have to; and it will turn out that we can supply such conditions. Kolnai makes his goal that of "seeking to grasp the essence, the significance and the intention of disgust, and also what might be called the law of cohesion of its object-realm" (p. 30)—and this well describes my own aim. In other words: what do all disgusting things have in common in virtue of which they are disgusting?

I shall follow Aurel Kolnai's pioneering phenomenological study, *On Disgust*, in classifying disgust as an *aversive* emotion, belonging together with fear and hatred.[4] All three emotions may be felt toward the same object—as it might be, in response to a loathsome monster in the form of a bloody vampire or a rotting cannibalistic zombie. But these three emotions are by no means identical. Fear may be described as a prudential emotion, hatred as a moral emotion, and disgust as an aesthetic emotion. Fear is prudential in that it operates to protect the person (or animal) from danger: it is prudent to fear what is dangerous to health or life. The natural expression of fear is self-protection—against damage to the self by the feared object. Flight is the obvious prime mode of self-protection, but so is armor or weaponry or a raised hand. One can also fear things that will cause no bodily damage, as with adverse economic circumstances or revelations that might destroy one's reputation; here, proximity to the body is immaterial. Not all damage to the person results from contact with the body by the dangerous object. Indeed, if the tissues of the body could be suitably hardened at will, avoidance of contact with the feared object would not necessarily be sought. Physical escape is a contingent mark of fear, prompted by the vulnerability of the body. Avoidance of contact is an instrumental aspect of fear, not its essence (as we shall see, disgust differs here).

Hatred can be said to be a moral emotion in the sense that it is not rational to hate someone who has not wronged you, or who you do not judge to have wronged you.[5] When you hate someone, you do so because of what you think he or she has done to you, where this something is judged to be wrong. If you

---

4. See Kolnai, pp. 29–47; also the appendix: "The Standard Modes of Aversion: Fear, Disgust and Hatred."

5. For a discussion of the belief component in hatred, see Robert C. Solomon, "Emotions and Choice," in *Mind and Cognition*. Solomon treats hatred as a type of moral judgment.

hate someone for having done a certain thing to you, such as maliciously destroying your good name, and it turns out that that person did no such thing, then you are rationally obliged to cease hating him or her. You need not fear a person in order to hate him, since the time may have passed when he could harm you. You can retrospectively hate someone, but it makes no sense to fear in retrospect—to fear someone for what he or she did in the past. Fear is future-directed; hatred is directed to the past. But it will be rational for the hated individual to fear you, because hatred is also an aggressive emotion, in the sense that it incites those who harbor it to wish harm to those they hate (this is not necessarily true for fear). Fear is defensive; hatred is aggressive. Fear is directed toward the self and its integrity, and it contains no necessary suggestion of moral condemnation of its object. But hatred is directed toward the external object in itself, and must contain a negative evaluation of that object. Both emotions may be called "aversive," but the aversion is of a quite different character in the two cases.[6]

Disgust, our main concern, is different again, though also aversive. Disgust is an aesthetic emotion in that its primary focus is the *appearance* of its object, not what that object can do or has done in the way of harm. You can be disgusted at something you neither fear nor hate—that you don't think will do you any harm and don't think has wronged you. Its natural expression is neither defensive nor aggressive; it is, rather, a response of *avoidance*. To be disgusted by something is, crucially, to want to avoid contact with it—either by sight

---

6. Note that fear is also evaluative in the sense that one has to regard harm to oneself as a bad thing, or else there will be no fear. Of course, that will generally be the case, but a person desiring his own death may well not fear what is about to cause it. There must be a normative element in fear, as also in disgust. In both cases, the aversion is backed by an evaluation; it is not merely brute. The evaluation may be instinctual and automatic, as with animal fear, but it is logically required.

or touch or smell or taste (but not, curiously, hearing[7]). However invulnerable you may feel with respect to a certain stench, and however blameless you take it (or its producer) to be, you still wish to escape its influence—to put distance between yourself and it. Putting your head in the sand is not, proverbially, a rational reaction to a feared object, but it is a perfectly sensible way to escape a disgusting stimulus (in fact, to do so in the face of fear just is to confuse fear with disgust). Disgust has everything to do with the condition of the senses and what they are delivering to consciousness, but that is not what fear and hatred are all about. You might, of course, fear that something will disgust you, since the feeling of disgust is, or can be, a kind of harm (the psychological kind); but disgust itself is not the same as fear, precisely because the disgusting stimulus need do you no further harm than that of merely eliciting disgust in you (by contrast, the feared object can cause more harm to you than merely causing the emotion of fear—if it did only that, you wouldn't feel *fear* at all). There is no contradiction in the idea that a deeply disgusting stimulus might be utterly harmless and judged by the subject to be so (I will be discussing examples shortly).[8]

7. Kolnai discusses hearing and disgust, pp. 48–49, suggesting that the reason for the absence of auditory disgust is that hearing does not "present" its objects as the other senses do—it merely provides signs of their presence. Since hearing lacks "substantial intentionality," it provides no immediate contact with the source of the sound. He notes the existence of sugary or sentimental music, but rightly observes that this is a matter of associations and a judgment of bad taste: "One would search in vain for any even approximately equivalent parallel in the aural sphere to something like a putrid smell, the feel of a flabby body, or of a belly ripped open" (p. 49).

8. Disgust is an inherently *unpleasant* emotion, so it is reasonable to fear experiencing it; but it is less clear that fear and hatred are constitutionally unpleasant in that way. Hatred is certainly not always experienced as unpleasant, and fear can occur in forms that are not clearly unpleasant, as with scary fairground rides. Disgust is unpleasant in somewhat the way pain is, without itself being pain, but hatred and fear are remote from pain as subjective states.

Kolnai expresses the contrast in traditional phenomenological terms, as that between *Dasein* and *Sosein*: between "being" and "so-being." Fear is directed toward its object as an existent thing, for only an existent thing can be really dangerous; so it is internal to fear that it presupposes that the feared object exists (whether or not it really does). Much the same can be said of hatred, for only an existent thing can wrong you. But disgust is directed more at "so-being"—that is, the phenomenal qualities possessed by the (intentional) object. The reality of an object is essential to its fearsomeness or its hatefulness, while the sensory appearance of the object is neither here nor there; but in the case of disgust the appearance takes up the foreground of the emotion, with existence relegated to a secondary status. It is how the object sensibly *seems* that is critical to its disgusting character, not how it might be in itself—even what it might do in the way of harm. We can state this intuitive contrast in a rather straightforward manner: fear and hatred presuppose the existence of their object (i.e., the subject of the emotion must believe the object to exist), but it is possible to be disgusted by an object in whose existence one does *not* believe. That is to say, you could believe yourself to be merely hallucinating a disgusting object and still be disgusted by it. Why? Because the sensory appearance could be the same whether or not the object exists. Suppose you become convinced that you are a brain in a vat (whether or not you really are): the range of your experience would still produce the same disgusting sights, tastes, and smells that it did before you became thus convinced. The *Sosein* would remain constant, though the (believed) *Dasein* has changed. You would no longer fear or hate those (believed) illusions, since no harm can come from mere illusions, but they would retain their power to repel. It is the same with beauty: an object does not cease to strike you as beautiful just because you believe it to be an illusion (think of an hallucinogenic drug that produced beautiful visions). Aesthetic emotions are geared to appearance and therefore don't require that the object actually exists.[9] Disgust is an "existence-independent" emotion, while fear and hatred are "existence-dependent" (with respect to the subject's beliefs). Macbeth can be disgusted by his bloody dagger, while all the while thinking it to be a mere figment of his imagination, but he cannot fear or hate Macduff while at the same time rejecting his reality.

This dependence on appearance in the case of disgust reveals itself in another contrast with the other two aversive emotions. An object can seem fearful and not be fearful or can be fearful and not seem fearful; and similarly for hatefulness, since there can be errors as to who has wronged you. Being dangerous or blameworthy is an objective property about which the appearances might be misleading. But it surely cannot be the case that an object can seem disgusting and not be, and be disgusting and not seem so; here, the reality and the appearance converge. To *be* disgusting is to *seem* so. It would be wholly bizarre to maintain that the range of things typically found disgusting by human beings are not really disgusting (to them), while some other class of objects found to be quite agreeable are in fact disgusting (to them). Yet these are logical possibilities for fear and hatred (despite the massiveness of the error that would have to be involved). To claim that feces are *really* non-disgusting for human beings, while diamonds are disgusting, is a preposterous proposition; skepticism cannot reach that far. But it is not conceptually outrageous to suppose that we are systematically mistaken about what is really dangerous to us or who has wronged us. This is simply because disgust concerns *Sosein*,

9. This is the Kantian doctrine that aesthetic experience is more or less indifferent to the actual existence of its object, being focused more on the qualities presented. If an artist could reliably generate merely intentional objects for your contemplation, and you knew their negative existential status, you could still experience aesthetic emotions in regard to them. The artist might merely stimulate your brain with electrodes to produce a virtual painting in your visual consciousness.

while fear and hatred concern *Dasein*—disgust is essentially appearance-sensitive.[10] This is not to say that the proper objects of disgust are *experiences* and not external objects. Indeed, that would be a category-mistake and quite false: as I shall explain later, psychological items such as experiences cannot be objects of disgust at all, still less be the familiar objects by which we take ourselves to be disgusted. The point is rather that the disgusting aspects of objects belong to their sensory appearance, not to what might lie behind that appearance—while this is not true for feared and hated objects. It is the "mode of presentation" of an object that provokes disgust, but the reference itself is what is feared or hated, no matter how it presents itself. We are repelled by feces qua a specific *Sosein*: but lions are scary in their *Dasein*, no matter how they may perceptually strike you. This is why no one needs to *tell* us to be disgusted by feces, but advice as to the dangers of lions can be very useful. Appearances are decisive in the one case, but possibly deceptive in the other. It is what something objectively *does* that makes it an object of fear or hatred; it is how something subjectively *seems* that makes it an object of disgust.

A final preliminary point: the primary focus of disgust is proximity, contact—we seek to avoid being close to what disgusts us. More specifically, perception of such closeness is what controls the emotion. Our aversion is primarily to the invasion of the disgusting object into our consciousness, mediated by the body. So we can say that our aversive concern is with our state of mind in the first instance: we want, in short, to avoid certain states of consciousness. This is not so

---

10. In fact, we can say that it is the sensory *appearance* of feces that is disgusting, not feces themselves, because not everything about feces is disgusting (say, the atomic structure of the constituent molecules), but it would be wrong to say that it is the appearance of things that is fearful or hateful (as a general rule anyway). This is why something with the appearance of feces that is not in fact feces will provoke the disgust reaction.

for fear and hatred, where the aversion concerns more bodily matters: we avoid the object that is actually dangerous to the body. Physical harm is not the aversive stimulus where disgust is concerned; we are not (necessarily) concerned that the disgusting object will harm our body—and if it might, fear is the appropriate response. What we seek to avoid is a penetration of consciousness itself—we shun certain experiences. Thus, it makes sense to hold one's nose in the presence of a loathsome odor, but it makes no sense to do so in the presence of a looming fist. We fear the broken nose (and hate the nose breaker), but we are disgusted at the smell as it invades olfactory consciousness. In this sense, disgust is consciousness-centered, not body-centered.[11] A person deprived of all forms of sensory experience would be spared the emotion of disgust, but he might have as much to fear and hate as the next man. We are disgustedly averse to external objects only *in as much* as they affect our perceptual consciousness in a certain noxious way. We thus seek to avoid the *kind* of contact with the object that will lead to this unwelcome invasion of consciousness. When disgusted by a smell, we seek to move away from the proximate source of the smell, or otherwise block the contact it is imposing on us in order to preserve our disgust-free state of consciousness; we sever the perceptual contact precisely in order to keep consciousness "clean." This is a very different matter from the kind of project we undertake when confronted by a fearful or hateful object; here, our focus is more outer-directed, externally anchored.

---

11. So the intention of disgust is reflexive in a way: in disgust, consciousness seeks to avoid a state of itself—namely, perception of the eliciting stimulus. When we endure a bad smell, say, our urge is to change a conscious state of ourselves. By contrast, in fear we do not self-reflexively seek to eliminate fear itself or the mental states that cause it. Fundamentally, disgust incites us to remove the state of disgust itself (as pain incites us to remove the pain itself). No doubt this is connected to the intrinsic unpleasantness of disgust.

In sum: disgust is a sui generis aversive emotion, importantly different from its aversive cousins. And this uniqueness is what makes it peculiarly problematic philosophically. The question, simply put, is this: Why should we be so averse to what is actually not intrinsically harmful to us? Disgust identifies its objects independently of their harmfulness, irrespective of it; so to what other trait of objects is it responsive? In virtue of *what* do we find disgusting things disgusting? What does the aversive character of the disgusting object consist in, if not in its potential for harm? We are naturally averse to what might harm us or has wronged us, but what has the disgusting object done to us that could provoke our extreme aversive response to it?[12] What is disgust's raison d'être? What does disgust *mean*? What is its pith and point?

12. One further difference should be noted: fear and hatred are purely and wholly aversive emotions, but disgust can have an attractive component (as I shall explain later)—there can be ambivalence to it. Disgust has a more complex "tonality" than fear and hatred. In addition, disgust can be described as a *sensation* more naturally than fear and hatred can: it is a way of sensing an object, while fear and hatred could not be so characterized. Disgust has a foot in both the perceptual and the affective.

2

The Elicitors of Disgust

TO BEGIN TO ANSWER our question, to resolve the puzzle of disgust, we must look at the class of stimuli that elicit disgust. I shall proceed by listing a number of categories of disgusting phenomena, accompanied by a pairing with relevant non-disgusting entities.[1] The list provides the data for any plausible theory of the disgusting, and what is striking is how heterogeneous the class is. This heterogeneity poses a problem for the most initially attractive theories, forcing a subtler and more elaborate account of the disgusting, which will finally emerge. The goal is to find a theory that unifies the varieties of disgust.

(1) Presumably the paradigm of the disgusting object is the rotting corpse, human or animal (but especially human). Not so much—or at all—the fresh corpse of the very recently deceased, but the corpse as it undergoes the process of putrefaction or decay: the changes in the texture, color, and smell of the flesh as the forces of decomposition impose their gruesome transformation

---

1. See also the lists compiled by Kolnai, pp. 52–72, and Miller, chap. 5. Their lists and mine are quite similar, despite some differences of emphasis, with one exception: they include the profligate, swarming nature of living things, especially insects. I don't find this very intuitive, because it seems to me that the totality inherits its disgustingness from its members; in the case of herds of cattle or flocks of birds I don't detect a disgust response. Nor do I find an increase of disgust when I see or contemplate large human populations. So I don't see profligate life as disgusting as such. If you do, then by all means add this category to the list.

on the once-living tissues of the body. As we now know, bacteria play the leading role in this transition to the disgusting—though this knowledge can hardly be supposed to be the basis of the emotion, since the emotion predates the knowledge. The infestation of maggots in the later stages occasions special horror. Bodily contact with a putrefying corpse is felt to be particularly repellent, as well as the odor produced, but the sight too can provoke strong disgust reactions—nausea and vomiting being the most obvious. It is clearly not fear that prompts such an aversion, since we generally are not afraid of what a dead body might do to us; rather, it is the sensory appearance of the decaying body that revolts and disturbs. If we could shut down our senses in the presence of a corpse, we could eliminate or mitigate the disgust we feel—though many other attitudes and emotions would persist. We feel horror not terror; we are appalled not afraid. Cannibalism and necrophilia are no doubt repellent to most people, even in the case of the recently dead; but it is surely an exceptional human being who can contemplate such activities in the case of a putrefied corpse! Putrefying flesh is reliably repulsive, always and everywhere. The normal reaction to the rotting corpse is either to escape its presence (and hence its sensory impact) or to dispose of it in such a way that it can no longer offend human consciousness (say, by burning or burying it). There also appears to be a curve of disgustingness for the corpse, rising to a high point relatively soon after death, a matter of days or weeks maybe, but declining as the process of decay reaches its later stages; two weeks, say, is a good deal worse than a year, under normal conditions. Disgust peaks at a certain point, thereafter lessening—yet the corpse is no less a corpse.[2]

What holds true for the whole body also holds for parts of it: a rotting body part elicits disgust, even when the rest of the

2. So it is the specific appearance of a corpse at a particular time that disgusts us, not the corpse as such; at any rate, the disgust varies with the specific appearance. We want to know, then, what it is about *that* appearance that occasions disgust.

body is healthy—gangrenous limbs being a prime example. This tells us that the mere absence of life is not what appalls in the case of the corpse, since the gangrene patient may be very much alive and under no immediate threat of death. It is the intrinsic perceptual condition of the limb that provokes disgust: its smell, its sight, and its touch. It may be, indeed, that a decaying body part is found *more* disgusting than a decaying whole body—for reasons we must inquire into later. Amputation is the usual treatment for such a condition, given that the decay cannot be reversed, and then incineration or burial of the offending limb. Certainly, the idea of possessing such a decaying body part oneself strikes us as especially loathsome (this cannot be so for the rotting corpse, for obvious reasons).[3]

Then there are zombies, lepers, and vampires (among other legendary monsters). The animated rotting corpse strikes dread into us, especially in the light of its ability to move and touch us against our will, even if its intentions are, so to speak, honorable. The still-living corpse, with flesh rotting and reeking, is a strong elicitor of disgust, even if only at the movies. Lepers have always been shunned, and not merely because of a fear of contagion; it is their flesh itself that we cannot stand, as it decomposes on their poor bones. Again, putrefying flesh on the living individual seems particularly potent as an agent of disgust. Vampires are traditionally found disgusting—mainly because of their association with blood, but also because of their typical depiction as clammy, cold, pale, and coffin-occupying.[4] They have

3. Imagine a disease that rots the body from the extremities to the core, hands and feet first. This combination of the living and putrefying seems particularly nasty, not just medically, but aesthetically and emotionally.

4. That is, the traditional vampire, made famous by *Nosferatu*; recent vampires of popular culture are trending more to the sexy and attractive, as in *True Blood*. I don't think this new vampire genre undermines the basic idea of the disgusting vampire, however, because the vampire is still associated with disgust in the form of corpses and blood. The creators are working more with ambivalence than outright unqualified revulsion, but the latter is still there in the background.

returned from the dead, so are really a species of zombie, even though they behave like living beings, and their flesh is immediately suspect (with its sickly pallor). Their consanguinity with bats is a further count against them, bats being deemed repulsive too. The vampire occupies ambiguous ground between the dead corpse and the living organism—neither dead nor alive, a kind of death-in-life. The vampire mingles categories.

Under this heading, we can add bodily partition as a source of disgust. It is not a form of decay, obviously, but it shares a degradation of the body that prompts a very similar reaction to that produced by putrefying corpses. A decapitated or dismembered body is far more repellent than a merely dead one, and not merely because of the presence of spilled blood; the separation of head and trunk is in itself horrifying. Nor need a decapitated body smell bad in order to excite disgust. Much the same is true, though less so, of severed limbs; and the amputee, unfortunately, must share in the revulsion we standardly feel for the body in a state of partition, dead or alive (this is not to say that such reactions cannot be overcome). Perhaps the most extreme form of disgust-inducing bodily partition is castration, in which also the disgust generally occasioned by the male genitals attaches itself to the fact of severance. The sight of a lopped-off penis, or of the loins following such an operation, is certainly high on the list of disgust elicitors. Even the severed foreskin has a grisly aspect. Breast removal shares in the uneasiness. A sliced-off nose is hard to bear. The body may not be rotting in such cases, but it is certainly in disarray and decline, dramatically lacking in its customary wholeness and unity. This is not the healthy normal body, intact and functioning, but the body as damaged and sundered; it accordingly prompts the shudder we feel when the body is otherwise falling to pieces.[5] One of the

---

5. Even a missing finger or toe can occasion mild revulsion, let alone a whole limb—though not the "amputation" of a fingernail or hair from the head. The

central horrors of the decaying corpse must surely be its propensity literally to fall apart under mild pressure. The deliquescence of the body excites extreme revulsion. Fragmentation and liquefaction of the firm body are strong disgust stimuli.

It is noteworthy that not all manifestations of bodily extinction are deemed disgusting. The skeleton is an interesting case: it may provoke a cold shiver and be generally shunned, but it does not appear intrinsically disgusting—so long, at least, as it is completely stripped of the remnants of flesh. Bare bones don't prompt disgust, unlike the decaying tissue that may recently have covered them. The skeleton strikes us as "clean"— white, dry, hard. Yet a mere fleck of flesh on a skeleton is enough to produce the disgust reaction. Bone *marrow* can, I think, provoke disgust, but the bone itself seems not to be disgusting, though it can be found offensive in other ways. Oddly, too, preserved bodies seem low on the disgust scale, especially those that are cryogenically preserved; freezing solid seems to forestall or reduce the disgust reaction, at least to some degree. In such cases, the process of decay has been artificially arrested even before it has begun, so the flesh has not attained that state of decline that we find most appalling: it just seems like a block of ice, odorless, unchanging, antiseptic. The flesh remains, but it is suspended in time, not subject to the degrading forces of the biological world. And it should also be noted that dead plants are not generally found disgusting, even if biological decline has set in: a crumpled brown leaf or a faded flower do not stir our sense of the disgusting. Organic tissue is here losing the signs of life, soon to lose all form, but that, by itself, seems innocuous, even welcome (we quite like dried dead wood, as in furniture). The drooping rose may strike us as sad, emblematic of mortality,

---

loss of any body part, even if small, excites the general idea of bodily dismemberment, and hence the fragility of the whole body; it therefore acts as a symbol of something larger and more catastrophic.

but it never occasions the nausea that a dead rat can evoke. This fact will be significant when we come to formulating a general theory of the disgusting.

(2) A second major category of disgust elicitors is that of bodily substances, particularly those we deem "waste products." These include: feces, urine, menstrual blood, mucus, vomit, earwax, pus, saliva, semen, skin grease, birth fluids, dandruff, bad breath, stale sweat. These no doubt vary in their degree of disgustingness, and context can mitigate the disgust reaction, but some items on the list are universally and robustly condemned as disgusting—the chief among these being feces. Nobody (save the most hardened or perverse) can tolerate the salient presence of human shit. We can't stand the sight of it, the touch of it, or (notoriously) the smell of it. Shit appalls and repels, no question about it (though a qualification will later be entered). Urine is infinitely preferable, despite its physiological propinquity.[6] Vomit comes pretty close, it's true, but even vomit lacks the visceral (!) power of excrement, especially human excrement. The disgustingness of human shit to human beings is, indeed, one of the great sources of misery in the world, in view of the relative backwardness of much of the world's toilet facilities.[7] And tyrants intent on maximizing human suffering often resort to putting people and their bodily waste on excruciatingly intimate terms—making people live in shit, literally. We thus avoid the proximity of something to which we are so irremediably and naturally proximate. In general, the secretions and

6. Urine is mainly composed of water and apt to be clear and transparent; it thus approximates to the inorganic water we find elsewhere, which we find not disgusting at all. Urine is disgusting in proportion to its opacity and odor, i.e., its degree of diluteness—the more watery the better.

7. Rose George's *The Big Necessity* is a powerful indictment of the world's inability to provide adequate toilet facilities for the majority of mankind. Disease is the major problem, but human disgust follows close behind. The cause is unpopular partly because people don't want to have to wallow too much in the disgusting issue of human excrement. Movie stars and politicians leave it alone.

excretions of the human body, with their proprietary orifices (of which more below), are the cause of much revulsion, actual and potential. The living human body is a rich repository—a factory—of dischargeable disgust materials. On a daily, even hourly, basis we must manage and contain the polluting substances generated by our own organic existence, as the body leaks and expels its natural products. The body spews forth its organic materials, what it needs to flourish and survive—and meanwhile we recoil. These vital substances are the objects of our steady revulsion, biologically necessary as they are. Semen, say, without which human life is impossible, is regarded with distaste, or even outright disgust—as if there were something *wrong* with the stuff. Why should we be revolted by something so harmless and so vital to life? Isn't semen something to savor and celebrate? Much the same can be said of menstrual blood, another source of intense taboo and revulsion. We seem as disgusted by the body in the full flight of life, squeezing and pumping, as we are by its quiet dissolution in death.[8]

Do we regard all bodily secretions as infernal in this way? By no means: we make exceptions for tears, fresh sweat, and moistened lips. Tears are the interesting case, since torrents of them, spilling from the eyes, do not revolt our generally delicate sensibilities. They have the advantage of clarity and lack of odor, though they can become sticky and even slimy; one wonders what we would make of tears if they gave off the smell of urine or if their color were an organic brown. Watery eyes can stimulate a pang of disgust, especially if they are a symptom of illness, and other secretions of the eyes can be disgusting (blood, jelly); yet tears are given a free pass, in normal conditions. We even

8. The healthy is thus as disgusting as the diseased, and the closer to life's vital roots the more disgusting—with tears and sweat being less revolting than semen and menses. Note the contrast between the first two categories of disgust objects: the first relating to death, the second to life. Opposite poles produce the same emotion: the non-excreting dead body and the excreting living body.

rush to embrace the tearful. Nor does anyone worry much about saliva on the teeth and in the mouth's interior. Sweat seems tolerated when performing its proper function, but stale remnants of it are frowned upon. So it would be wrong to say that we are disgusted by all bodily secretions, and there is definitely a hierarchy of disgust relating to different types of substance—excrement being gloriously at the pinnacle. Distinctions are clearly made in our pattern of aversive emotional response—but on what basis?

(3) We do not confine our disgust reactions to the fluids and semi-solids of the porous body; we are also offended by things that grow *on* (or with) the body—things that decorate its smooth surface or shape its contours. In this category we can count blemishes and disfigurements, abnormalities and excrescences. Thus: pimples, acne, boils, warts, wounds, deformities, scabs, rashes, skin tags, burns, growths, tumors, cysts, swellings, birth marks, moles, misplaced hair, obesity, disproportion, flab, folds, loose skin, wrinkles, cellulite, varicose veins, discolorations, and lumps. The skin is a virtual treasure-trove of disgust objects—and that is only when observed with the naked eye. Things take on an even more vicious hue when the skin is viewed up close—say, through a microscope—when the smoothest and loveliest skin is seen as dimpled and glandular, rough and greasy, home to nasty little creatures. But, setting that close-up view aside, the human skin is the site of innumerable potent loci of disgust, and one small pimple, with its tiny raised center of white, can be enough to provoke a disgust reaction to an otherwise beautiful face. The skin is a rich and varied source of disgusting stimuli, despite its aesthetic (and erotic) appeal. No wonder there is a thriving cosmetics industry devoted to minimizing its disgust potential, not to speak of the attractions of plastic surgery. Of particular interest in this long list are signs of age and errant hair. Skin that was once taut and firm becomes loose, sagging, wrinkled, and folded; surface beauty departs and

the eye rebels at what age does to the flesh and its paper-thin envelope. Instead of seeing here the signs of a fine maturity, parallel to the maturing of the soul that dwells within, we tend to experience disgust and depression—as if the flesh and skin have betrayed us, become corrupted. That hardly seems fair. Instead of wanting to touch, we want to avoid. In some quarters, the ugly old woman is the very apogee of the disgusting, as if age has turned her from disgust's opposite to disgust's avatar; the breasts, in particular, have undergone an atrocious demotion (the pot belly of the middle-aged male, where once was a flat midsection, is a close analogy).[9] Disgust and age march inexorably together, and the skin operates as reliable timekeeper.

As to hair, we maintain remarkably finicky standards of what is acceptable and unacceptable, and here too whole industries ply their anti-disgust trade. Hair on the head is fine, of course, though it must not sprout from too far down the forehead or intrude unduly on the neck. Confined to the scalp it is even deemed highly attractive, and the thicker the better.[10] But woe betide the eyebrows if they partake of such luxuriance: they must remain thin and separated, by regular depilation if necessary, however painful. Ears and nose must be clear of bristling hair (here too age plays its insidious role). The beard is acceptable in men—but there are definite limits on how far it may grow down the neck (think of a beard sprouting from the upper chest). The

9. Menninghaus has a whole section entitled "The Ugly Old Lady" (pp. 84–91). He writes: "This phantasm [the old lady] conventionally brings together folds and wrinkles, warts, larger than usual openings of the body (i.e., mouth and anus), foul, black teeth, sunk-in hollows instead of beautiful swellings, drooping breasts, stinking breath, revolting habits, and a proximity to both death and putrefaction" (p. 84). That, at any rate, is the stereotype of the old lady as she figures in various cultural traditions, fair and accurate or not.

10. But if the hair becomes too long, so that it can be sat on or trails on the ground, then some disgust reaction is likely, and of course it must not become dirty or greasy or louse-ridden. Even the most lustrous head hair turns offensive once it becomes detached from the scalp and enters the mouth—or gets into food.

chest may be hirsute in the male, within reason, but the back is generally deemed an inappropriate location for hair to proliferate; the shoulders are an area of some uncertainty, but must not be thickly pelted. Then we reach the danger zone of the pubic hair, which has undergone something of a cultural transformation, notably in the female (though increasingly in the male). Where once copious natural foliage was deemed acceptable, we now witness a definite disgust reaction to nature's furry bounty; these days the pubic hair must be trimmed and tamed, possibly entirely removed, and on no account permitted to descend down the inner thigh. Nor must it proceed backward to other regions regarded as sites of revulsion. Pubic hair, like the rain forests, is fast disappearing, driven away by the strong force of human disgust, as it deepens and mutates. Soon it may reach the advanced state of depletion experienced by hair on the female leg (and how far behind is the male leg?): the female leg must not be allowed its natural allotment of hair—it must be preternaturally bald, alabaster-smooth. Hair on the female foot, too, is not generally permitted, for fear of instant aversion; the toes must be wholly innocent of it. The female is allowed very little in the way of bodily hair, at least at this point of history, except for an enormous flowing growth on the top of her head; the male generally manifests less on top, but is allowed a greater share elsewhere. In both cases, hair has its strictly enforced boundaries, from which it must not stray. We should be struck by the apparent arbitrariness of these arrangements and wonder at their origins and meaning (they are scarcely the result simply of passing fashions, like bell-bottom trousers or particular hair *styles*)[11]. The large

---

11. Baldness can take on a disgusting aspect too, especially if it is the result of disease or is less than characteristic (e.g., baldness from radiation treatment). On different parts of the body, hair must reach only certain lengths or risk censure—the hands should have shorter hair than the armpits, say. The hair on monkeys and apes strikes many as unappealing (and hairy men are described as having apelike backs): but would a bald ape be preferable?

hairy mole on the wrinkled face concentrates these fierce aversive passions, focusing the feelings of disgust that surround our peculiar attitudes to human skin.

No doubt much more could be said about the items on my lengthy list, but I think we have enough to go on with, and it is now time to enumerate the positive aspects of skin-covered flesh. What do we find distinctly non-disgusting? In the first place, firm or toned flesh with homogeneous skin, both in respect of color and texture. Big muscles are fine, though some misgivings develop in the case of extremely "vascular" bodybuilders; we certainly don't feel any aversion to muscle development beyond the "normal." Slimness is a good thing, but not to the point of the skeletal; the bones must never show conspicuously through. Freckles are perfectly acceptable, but extreme density or spread might occasion a wince, and they must not protrude in the manner of moles. The callous, perhaps surprisingly, is tolerated, especially if acquired through sport or "honest work"; it may constitute itself as a raised surface and a tactile anomaly, but we do not recoil from contact with it (e.g., in shaking the hand of a brick layer or tennis player). Tattoos, despite their discontinuities of coloration, analogous to birth marks, are regarded with equanimity, though here cultural changes have played a significant part in the tolerance of the tattoo. Piercings hover on the edge and can slide easily toward the disgusting (the tongue, the nipples, the genitals), but a pair of earrings inserted through pierced lobes have never been known to excite much in the way of revulsion. Nor has ordinary make-up raised the talons of disgust, even when it has broken every rule of normality. All these instances show that it cannot be a matter of what is normal or abnormal, natural or unnatural, that determines the contours of disgust— even if those notoriously slippery words could be given precise meaning. The acceptable items are not "normal" in any well-defined biological or statistical sense, and the unacceptable items are often common and biologically mandated (such as aging).[12] Yet, we insist on a firm line of demarcation: freckles yes, warts no; big muscles yes, big bellies no; hairy scalps yes, hairy necks no. Of all this we would like some account. It certainly doesn't appear that shape or material or color plays much of a role—the primary and secondary qualities of the formations in question. Something subtler must be afoot.

(4) We have so far considered the exterior of the body, in life and death: what about the interior? Here, things look especially dark and grim. Once we plunge beneath the surface of the skin, the body reveals itself as a disgusting assemblage of grisly organs, damp tissues, and noisome fluids (blood, bile, gurgling foodstuffs). Only the bones offer any relief in this foul landscape, and they are so enveloped by the loathsome that their white purity is all but smothered. The heart, the liver, the lungs, the kidneys, the intestines, and the *brain*—none of this is remotely pleasing to the senses. We can stand the thought of these soggy monstrosities when they are ensconced safely inside the body's fragile envelope, but once they are brought out into the open—in surgery or trauma—disgust beats its drum loud. Few things are more revolting to us than disembowelment, when the intestines are exposed and ripped from the still-living body; but the mere sight of a pulsating bloody heart is enough to turn most people's stomachs. The sight of all this is awful enough, but the prospect of inserting a naked hand (or face!) into the body's gory interior fills most of us with dread (surgeons must develop a special callous of the mind). Part of the horror of the body's orifices derives from this threat of exposure of the body's internal landscape—the butcher's shop that lies within each of

---

12. In general, disgust items are entirely "normal" and "natural"; anti-disgust measures are typically *ab*normal, requiring some invention and technology. The disgusting aspects of the body are often integral to basic life processes, having nothing to do with disease or breakdown.

us. (The vagina seems particularly susceptible to this anxiety, because inside and outside meet here with such vividness). The brain, so vital to our higher attributes, can scarcely be contemplated in its physical actuality: to see or touch (or taste!) a human brain is more than most people can bear (I have queasily held a pickled one in my bare hands). One wonders what we would make of ourselves if our outer covering were transparent, affording us a clear view of the anatomical wetware within. A simple cut, with the blood flowing, is already an insight into the interior that we could do without, and a major gash, with the muscle sliced open, is impossible to face calmly. We must keep the insides hidden and not dwell too much on their reality; the mere removal of a cheek from the face is enough to bring on convulsions of disgust to the unhardened. The skin acts as a disgust-averting device of modesty, a kind of veil. Once again, human viciousness has sought to exploit this natural horror, with punishments and ordeals that evoke disgust in both victim and audience (as if the pain were not enough): beheading, evisceration, burning, laceration, and skinning. Beauty, they say, is skin deep (and compromised even there); inside everyone is as revolting as anyone else—and we all know it.[13] And notice: the disgust that prevails here takes as its target perfectly normal living processes—nothing dead or decaying or abnormal or diseased or poisonous. A robust and sturdy liver, doing its job perfectly, can prompt as much physical disgust as the most wretched of earth's creatures. In fact, dead and desiccated organs probably occasion less disgust than humid and living ones; here the freshness itself can take on a disgusting sheen.

---

13. An interesting irony here is that the soul is often described as "within" or "inner," and yet it is the paradigm of the non-disgusting entity, while the literal bodily interior is strongly disgust-laden; for some reason we don't sense a clash in these conceptions. The bodily exterior acts as a misleading mask both with respect to the indwelling soul and the internal organs—yet these belong at opposite ends of the disgust spectrum.

Are any bodily organs exempt from this general ban? Well, the skin is an organ and it offers less in the way of disgust potential, at any rate when clothing the body (it quickly turns disgusting once stripped from the body). With animals, fur is typically quite free of disgust, but the skin may prompt disgust, depending on the details of the case (elephants OK, snakes not so much). Apart from the skin, the eyes seem most distant from the domain of disgust; indeed, eyes can be gazed at, and into, with relative impunity. Yet even they walk a fine line: bloodshot or dripping they lose their luster, and removal creates an instant horror story (think of Gloucester in *King Lear*). Still, the eyes are a good deal better regarded than the kidneys—though what would our feelings be were the function of the kidneys performed by organs with the physical appearance of the eyes? The mouth is also an ambiguous case: it can clearly be found attractive and invite intimate contact of several sorts, but it also offers access to a bodily interior that we abruptly rebel against. Then there is the digestive function of the mouth and its integral relation to the anus (input and output of the same system, basically). The lips are generally in the clear, but the tongue can quickly assume a disgusting aspect, and the throat is manifestly a route to the unmentionable. Our attitude toward the mouth is clearly highly ambivalent, given its several functions and uses, but it is not an organ that altogether escapes the tentacles of disgust; there is too much of the bodily interior about it. The same might be said of the genital organs, especially the female: ingress to the interior is part of their gross anatomy, though they also occupy a superficial position on the body. The genitals—about which we shall have to enquire further—have such a rich and complex psychology that primitive disgust reactions take on a more sophisticated form in their case. In any case, the vagina shares with the mouth (with which it is often compared) a disturbingly ready access to the body's gruesome interior, and must inherit the reactions that attach themselves to that interior.

The penis may be said to do the same in a very attenuated form, because it too presents an aperture with the bodily interior at its inward end; not only that, but it carries something from the interior, itself found disgusting, to the exterior—namely semen (urine too, of course). In semen, something of the body's gooey and secretive interior finds its way to the outside world, with the penis as its conduit; thereby the penis has its dubious dealings with the disgusting inside. Ditto the anus, obviously. There is really no sharp line, anatomical or affective, separating the body's interior from its exterior, with breaches at several zones, and so disgust cannot easily confine itself topographically: it is apt to take in the whole organism, with only a diminution of intensity at the juncture of the skin. The exterior, after all, is only the exterior *of* that interior.[14]

(5) So far, the human body has been our prime focus, but we are disgusted by a great deal besides that. To say that we are disgusted by human beings as such—as a species—would be an exaggeration; our disgust reactions are more selective than that. But we do speak of disgust at other animal species in an unselective style; we apply a broader brush in their case, as if their whole identity is disgusting to us, not merely certain of their traits. There may be some individual variation, even within late-capitalist Western culture, but the following animal species excite fairly widespread revulsion: insects in general, but especially cockroaches, flies, and spiders, snakes and other reptiles, rats, bats, pigs, mice, slugs, earthworms, maggots, tapeworms and other parasitic worms, bacteria in the form of mould, jellyfish, the octopi, oysters, and no doubt others. Again, the intensity of disgust may vary over these species, but the phenomenon

---

14. The body's epidermal envelope also *contains* the revolting innards, keeping them from slopping out—as if the insides were pressing for release. This is very true of blood, which leaks at the slightest cut. It is hard for us to keep thoughts of the inside away from perception of the outside, so the disgust is apt to spread outward to the bodily surface.

is robust and can be very strong. It covers many species and takes in a number of phyla, from bivalves to insects to mammals. The list can seem arbitrary from a zoological or even a prudential point of view (some of these disgust objects are harmless, others dangerous), raising the question of what unites these disparate fauna. Some come into our homes to steal our food, while some do not. Some carry disease, but others don't. Some are slimy, but not all. It looks like a wildly mixed bunch. Are we just hopelessly irrational and confused, finding commonalities where none exist? Is the definition of the disgusting just a pointless disjunction? A skeptic may be forgiven for so thinking, given the range of items that we have hitherto identified. We shall see.

It would be simpler if we could just say that we find animals in general disgusting, but we clearly don't. Some of them we even like to keep as pets, and stroke, and sit on our lap; we enjoy the physical contact, we don't abhor it. We are not generally averse to cats, dogs, birds, rabbits, guinea pigs, deer, and elephants—and so on through a long list. True, we may find certain of their traits disgusting—as we do our fellow humans—but we do not object to their very presence, except for reasons of safety; people don't find lions disgusting, as they commonly do pigs and rats, even though they are scared to death of them. The rear end of certain primates may offend our delicate sensibilities, but we don't regard these animals as disgusting tout court. Every animal must defecate, and thus to that extent attract our disgust reactions, but that has nothing to do with our revulsion to worms, say. There must be something about certain animals in the round, and not others, that underlies our responses—unless we are seriously off the rails. Once again, these loathed objects can be fit and healthy, in the prime of life, perfectly harmless, in no way a threat, and *still* we can't stand to be near them (consider your feelings about the common slug making its lazy way up your bare leg). Worms in general seem to excite special antipathy, no matter how harmless they may be, but the kind that live inside our bodies (or those that dine on our deceased flesh) are deemed the most disgusting of all. I recall when I first heard about the tapeworm, at around the age of ten, and could scarcely sleep for a week, my stomach perpetually perturbed—might there be one of the dreaded things lurking in there? Surely that was the most disgusting thing imaginable—especially when its vile head emerged, well fed and hearty, from the unhappy victim's anus. Even if such a parasite could cause you no real harm, perhaps allowing you to consume more food without getting fat, or clean out your insides, it was still a horrifying notion. Whence the horror? Why does this strike us as so revolting—aesthetically, viscerally, *existentially*—while the bite of a dog is simply something to be feared? What explains the disgusting *Sosein*? What, I ask, is the metaphysics of the worm?[15]

(6) If animals can be disgusting, what about plants? Here the disgust gradient starts to shade to zero, but it can still sometimes get a grip. Certainly, decaying plants can excite disgust, especially if those plants are intended to be eaten (e.g. the soggy rotten cucumber in the back of the fridge). Mould on vegetables is a clear disgust object. Here we have an analogy with the putrefying animal body: the once-living organism now subject to forces of decay and breakdown—soft, smelly, discolored. But healthy plants can sometimes occasion disgust too, even if it is relatively

---

15. Once I was on beautiful Harbor Island in the Caribbean eating lunch overlooking the water. I looked down to see what seemed like lengths of white mooring rope in the water, swaying with the current, looking rather frayed and flimsy. After a while I detected autonomous movement and realized that I was looking, not at ropes, but at worms—long and white, dining off muck on the ocean floor. Suddenly they began to appear to me exactly like human intestines in the water, and I was hit with a strong access jolt of disgust—putting me off lunch completely. Imagine if they *had* been human intestines, dumped there somehow: that would have been truly revolting. But these giant white worms of the sea—like long ragged maggots—were bad enough. The dead had come to life before my blinking eyes.

mild: algae, seaweed, and fungus can prompt an aversive reaction. Sliminess is negatively tagged, and some plants seem naturally dirty (mushrooms and toadstools often have dirt clinging to them). Parasitic plants, like tree fungus, can also make us feel queasy. We certainly are repelled by plant forms that live on the human body, such as fungus between the toes (athlete's foot); grass that grew out of our skin would surely excite strong revulsion. So the botanical world is not devoid of disgust stimuli, even if not so forcefully as the animal world. Still, for the most part, plants are not felt to be repulsive in the way animals are. Quite the contrary: flowers and trees, grass and cacti—none of these carries even a hint of the disgusting. They don't even have specific traits that excite our aversion; the interiors are just as innocuous as the exteriors, and the decaying plant is not treated as a rotting corpse. Even when a plant smells offensive, this does not typically make us feel nauseous, and generally the smell of plants is pleasant or neutral. A rose is the very antithesis of the disgust object—nothing remotely like a rat (it is even hard to accept that a rose could have been *called* a "rat" and a rat a "rose"). Given this general acceptability, why do we single *any* plants out as even mildly noxious? Poisonous plants are rightly singled out for their danger, and are contrasted with nourishing plants, but that is not the disgusting/non-disgusting distinction: poisonous plants are not ipso facto found disgusting, and some nourishing plants (like seaweed) are found by many to be disgusting as potential food. Sliminess may be cited, but can that be what the disgustingness consists in? Not everything disgusting is slimy. And why should sliminess be a problem anyway? We need a deeper analysis.[16]

(7) The next category is no sort of organism or organism part or trait (except in the most extended sense): it is simply

16. What about sap oozing from a tree trunk? Can that occasion disgust? Maybe, but I suspect this is because it reminds us of mucus and other bodily secretions; it seems distinctly secondary as a disgust object—requiring some active seeing-as.

dirt. The concept is not a scientific one; there is no natural kind of dirt. Rather, dirt is a category defined according to our affective responses: dirt is what we *find* dirty, more or less. The primary kind of dirt is the kind that clings to the skin and takes some effort to remove, say with soap and water. But that can hardly be the definition, since cosmetic makeup shares that characteristic—as well as war paint, perfume, and soap itself (which is why we smell of it after recent application). For something to qualify as dirt it has to evoke repulsion and a desire to erase it, if not in the dirty individual then at least in his associates (consider a grubby child and his more fastidious parents). Dust and grime surrounds us, and as we make contact with the world it rubs off on us; hands and feet become, as we unreflectively say, dirty, even filthy. The worst kind of dirt is undoubtedly fecal matter, but other sorts of matter qualify too (it's not the quantity that counts so much as the quality). This dirty matter need not, significantly, be organic, as everything considered heretofore has been: there is purely chemical dirt, as when a fine dust of some metal clings to the body (you can get quite dirty messing with rusty objects). Dirt typically changes the color of the body, as well as its smell (and taste); and it is apt to be sticky. Dirt deriving from the body's own secretions and excretions is greatly frowned upon, cleanliness being next to godliness and all that: to be smeared with one's own feces is not, as a general rule, tolerated in polite society. Personal hygiene, as it is called, is a systematic effort to manage the dirt that flows outward from our mucky insides—sweat, urine, excrement, mucus, ear wax, and so on. Exogenous dirt, while not so heinous, is still deplored and will earn you banishment from civilized company if left unchecked; it is unwise to show up for an intimate date with muck on your face and grime under your nails—no matter how "harmless" such dirt may be (coal miners have a difficult time here, not to mention sanitation workers). A certain amount of accumulated dirt is unavoidable as the day progresses, even for the most personally fastidious, but we are expected to make every effort to minimize it and to undertake a wholesale scrub down every twenty-four hours or so (well, maybe not so frequently in England). If sweat is abundant after athletic exertion, we are required to wash it off forthwith, which can entail a lot of showering for tennis players and others. Of course, it is all a matter of degree, since the microscope will discover dirt in the most "hygienic" of persons, and dirt comes to us from the air at every moment of the day in the form of pollution, pollen, and what not. Still, it must not become conspicuous, and must be quickly expunged. But again, I ask, *why* are we thus fastidious? What is it about dirt that repels us so? Some animals relish being covered in mud; pigs wallow in all manner of gunk. But we become hysterically disgusted at the mere hint of dark matter under the fingernails, harmless as it may be (though we don't mind dark nail polish *on* the fingernails). Moreover, not only do we deplore dirt on the body; we also can't stand it in our surroundings, even if there is no prospect of its being transferred to the body. One's house must be kept properly clean, swept and scrubbed, whether or not the dirt might contaminate the inhabitants; cobwebs high in the ceiling are not exempt from revulsion. For some extremists, untidiness alone is a form of dirtiness, as with scattered books or papers. We must "clean up the mess," as we are required to clean the besmirched body. Dirty cooking utensils particularly cry out to be scrubbed and cleansed. The fridge or oven can easily become an epicenter of frightful dirtiness without any drastic infusion of antecedently filthy matter. Dirt encroaches on us constantly; it is a battle to keep it at bay. Disgust is what drives our efforts—all that wiping, scrubbing, sweeping, polishing.

It might seem that this category of the disgusting is cut and dried, with no anomalous exceptions. But matters are not quite so simple: I have already mentioned make-up, a form of bodily smearing that *enhances* attractiveness; but there is also hair gel, moisturizer, skin rejuvenator, perfume, sunscreen, and fake tan. Left too long, these can enter the category of the dirty, but freshly applied they occasion no complaint. Nor do we regard clothes as a species of bodily dirt, though they can cling to the skin in the manner of dirt. Is it because dirt must be small and separable? But would we find a sweater disgusting that was sprayed onto the body a particle at a time (think of body paint)? Clothes can get dirty, but no one thinks of clothes *as* a form of dirt—as just a large and colorful kind of dirt that can be removed by simply undressing. At what point, if any, does a worn and ragged shirt enter the category of dirt, or dingy forlorn (but clean!) underwear? Is a Band-Aid ever a kind of dirt, or wart removal ointment? What about bits of fluff in the navel? The category can get fuzzy at the edges, with some borderline cases. Certainly, it is not merely a matter of clinging matter, or else wall hangings would be as bad as cobwebs and face powder as bad as coal dust. Hair isn't dirt, after all, despite its superficial formal resemblance— though it becomes dirt once it has been cut or shaved. The category of the dirty must be delimited by something other than mere physical constitution or simple proximity to the body. Dirt is not a category of matter of interest to the physicist. Dirt must be defined, roughly, as loose matter that is found disgusting: but what *is* it to be disgusting? Things are not found disgusting because they are dirty; they are deemed dirty because they are found disgusting. This is why it is no explanatory help to say that corpses, feces and worms are disgusting because they are dirty, for we lack any account of what dirtiness is that is independent of the category of the disgusting.[17]

---

17. Kolnai has a fine discussion of dirt, pp. 55–56: he writes that there is an "unmistakable intentional relation to life, and to life's ebbs and flows. Hands become dirty through manual activity, underclothes through being worn. And there is often sweat that plays an agglutinating role in the formation of dirt. Dirt is, to an extent, simply the presence, the non-obliteration, of traces of life."

(8) So far, the modalities of the disgusting have been sensory in character: the sight or smell or feel of something is what disgusts. But that does not exhaust the field: forms of behavior can be found disgusting too. It is not clear whether all such cases qualify as moral disgust in the strict sense, though they certainly shade into moral disgust, but they are more "abstract" than what we have considered hitherto—more a matter of conception than perception. It is not how the activity perceptually seems to the disgusted subject that counts, but the nature of the activity itself—the very idea of it. I am thinking primarily of disgust with respect to sexual practices regarded as "deviant." Such reactions vary with the prevailing state of opinion regarding the practices in question, but the following have at various times been felt by many to be disgusting: interspecies sex, pedophilia, homosexuality, anal sex, oral sex, masturbation, "French kissing," non-missionary-position intercourse, sex purely for pleasure not procreation. Although in most of these cases, the judgment of disgustingness has been accompanied by a moral evaluation, it is important to see that two distinct attitudes are involved: the aesthetic attitude of disgust and the moral attitude of condemnation. No doubt many people have confused the two, moving from their sense of aesthetic revulsion to a moral judgment.[18] But that is a clear non sequitur: things can be found utterly disgusting and yet not have anything morally to be said against them. For one thing, not everyone agrees that these practices are disgusting—but moral judgments cannot have such relativity built into them. More significant from our point of view, it is quite consistent to judge that an activity is disgusting (so far as the judger is concerned) and also to judge that it is morally permissible: for example, a heterosexual

18. For a good discussion of disgust in relation to morality and the law, see Martha Nussbaum's *Hiding From Humanity: Disgust, Shame, and the Law.* She rightly distinguishes sharply between the disgusting and the immoral.

may find the idea of homosexual sex disgusting, in that he or she would be repelled by it in his or her own case, while at the same time judging that it is entirely morally acceptable. I recognize that others may not share my aesthetic attitudes—my field of disgust objects—and that what is morally permissible cannot be determined from what I happen to find disgusting. Even if everyone found a certain activity disgusting, say eating live worms, that is no *moral* ground for condemning it, if some people wish to engage in what actually disgusts them (they might do it from a desire to demonstrate self-mastery). So, the examples cited in this section are intended only to exemplify disgust in the *non*-moral sense (next I will consider moral disgust strictly so called). With that clarified, we can say that disgust at perceived sexual "deviance" can be added to the varieties of disgust distinguished so far.

A few remarks about these cases may be made. First, some of these activities are associated with body parts already on the list of disgust-inducing items, notably the anus, and thus may be supposed to inherit their disgust-value from those parts. But that cannot be the whole story, because other sexual activities deemed disgustingly deviant do not involve such antecedently disgusting parts, and even in the case of anal sex the disgust is not merely a disgust at the part itself but at what is being *done* to it, that is, the nature of the activity. So this category is not reducible to the previously identified categories (note that the revulsion to interspecies sex does not depend on the object species itself being found disgusting—sheep are not normally regarded as inherently disgusting). Second, it should not be ruled out that part of the appeal of the practices listed might depend precisely *on* their being felt as disgusting. People could engage in them, not in spite of their disgustingness, but because of it. Part of the attraction *is* the repulsion (I shall have more to say about the attraction of the disgusting later). Third, the disgust reaction here is conspicuously variable from culture to culture and time to time, as well as from individual to individual. Clearly, homosexual sex is not disgusting to those who desire it; indeed, heterosexual sex might be disgusting to someone with no desire for it—and similarly with respect to other types of "deviant" sex. Attitudes toward oral sex and masturbation have proved remarkably plastic, compared to the rigidity of earlier times. So the data here are not very robust or absolute. Such disgust does not seem as primitive and ineradicable as the other kinds, depending more on contingent beliefs and cultural assumptions—or simple prejudices. Still, any general theory of disgust should have something to say about the possibility of such reactions—finding in them some kinship to more central cases, even if remote or tangential. For it is at least true that people have *found* such things disgusting, whether they objectively are or not—and their emotion presumably has some sort of intelligible basis.

If we ask what sexual activities are most free of the disgust reactions prompted by the activities listed above, then it would appear that missionary-position intercourse for purposes of procreation earns the most points (though some may wince even at that). Those who declare themselves genuinely disgusted by homosexual sex, say, may well have no problems with heterosexual sex at all. Yet, from a more objective perspective, it is hard to see what could make the difference—that is, if we focus purely on the dynamics and *Sosein* of the activity (orifices and thrusting, basically). Why such selective revulsion at a certain rhythmic action directed at one orifice rather than another? Why should masturbation be an object of revulsion, harmless and tidy as it is, while penis-in-vagina ejaculation is regarded as perfectly above board? Why should the latter be *aesthetically* preferable to the former? Mere mechanics cannot be the answer: friction and hydraulics are deployed in both cases. It would be nice to find something to differentiate the two, at least in the minds of those who have differential disgust reactions to the cases—something that unites this category with the others. The felt kinship should be explicable, if not rationally defensible.[19]

(9) Lastly, we must consider moral disgust proper—the kind we feel when we condemn an action with special venom. In this category, I want to include what might be called intellectual disgust—the kind we feel (some of us) about intellectual performances that fall well short of proper intellectual standards. The category thus ranges from our reactions to, say, a particularly deplorable financial fraud to what we feel about a piece of shabby writing (possibly our own). Here is a representative list of the kinds of vice that typically excite such reactions: cheating, corruption, cruelty, bullying, deception, selfishness, hypocrisy; confusion, sloppiness, laziness, pretentiousness, evasiveness, obscurity, sophistry, prolixity, cliché, plagiarism, bad grammar. Flinging a piece of shoddy writing across the room, so as to remove it from one's sight, would be a clear case of intellectual or literary disgust (for some reason student essays come to mind at this point). Revulsion at the sight of a notorious criminal might be another case; Hitler's visage can prompt such a reaction. I think it is pretty obvious that these kinds of disgust are derivative from the basic sensory cases and may even be metaphorical in character; certainly, we should not begin with these and attempt to work back to the non-moral cases cited above. The point of this kind of disgust talk is to evince our strong disapproval of some agent, drawing an analogy to the basic cases of disgust: "that makes me *sick*," we say, though there is no real prospect of actual vomiting—as there might

---

19. This is a problematic area, with much individual and group variation. Even if there is no solid basis to the differentiation made, I assume that people at least *attribute* some distinguishing property to the cases they purport to find disgusting. As we will see, it is possible to subsume these reactions under a general theory, arbitrary though they may initially seem.

well be for corpses, feces, and so on. I therefore think that moral and intellectual disgust are only marginally relevant to developing a general theory of disgust, interesting as they may be in their own right, so I won't be saying much more about such disgust in this study.[20] From our point of view, what is most significant is the way primitive disgust has reached out beyond its original borders to shape the way we evaluate things at another level, thus demonstrating the psychological power of that emotion in our lives. The perceptual-affective system has become recruited by the moral faculty, though its original basis is entirely non-moral. We would not be morally disgusted by things unless we were *already* capable of physical disgust. Disgust is an emotion that easily spreads itself wide, influencing the way we negotiate many things seemingly remote from its original primary domain. We are a disgust-obsessed species. Our psyche is saturated with disgust reactions at many levels, from food and the body to moral and intellectual value. Disgust is protean and recurrent—cropping up all over the place.[21]

And what do we find non-disgusting in the intellectual and moral spheres? I suggest: truthfulness, clarity, concision, rigor, elegance, hard work; and honesty, kindness, integrity, generosity— the traditional virtues. It is hard to imagine anyone reacting to these qualities with disgust, however fanciful we are in contriving an alien psychology. How could someone know what

20. For further discussion of moral disgust, see Miller, chap. 8, Kolnai, chap. 4, and Nussbaum, passim. One obvious difference between simple physical disgust and moral disgust is that the former implies no notion of *blame*, but the latter does.

21. I am in effect suggesting that disgust has the pervasiveness in the human psyche that Freud attributed to sex, affecting sensation, memory, imagination, emotion, dreams, art, humor, morality, religion, politics, and so on. (I discuss the pervasiveness fully in Part Two of this book.) It is the background hum of human consciousness, a kind of universal systemic unease, and ready to erupt at any moment. The "disgust drive" has the same kind of potency Freud found in the "sex drive"—a powerful, protean, and ramifying psychic force.

truthfulness is and yet feel it to be a disgusting character trait? (We can, by contrast, imagine a type of mind not disgusted by, say, rotting corpses—the kind possessed by vultures, one assumes.) It is clearly impossible to be morally disgusted by something of which one morally approves—though the two attitudes are notionally distinct. The moral sense has adopted the preexisting disgust sensibility and now they march in parallel. In any case, I shall not be much concerned with moral disgust from now on.

3

The Architecture of Disgust

I HAVE NOW ASSEMBLED the data of disgust; next I must try to discern some general patterns, before turning to the task of finding an explanatory theory. What general characteristics stand out in all the variety?

(i) Disgust is "contact-sensitive." If we ask what disgust makes us averse to, then the short answer is *contact*. It does not make us averse to danger, as fear does, but to what may be called *contamination*—not in the medical sense of germs and disease, but in the sense of feeling oneself to be invaded, violated, made unclean. In this respect, touch is its primary sense modality: the disgust object is primarily an object by which we do not want to be touched. You may catch sight of a corpse or a mound of excrement and feel a growing disgust, but what you mainly dread is physical contact with these things and the residue that would remain on your body. The same is true of disgusting animal species. It is physical propinquity that disgust seeks above all to avoid. And not just on you, but also *in* you: the worst of all is ingestion of the disgusting object—on the tongue, the lips, in the throat, inside the stomach. The farther from the mouth the shunned contact is, the more bearable it feels; hence the foot is the part of the body whose contamination we can tolerate most equably (and, of course, it is nearest to the dirty ground). Eating a loathsome bug is considerably more revolting than having one crawl on your skin, though that can be traumatic enough too. A quick survey of the categories of disgust I listed earlier will confirm this generalization. Touch is the strongest form of intimacy, and we don't want to get intimate with what we find disgusting. Smell and taste are interesting in this regard. It is quite true that these two senses are also highly sensitive to disgust stimuli; smell may be the sense that first alerts us to something disgusting in the offing—"what's that awful smell?" But both smell and taste are tactile senses in quite literal respects, unlike sight and hearing. Taste obviously is, because the object cannot be tasted unless you are in direct contact with it: it must be on your tongue, in your mouth—there can be no "tasting at a distance." Also: a disgusting stimulus may not in fact taste bad; what repels is the fact that this revolting thing is in contact with that most sensitive of bodily zones—the mouth. It would be little consolation to discover that cadaver and excrement don't actually taste too terrible! Smell, too, is a contact sense, because particles of the stimulus actually reach the nostrils: parts of the disgusting object, which may be some distance away, are actually present inside the nose. The closer such a stimulus gets, and the stronger the smell, the more of the object enters the subject's body through the nasal cavity. Accordingly, we plug up the nose to prevent olfactory contact. Subjectively speaking, a nasty smell is felt as an intrusion on the body, a kind of suffusion or saturation—while this is not true of vision or hearing. If the worst thing is to be covered from head to toe in the foul matter of the disgusting object, then at the other end of the scale we have the local bodily contamination provided by smell. The nose is literally touched and occupied by the smelly object. This is why we suck a pleasant odor inward through the nose but expel an unpleasant smell by blowing outward—we are repelling the contact in the latter case.

The natural response to a disgusting object is thus to put it beyond the scope of the sense of touch (think of the "untouchables" of the Indian caste system). We imprison people or animals we are afraid of, so as to prevent them doing us harm; but for disgusting objects we "dispose of" them. We bury or burn them or convert them into something we can live with. We render them incapable of touching us—by smell, taste, or the tactile sense proper. It is possible to be harmed by something at a distance and out of sensory range, but it is not possible to be disgusted by such a thing (except through the intermediary of memory). We might even postulate that disgust obeys an inverse square law: the disgust value of a stimulus varies with the square of the distance between subject and object (this might be experimentally tested, but common observation suggests that it is approximately true). The closer something comes, the greater the disgust reaction; thus, the disgusted subject seeks distance between herself and what disgusts her. And the nearer a thing is the greater the chance that it will reach out and touch you. Viewing a corpse through a telescope (and knowing that you are so viewing it) will then provoke less of a disgust reaction than seeing it up close, despite the possible ocular identity of the image. Perhaps we can conjecture at this point that the reason touch is so crucial here is that to touch something is to mingle with it—to have one's own nature or identity mixed up with that of the impinging object. To be smeared with shit, say, is not only to be in contact with the stuff, but also to have it constitute what one is (at least until soap and water become available). Putrefying flesh in contact with one's own is too much like one's own flesh taking on the identity of the flesh that touches it. Thus the residue is as appalling as the initiating contact: the disgusting object has left its mark on you, shaping you, transforming you. Imagine if contact with feces initiated a process in which one's own flesh turned to shit, quite literally; that would be the ultimate disgust nightmare. But even the local smear is uncomfortably close to this. We feel that the property of disgustingness is contagious and spreads by physical contact; we thus fear a metamorphosis to the disgusting following contact with it. We protect ourselves from such a metamorphosis by keeping the necessary distance. This type of fantasy thinking may be precisely that, but this doesn't mean it has no hold on us—and anyway there is literal truth to it, in that to be smeared with shit *is* to smell of (and like) shit. Besides, we are *already* disgusting beings, even before the touch of the alien disgusting; so it is not bizarre to think of ourselves as constitutionally prone to disgust-ingness. We have shit inside us constantly; our bodies are, funda-mentally, made of shit (via the process of digestion); and we directly touch shit on a daily basis, if only with the anus. We may not be decaying now exactly, but we assuredly will; our living bodies are eminently decay-able: so the touch of an actually decaying body is only contributing to what is inevitable and inherent. If my relation to my own body is the limit case of touch-ing, then I am always touching a disgusting body, as well as being constituted of one. If we dread the touch of the disgusting, we must reckon with that disgusting body with which we are always and everywhere in touch. The metamorphosis has already occurred (I return to this theme later).[1]

(ii) Disgust is a "sense-based" emotion. Fear results from beliefs about an object, to the effect that it is dangerous; its sensory appearance is as may be. But disgust is not belief-based in this way; it is triggered by, and focused on, the sensory appear-ance of the stimulus. The predicates used to justify the emotion are accordingly sensory predicates: "slimy," "smelly," "grotesque," and so on. The object makes its sensory appearance and the dis-gust response occurs; there can be no disgust before, or inde-pendently of, the sensory presentation.[2] The look, feel, taste, or smell of something determines its disgust value, not its functional or dynamic properties. It is, in this way, a primitive

1. On touch and disgust, see Miller, pp. 60–66, and Kolnai, pp. 39–45. Kolnai sug-gests that the disgusting object has a way of forcing itself on us, reaching out to us: "The disgusting object grins and smirks and stinks menacingly at us" (p. 41). It seems active and willed in its propensity to make contact with us.

2. I suppose we should include sensory imagination here too, as when I form a mental image of a disgusting object. Certainly, memory images of disgusting things can evoke the feeling of disgust quite easily.

perceptual emotion. Its behavioral expression is also primitive and non-cognitive: bodily recoil, wrinkled nose, gaping mouth, and nausea. When we are disgusted by something we do not simply make an intellectual judgment; the body is centrally implicated. We might almost say that *my body* is disgusted—as it retches and recoils. Yet, as we shall see, it is not an innate reflex, like the body's response to other noxious stimuli, such as the smell of chlorine or the taste of sour or bitter fruit. Disgust is a sensory-somatic emotion, but there is (as we shall see) a degree of cognitive sophistication to it. In any case, it is rooted in the senses, despite the way it seems to carve up the world in perceptually arbitrary ways. This is one of its puzzles: how can disgust be sense-based and yet sensitive to higher-order classifications (which we have yet to identify)?

As has often been remarked, disgust does not distribute itself across all the senses, or all equally. Different enquirers have made different choices as to the primary sense modality for disgust—some say taste, others smell, yet others select touch[3]— but all seem agreed that hearing is free of disgust triggers, except by association with other senses. Hearing something can make us afraid, but no auditory stimulus seems to elicit human disgust. To be sure, sounds can be grating, chaotic, unpleasant, and ugly—but has anyone ever vomited to a foul sound? Nor is it clear why. Can we imagine a being that responds aversively to sound as we do to visual stimuli or to olfactory stimuli? It can hardly be simply that hearing is less developed in us than vision, since smell is even more limited but a rich source of disgust. Could an intelligent bat, with its refined sonar sense, experience sounds as disgusting, as we do sights? It sends out an auditory

3. Darwin favored taste, as we see shortly. Kolnai finds smell central, writing: "For the true place of origin of disgust is the sense of smell. Disgusting smell-types present more solid unities and are less in need of associative appendages than other disgusting formations" (p. 50). Miller especially stresses contamination by touch: see chap. 4.

signal that encounters a decaying body; this signal's echo is then interpreted as a rich auditory image of that body; thereupon the bat experiences a queasy feeling in its stomach and announces its disgust. There seems no conceptual reason why not, and yet the idea seems farfetched. Is this just because of our limited imaginative grasp on the possibilities of bats' sonar experience? I don't know. I don't know what it would be like to be an aurally disgusted bat. Is it the qualia of experience that prompt disgust or the information contained in the experience? One feels that it is the precise smell of shit that evokes disgust, but maybe the same reaction could occur in a being that sensed shit differently. Fortunately, I have no need to answer such questions here.[4] As things stand, at any rate, humans do not respond with disgust to the deliverances of their auditory system (putting aside possibilities of psychological association or synesthesia). One may respond with moral or intellectual disgust, perhaps, as with a piece of music one particularly deplores, but that is not the same as reacting with the characteristic symptoms of physical disgust. Sounds don't literally nauseate; their phenomenology is disgust-free.

(iii) Disgust is, importantly, both an aversive *and* an attractive emotion. It repels us from its object, and this is surely its primary character, but it can also draw us to that object.[5] The attraction can take various forms, and the combination of

---

4. There does seem to be something to the thought that hearing fails to bring the object of perception *into* consciousness, as a presented reality, no matter how fine-grained and detailed it might be. When I hear an insect scratch the insect itself is not present in my awareness; rather, I *infer* its presence from the sound that I directly apprehend—we hear the sound not its source. So maybe bats have this kind of indirect awareness of their aurally identified objects: what they hear is the sound of an object, not an object (but we touch, see, smell, and taste objects themselves).

5. Kolnai appreciates this from the start, speaking of the "macabre allure" (p. 42) of disgusting objects; they invite our attention and seek to keep it. Simultaneously, the object draws the senses in, magnetically, and also repels them.

attraction with repulsion can be complex and subtle. This ambivalence is perhaps at its sharpest in the case of sex: we tend to find the sexual organs of the other repulsive in certain ways, and yet we can be strongly attracted to them. The peculiar phenomenology of sex (at least as many people experience it) reflects this attraction-repulsion dynamic: an element of trepidation accompanies the urge to touch, probe, and stimulate the other's genitals. Juices and ejaculate excite both sexual excitement and sexual restraint, or at least hesitation (sometimes dread). Unalloyed beauty is not to be found there, yet the senses are heightened and stimulated. The characteristic of sex is to want something urgently that generally elicits aversion. This truth becomes most apparent when sexual desire has ebbed, especially when it has been sated beyond surplus; then sexual disgust becomes all too accessible. The same is true of the mouth and kissing: we are naturally repelled by the moist and odoriferous mouth of the other, as we are by the anus, but this repulsion can be overcome if the attraction is strong enough. We won't kiss just anyone! Sexual attraction is the overcoming of a prior standing aversion, for disgust-prone humans, and the aversion persists in the overcoming, as a background condition. The character of sexual pleasure (its unique charm, we might say) lies precisely in this attraction-in-repulsion—not unlike the pleasure of eating a raw oyster, as has often been remarked. The ambivalence is part of the point.[6]

Nor is this kind of ambivalence confined to sex. Death and feces have their fascination for the human psyche, in the teeth of their repugnance—as do disease, injury, deformity, and other disgust-inducing conditions. Here is where the notion of "morbid fascination" comes in—unhealthy curiosity, sticking your nose

---

6. My remarks here are, I know, sketchy and jejune, and wholly unoriginal. I am attempting only to allude to a familiar phenomenon that could be discussed in much greater depth.

where it doesn't belong. People find themselves mesmerized by the dead body, drawn to it against their will, even as their stomach turns queasy. The bloody car accident invites the prolonged stare, along with the heaving of the innards. Even a pile of dung, human or animal, carries its quantum of fascination—so intimate, so elemental, so curiously assertive. We have to stop and look—a momentary sniff might even be indicated. Then we turn abruptly away—only to turn back after a calming interval. The disgusting exerts its demonic pull, even as it thrusts us away. We feel conflicted, confused, and disturbed. The vampire embodies this kind of ambivalence perfectly: the magnetically attractive corpse, the romantic sucker of blood, with his morbidly sepulchral beauty. There is, after all, something exciting about the disgusting, something beyond the humdrum: the disgusting is stirring, vital. Disgust sticks in the memory and vivifies the senses, even when—especially when—it is deemed most repellent. Disgust is not boring. It has a kind of negative glamour. And the human psyche is drawn to the interesting and exceptional—the charged object, with its magical potency. We are stunned at our capacity to be convulsed by the disgusting object; we marvel at its strange power. All this is compatible with feelings of intense revulsion. Consider the horrified fascination of watching a vulture tear at the gizzards of its carrion, or a cow giving messy birth, or certain types of transgressive pornography. We gaze between our fingers, stimulated and appalled simultaneously. It is hard to think of a single aversive disgust object that does not simultaneously grab the attention. We find no beauty there, nothing to invite our positive evaluation; yet we are gripped and subdued by the disgusting object, compelled to absorb its grisly pantomime. There is something almost *gleeful* in the disgust object, as it obtrudes itself importunately on our attention—a kind of wickedly shameless exhibitionism. It seems to cast a spell on us, hypnotizing us. An uncanny aura surrounds it, drawing in the senses. "Why am I staring?" we ask ourselves, and can provide no answer. Yet this undeniable fascination has its firm limits (for most of us): the strong aversion triumphs in the end, perhaps permitting only a rapid glance through half-closed eyes. We have to *know*, but we don't want to drown in the disgusting spectacle. We can only take so much of it.[7]

Certain perversions seem to result from an inability to suppress the attraction, the curiosity. Necrophilia, coprophilia, and fetishism of various stripes are cases in which aversion is eclipsed by attraction. The disgusting becomes wholly or mainly attractive, with the aversive element in retreat or silenced. Such conditions appear as extreme cases of the norm; indeed, what is arguably abnormal is the total *lack* of any attractive component in disgust-inducing situations. We are all, if you will forgive me for saying so, mildly perverted, at least potentially or on some occasions. That is, we are all fascinated by what disturbs us most, by our own responsiveness to the gross and repugnant. Some balance is required, some self-discipline; we must not succumb to the temptation to eyeball and rubberneck. We must not let our taste for novelty and excitement numb our natural sense of the disgusting; that way lies insanity or even worse. (At the same time, an ability to control disgust reactions is essential in doctors, nurses, sanitations workers, and others.) In this way the phenomena of disgust issue a challenge to character, and a complex one at that: we shouldn't feel too little of it or too much—disgust-deficiency or disgust-superfluity. We must seek the aversive mean.

---

7. We call disgust an aversive emotion, subsequently noting its attractive aspect. But a possible theoretical position is that it is an attractive emotion with an aversive overlay. Part of the psyche genuinely likes the disgusting object (we might call this part the *id*), while another part (let's call it the *superego*) dislikes it: both have their proprietary preferences. We thus have a split psyche. Such a position might maintain that the more ancient id part of the psyche is attracted, while the more recent superego part has placed strictures on the base attraction. This may be a disquieting position, but is not one to be ruled out a priori. The attractive aspect does seem quite deep-seated and robust.

(iv) Disgust exhibits a self-other asymmetry. I am naturally more repulsed by you than I am by myself, other things being equal—and yet I doubt that I am less objectively repulsive.[8] What I tolerate in myself I cannot tolerate in others. Am I then an incorrigible narcissist? If I am, then so is everyone else. Consider your attitude toward your body's waste products, compared with your attitude toward those of other people. It is a truism that your shit doesn't smell as bad to you as it does to other people, and the same is true of the revolting qualities of the other items on our list. Even dirty hands elicit a different reaction according as they belong to you or someone else. In a way, this is paradoxical—for by definition your own body is closer to you than that of others. Dirt on my hands is already *on me* and it may easily be transferred to other parts of my body, say my mouth; yet I seem far more obsessed with your dirty hands, especially if it is you making the sandwiches. It is as if I think my dirt is cleaner than your dirt! One's own genitals seem quite low on the disgust scale compared to the genitals of others; likewise for armpits, fingernails, nose, ears, and so on. It is true that self-disgust can arise in me, especially if illness or disease is involved (a gangrenous leg would not be regarded with complacence), but in general I seem remarkably unmoved where my own disgustingness is concerned. True, one's own feces are not accepted as mere lumps of neutral matter, fit for self handling and self application; the habitual narcissism does not extend that far. But one finds their proximity far less off-putting than the feces of other people. Runny noses tell the same story. A survey that asked people which they would prefer to confront—their own feces at 5 feet or someone else's at 20 feet—would produce a predictable result.

What is the ground of this asymmetry? Obviously it cannot be that one's own disgust objects are further way from one than

8. I have not seen this point made by others, not explicitly anyway; yet it seems quite obvious. It poses a difficult theoretical challenge.

other people's (hence the paradox)—which would explain why I regard X's products as less repulsive than Y's, given that X is farther away from me than Y. The natural answer to the puzzle is that I am simply more *used* to my own products: I am habituated to them, by dint of sheer repetition. But I don't think this explanation works. I can report that I have not become habituated to my own bodily products over time—they seem about the same in disgust value to me now as they did thirty or more years ago. There has been no general falling off of self-directed disgust by sheer repetition. Nor have I become more at ease in the presence of other people's products the longer I have lived; again, this has remained pretty constant for decades. Repetition has not lessened my disgust responses in either case. Moreover, professionals whose daily job is to tend to the bodies of the sick and old, and who seem to become somewhat accustomed to what may initially have appalled them, *still* show the asymmetry in question. The trained nurse, all bedpans and sponge baths, may have become habituated to the excretions of the body, maintaining a steady stomach where lesser mortals would quiver, but I am morally certain she still regards her own body with greater equanimity than the thousandth incontinent patient to whom she has attended. In fact, I suspect that her composure in the presence of the disgusting is more a matter of behavioral suppression than deep affective modification. Certainly, one's own composure about one's own body is not the result of rigorous training and iron self-control. On the contrary, it comes naturally and requires no effort: it isn't that I have had to *force* myself to tolerate my own feces because I know that every day for the rest of my life I will have to be in their aromatic presence. Neither have I experienced any process of involuntary habituation—any more than food has come to taste less pleasant to me simply because I have eaten a lot of it over the years. In fact, disgust reactions to stimuli in general seem pretty robust over a lifetime, with hardly any habituation effect at all. So the asymmetry has nothing to do with the greater frequency or proximity of my contacts with my own disgusting nature.[9]

The asymmetry thus appears firm and universal, not reflective of contingent facts about frequency of contact and the like. It is simply the known fact that the products come *from me* that makes the difference—that they are *mine*.[10] If someone tricked me into believing that what are in fact my own feces belong to someone else and invited me to register my disgust reaction to them, then I am sure it would be for me just as if the material in question did come from another person; and similarly, if I were led to believe that someone else's were mine. It is not as if one's excretory products carry the unmistakable mark of one's identity upon them; rather, one's fallible belief about their origin is what makes them acceptable or unacceptable. The explanatory question raised is why this belief about origin should be determinative of our disgust reactions, since the sensory impact of the substances would be the same no matter what their origin. The reaction is indisputably sensory in its target, but beliefs about non-sensory facts constrain and

9. Suppose I have been artificially deprived of sensory contact with my own feces, but exposed to the feces of others: then my frequency of perceptual contact has been greater in the latter case than the former. Would I then, upon initial exposure to my feces, find them more repulsive than the feces of others, because of a habituation effect? Somehow I doubt it: it is the fact that I know whose is whose that counts, not the statistical frequency of contact.

10. Might it be that I have a stronger sense of my own psychological identity than I have of other people's, and that I regard my waste products as more *extraneous* to my identity than I do in the case of others? *I* am not to be intimately associated with the waste products produced my body, but other people are more identified by me with their waste products. I think of others as more body and myself as more mind, so I take myself to be further removed ontologically from my body than other people are from theirs (as I apprehend them). Accordingly, I find my body less offensive, because less constitutive of what I am. There is a clear asymmetry here, but whether it really explains the asymmetry of disgust is less clear; still, the suggestion is worth considering.

modify the affective reaction to the sensory stimulus: the stimulus somehow *smells* different given one's belief about who produced it—or at any rate, the smell is differently registered in the two cases. Again, one would hope that a good theory of the disgusting could shed light on this curious asymmetry (I have some ideas, to be developed later, but the question remains perplexing). We need to find some deep structural reason for the asymmetry—something about the different *meanings* of disgust objects according to whether they belong to me or someone else. Clearly, nothing about their intrinsic material composition or perceptual *Sosein* will work, since that will be constant across different individuals; the difference will have to reside in the mere fact of personal origin and whatever significance this can be seen to have.

(v) Disgust is a response to biological, not inanimate, objects. This has been implicit in everything that has gone before. Animal organisms are the prime focus of disgust, with plants trailing a distant second. It is quite different with fear and distaste: it is entirely possible to fear machines and mountains, seas and precipices, and also possible to react with distaste to chemicals that are bad for you—as with a bitter taste. But it is not possible to be disgusted by such things. This is a very significant fact about disgust, which must condition any account of its nature. It begins to suggest a strong cognitive component to the emotion, despite its perceptual focus, given that the mind must be registering the distinction between organic and inorganic in regulating our disgust responses. Of course, it is possible to provoke disgust with inorganic materials so long as these materials simulate the organic; what seems impossible is to produce disgust with something recognized by the subject to be inorganic—as it might be, bits of metal and plastic. An impression of life substances must be present in the disgusting stimulus. This fact must strike us as significant, because certain objects that share many of the physical features of disgusting things are not themselves found disgusting—I mean things that are greasy, slimy, sticky, dirty, leaking, deformed, decaying, and so on. Take a car that is peeling and rusting, with oil leaking from the engine, beaten up, scratched, with ripped seats, maybe sticky and dirty: it would be an offense to the senses, perhaps, but would it elicit genuine disgust? Would a car enthusiast find himself feeling nauseous in its presence, as if to a rotting corpse? I very much doubt it. The "decaying" car lacks living tissue, with all that this implies; it may sadden but it cannot disgust. The ruins of old buildings are much the same, or cratered rocky surfaces, or spewing volcanoes, or decrepit statues, or soaked blankets. There are some perceptual resemblances to disgusting organisms here, but the substrate of organic tissue is missing, crucially so. The putrefying corpse is in a different affective category from that of crumbling buildings and collapsing bridges. Even a robot, built to look like a man, will not elicit disgust, no matter how much it may leak (so long as the leaking substance is not organic). Rusting is never the equivalent of putrefaction. The inorganic can only excite disgust if it is made to mimic the organic, fooling the audience (as with fake blood or plastic do-do); but this is quite hard to accomplish (fake blood is usually made with an organic material), and it shows the utter dependence of the disgusting on the perceived-to-be-organic. Fear and hatred can go beyond the organic (one might conceivably hate a conscious robot, made of metal, for its evil acts), but disgust is more selective in its chosen objects. In this, I think, lies an important clue to what makes disgust the emotion it is. Disgust and organic life go hand in hand.[11]

11. This point is often remarked on by writers on disgust, but its theoretical significance is less commonly appreciated. It pushes disgust in a more abstract cognitive direction, away from simple sensory features; the conceptual distinction between life and non-life is integral to it. How the concept of organic life should be defined is a further question, and not an easy one (are reproduction and digestion sufficient conditions?).

(vi) Disgust is not, apparently, experienced by animals and small children.[12] This fact subverts the natural idea that disgust is simply a response to the sensory quality of the disgusting stimulus. Consider feces again: adult humans tend to find them excruciatingly repulsive, but animals and children don't—yet the sensory stimulus is surely the same for both groups. Animals will home in for the intimate sniff, quite unperturbed, while human infants think nothing of playing barehanded with shit: but surely the stuff looks, feels, and smells the same to all concerned. Sometimes it is assumed that this shows that disgust must be learned, that it is not instinctive or innate. That doesn't exactly follow from the data, however: from the fact that children don't show disgust reactions till between 3 and 7 years it cannot be inferred that there is no genetic basis for the emotion, since it is quite common for genetic programs to begin manifesting themselves some years after birth—as with language development and puberty. It may be genetically determined that the disgust faculty will start to operate at a certain stage of childhood development, having initially gone through a kind of latency period. To settle the question of innateness we would need further data from individuals not subject to toilet training and so on. Even if no disgust reaction were found to develop spontaneously in children (say, feral children), it still would not follow that the faculty is learned not innate, since the innate program might need a triggering outside stimulus to manifest itself, as with normal language development. I myself suspect that it is innately based, because of its resilience, universality,

12. It is interesting to connect the developmental theory of disgust with other aspects of the maturing child's mind, in particular the child's grasp of the concept of mind (as in "theory of mind" studies). Is there a correlation between the onset of disgust and a grasp of the concept of mind? My later reflections suggest that the two might well be intertwined, because of the way disgust embeds an understanding of the mind-body connection—but this will become clear only later.

and involuntariness. But we don't need to settle that empirical question here: what is important is that disgust emerges in humans, uniquely so, only at a certain stage of cognitive and affective development. Certain high-level psychological prerequisites are apparently required; it is not simply a reflex response to a nasty taste, bypassing all cognitive input. As will become clear later, I believe that disgust rests upon a fairly rich cognitive background, involving sophisticated conceptualizations. This background may or may not proceed from an innate basis—a kind of "universal disgust grammar"—but it has a much richer structure than a simple sensory-motor reflex, such as the eye blink or the automatic rejection of bitter-tasting substances. In my view, disgust rests upon certain *thoughts* about the world, specifically in relation to life and death. Thus the child reaches a stage of maturation in which certain conceptions take shape in his or her mind—certain facts about the world are recognized and understood—and this is the necessary backdrop to the emotion of disgust. I am skeptical of the idea that it is parental toilet training that is responsible for developing disgust—as if the child has to be bludgeoned or conditioned into believing that excrement is nasty and simply accepts what he or she is told. It is not a matter of the inculcation of habitual responses by reward and punishment. Rather, the child must come to grasp that certain facts obtain, and then appreciate that disgust is an *appropriate* reaction to these facts. My view is that the child spontaneously grasps certain general principles—a *schema*, if you like—and that he or she then generalizes these to a wide range of cases, in much the same way that grammatical principles are grasped and applied generally.[13] These principles

---

13. Obviously, I am following Chomsky here, suggesting that disgust rests upon innately specified abstract principles that constrain its development. We don't, then, learn to be disgusted, as we don't learn language; we merely add culturally specific detail to a universal innate mental structure.

go deep into the nature of things, and are quite abstract in character, metaphysical almost. The child is not just a repository of conditioned habits, operating separately and serially, that have been inculcated by adults during a course of training. The child has not been conditioned to respond to this and that with disgust, but not to certain other things; rather, he or she has worked out a general schema of disgust, quite abstract in character, that is then applied to a range of disparate phenomena.

That abstract schema allows for some plasticity in the final outcome (rather like the case of language). Thus a measure of individual and cultural variation will be exhibited in what is found disgusting (for example, in which things are deemed acceptable to eat), but the general shape of the disgust reaction will be universal and robust. In this, the case will be much like language and other innate cognitive systems. For instance, we would expect to find that putrefaction and excrement will be universal disgust objects, while there can be variation in which animals are found repellent, or which sexual practices. Like the psycholinguist, then, my task is to identify the general principles involved, thus obtaining a picture of the cognitive structures that come to exist in the child's mind as he or she begins to respond with disgust to assorted stimuli. Animals can be presumed to lack these structures, which is why they exhibit no disgust to speak of: they just don't *conceive* the world in a certain way. A specific cognitive set-up is required in order that perceptual stimuli shall elicit the aversive disgust reaction; the stimuli by themselves are not sufficient. So, although the disgust reaction is geared to sensory presentations as triggers, it incorporates non-sensory components that make the emotion possible. The perceptual stimuli have to be *interpreted* by the subject according to a certain conception of their meaning—of how they fit into the wider world. Not to put too fine a point on it, the stimuli have to be seen as *representing* something beyond themselves—as signs of a deeper truth.[14]

We can already see that a simple survival-based account of disgust will not work; the emotion cannot be explained by elementary considerations of biological utility. Disgust is not *useful* in the straightforward way that fear and distaste are. Animals have plenty to fear and accordingly fear abundantly—the emotion helps them avoid predators and the like. It is also useful to have taste buds that signal when something will be poisonous or non-nutritious, and animals are thus endowed too. But disgust is not adaptive in this way, which is why animals don't bother with it. In humans no obvious biological need is served by our disgust reactions, considered in their totality; the emotion instead reflects something about how we understand the world, and our place in it, and what kind of being we are. It is, in a sense, a *philosophical* emotion—a result of high-level conceptualization. Babies and animals, not being philosophers, have no time for it, but cognitively mature adult humans cannot escape being philosophers— and disgust comes with the philosophical territory. But this will become clear (I hope) when we come to consider the explanation of disgust—what the general principles are that underpin it. For now, I note the inaccessibility of disgust, in the form in which we adult humans possess it, to animals and infants, and observe that this must reflect something of its sophistication and cognitive presuppositions. Disgust is an *advanced* emotion—and hence a late arrival on the evolutionary and ontogenetic scene.[15]

---

14. I see this as part of a general thesis of "innate metaphysics" with a Kantian ring: that is, there is an innate system of quite abstract categories that enter into the formation of cognitions and emotions—concepts like *object*, *causation*, *organic*, *mind*, *space*, *time*, and so on. As will emerge, I think the cognitive component of disgust brings in these kinds of highly general concepts, which are probably innately laid down.

15. Disgust belongs with such emotions as shame, pride, and guilt in having a sophisticated conceptual underpinning, involving evaluations and self-representations. Animals and infants don't have these kinds of emotions either.

(vii) Disgust can claim to be "encapsulated." Just as visual illusions are not modifiable by knowledge or belief about the real state of things, so the disgust reaction cannot be altered simply by will or cognitive enhancement.[16] In other words, we can't help what disgusts us—just as we can't help seeing the lines of the Muller-Lyer illusion as unequal in length. I may tell myself that the decaying corpse I am now seeing and smelling is really quite harmless, that it would be better for me if I could retain my cool in its presence, but I won't be able thereby to turn off my disgust reaction. By contrast, if I come to believe that something I took to be dangerous is really quite harmless, then my fear will retreat; but nothing I can learn will enable me to quell the disgust I feel about an object that is turning my stomach. The disgustingness of a stimulus cannot be overridden by knowledge or belief or brute willpower.[17] I may think my life would be better if I could banish all disgust from it, and I may firmly believe that disgust is irrational and groundless, and yet I will be as susceptible as ever to the usual array of disgust objects. Nothing you can say to me can make me stop feeling disgusted, no matter how much I am persuaded by your words. Disgust is insulated from the rest of the psyche—an encapsulated module. In this, it is quite different from fear and hatred, as well as belief formation. Perhaps this is not surprising in the light of its perceptual character: we cannot help *seeing* the world a certain way, no matter what our beliefs about it may be. There is something

16. I am using Jerry Fodor's concept of encapsulation, developed in *The Modularity of Mind*. Paul Griffiths applies the concept to the case of emotions, including disgust, in *What Emotions Really Are: The Problem of Psychological Categories*. (I see no necessary conflict between the encapsulation thesis and the idea that disgust has complex cognitive presuppositions: it is not a type of belief or judgment.)

17. Paul Rozin's experiments confirm this picture: plastic feces and sterilized roaches still elicit disgust even when they are known to be such—the sensory *Sosein* is not so easily overridden. See the survey article "Disgust" by Rozin, Haidt and McCauley.

automatic about disgust, like feeling pain at a pinprick. It would not be wrong to speak of the disgust *reflex*. It works rather like jamming the fingers in the back of the throat.

It may be felt that this encapsulation thesis is at best exaggerated. Don't people sometimes overcome their initial natural disgust by sustained effort? Can't love work to mitigate or even suspend disgust? (It might also be wondered whether long-term, highly motivated effort might overcome visual illusions—so far as I know, there are no empirical data bearing on this question. I doubt it, though.) I think we have to be careful in interpreting such cases. To be sure, will power can help suppress the behavioral symptoms of disgust, and may even reduce strong initial disgust; but that is not to say that it can *nullify* disgust, that is, simply erase it from the psyche. The dedicated nurse can negotiate her feelings of disgust, not revealing them, bracketing them; but I doubt that she can simply eliminate them from her mind, or replace them with something positive. No amount of self-admonition to the effect that one *ought* not to feel disgust will simply make it disappear.[18] The case is somewhat like the sensation of vertigo: it wells up involuntarily and no amount of firm conviction of one's physical safety can make it go away. It would therefore be quite wrong to think of disgust as a kind of *judgment*, since judgments precisely are susceptible to revision from other judgments (they belong in the "central system"), but disgust is not sensitive to what the subject judges about the world at all. A disgusting odor, say, cannot be rendered affectively neutral by coming to believe that it emanates from something innocuous. Disgust, we may say, bypasses the rational faculties: it is reflexive, not deliberative. We do not *decide* to be disgusted, nor can we decide not to be.[19]

18. Miller's report of St. Catherine of Siena's self-induced ordeals of disgust is quite extraordinary and shows how hard it is to control the disgust response: see pp. 158–9

19. The fact that disgust can be characterized as a type of sensation fits with the encapsulation thesis. We might call it "affective perceiving"—we perceive in an

(viii) Disgustingness is not—perhaps surprisingly—a secondary quality, defined dispositionally. If I apply the predicate "disgusting" to an object, I do not attribute a property that is defined according to a disposition to produce the disgust response in some selected group of subjects. Disgustingness is not relational in this way. It isn't that a given type of object cannot produce disgust in one group and non-disgust in another group; my point is rather that in such a case one group will be right and the other wrong. Disgustingness, I contend, is an objective property, not a subjective or relative property.[20] Humans find feces disgusting and crystals non-disgusting; but suppose that Martians invert this pattern of response—feces are lovely for them, while crystals bring nausea and the other symptoms of disgust. Let us suppose that the Martians really do feel the very same sensation in the presence of crystals that we feel when confronted with feces. Should we say that neither of us is wrong in our reactions, since to *be* disgusting just is to *seem* disgusting (to normal subjects in a sufficiently large group etc.)? Do Martians speak the truth when they say, "Crystals are disgusting, but feces are not," just as we do when we say, "Feces are disgusting, but crystals are not"—since the property in question is defined relatively? I think that intuitively this is quite wrong—there is really nothing at all disgusting about crystals! The Martians are making some strange error of judgment, or are victims of an emotional pathology. We might discover that they also think gold is disgusting, or triangular shapes, while relishing

---

affective mode. Another example of this kind of psychological state is our experience of beauty: we perceive an object in the mode of responding affectively to its beauty. The perception and the emotion merge indissolubly together.

20. I know this will sound surprising at first, because disgustingness seems so close to being *found* disgusting; but bear with me, the connection is not as close as with typical secondary qualities.

the aroma of rotting flesh and dining on mucus pie. We can't deny that they feel that way, but we don't have to agree that they are getting things right (they might also disagree with us over the primary qualities of things—and here they might well be simply under an illusion). Intuitively, we want to say that crystals don't *merit* the disgust response, while feces and mucus do—thus signaling our conviction that the property of disgustingness is not to be defined subjectively. There is something about feces themselves that justifies the disgust response, and crystals lack that something; there is a "fact of the matter" about whether an object is really disgusting. The same can be said of the property of being fearsome, since a harmless object does not have that property, whether or not people are actually afraid of it. To be fearsome a thing has to be actually dangerous, to *merit* the fear response. But, it may be asked, what stands to the emotion of disgust as danger stands to fear? What *makes* an object inherently disgusting, independently of whether people are actually disgusted by it? Well, that is the question we are in the business of trying to answer: we are trying to find out what constitutes an object as disgusting. When we have an answer to that question, then we shall know what it is about certain objects that warrants the disgust response. And it will turn out that this is a perfectly objective property of things—a property possessed by feces but not by crystals. Accepting that correct theory, the Martians themselves might come to the view that they are indeed subject to a strange sort of delusion—they find things disgusting that objectively are not! (In fact, it is hard to see how they could make this kind of mistake to begin with, because it is so obvious that crystals, gold, and triangles are *not* disgusting.) Things are therefore not disgusting simply in virtue of the fact that people *take* them to be, with the possibility of equally correct but different modes of taking. There is something that *grounds* the disgust response, making it appropriate or inappropriate. Accordingly, disgustingness is not, upon careful analysis, a secondary quality.[21]

(ix) Disgust often gives rise to comedy and embarrassment. Scatological humor abounds, as do jokes about death and sex. We laugh about the things that disgust us. This is connected with the fact that disgusting things are often embarrassing things. Discomfort is the underlying factor. We joke about shit because we find it embarrassing and are discomforted by it.[22] Issues of respect and social status are bound up with it too. Farting in public is embarrassing, discomforting, and also funny—all too redolent of the disgusting body that is with us always. Why should these secondary emotions attach to disgust? Why is shit found to be so funny and discomforting? We would like our theory of the disgusting to shed light on these associations—to explain why the secondary emotions attach themselves to the underlying emotion of disgust. What are the background thoughts that generate disgust *such that* they also give rise to humor and embarrassment? What are we thinking in the area of disgust that naturally produces our feelings of disquiet and absurdity? What is the *content* of disgust that it should bring with it such troubled comedy? More pointedly, what does disgust force us to try to come to terms with? What sensitive psychic spot does it agitate? In the next section, I shall set about answering these questions.

21. Disgust is like shame, its close emotional cousin, in this respect: an act is not shameful because people are *in fact* ashamed of it—the act has to *warrant* shame (just as a joke is not funny simply because people laugh at it—it has to *merit* laughter). Something is (really) disgusting if and only if it is *right* to be disgusted at it. We need the idea of a normative response–dependent concept: the response enters the analysis of the concept, but in a de jure not a de facto way. This allows room for widespread errors about what is disgusting or not.

22. Freud famously regarded humor as the release of repression, centering on sexual desires. I too think humor springs from repression of taboos, but not (or not typically) sexual ones: it is the release of repression about what disgusts us. Sex comes into humor, not because we have erotic desires that are deemed unacceptable, but because (roughly) sex is an area of potential disgust. Instead of feeling helpless nausea at the disgusting object, we laugh at it, thus undermining its potency. We try to make fun of what viscerally alarms us.

4

Theories of Disgust

THE MAIN THEORETICAL CHALLENGE posed by disgust is the great variety of objects that can provoke it. It is hard to see how we can bring order to this variety without selecting some disgust objects as basic and viewing others as radiating out from the central core. But the danger here is selecting a subset of disgust objects that suits the theory that is favored by the theorist; the theory then becomes too narrow. The converse danger is striving to be all-inclusive, treating all disgust objects as on a par, and then finding that the theory is too broad, including more things than are strictly speaking disgusting. I hope I shall not be found guilty of either error if I suggest that the core examples of disgust are provided by: (i) putrefied flesh, (ii) feces, and (iii) wounds. Put in terms of processes, we have bodily decay, excretion, and injury to the body. By the last of these I mean to include not only sliced or ripped flesh but also diseases that affect the integrity of the flesh, such as leprosy. I then see the other cases as branching out from these three core areas, sometimes by close resemblance, sometimes more tenuously. At any rate, that is to be my working hypothesis, to be tested by examining all the cases earlier listed in the light of whatever theory we are considering. I don't think the risk of excessive narrowness will be too great if we insist on covering these three basic cases. I also think it is a mistake to single out one perceptual modality as primary, in the sense that all the others register disgust derivatively from that one: vision, taste, smell, and touch should all be accorded their rights in assessing any proposed theory; and only a strong argument should persuade us that one sense is basic and the rest derivative.[1] I think each sense could by itself register disgust in a subject, even if the other senses did not exist in that subject (not so for hearing, which really does register disgust only derivatively); so, for instance, there could be visual disgust in the absence of olfactory disgust, and vice versa. In other words, any theory of disgust needs to be evenhanded, both as to cases and as to sense modalities, though some selection of basic cases seems inevitable. With these conditions of adequacy in mind, let me now consider some theories, beginning with what I take to be the least plausible.

(a) The Taste-Toxicity Theory. This is the theory originally proposed by Darwin, and sanctioned by the etymology of the word. In *The Expression of Emotions in Man and Animals*, Darwin writes: "The term 'disgust,' in its simplest sense, means something offensive to the taste. It is curious how readily this feeling is excited by anything unusual in the appearance, odour, or nature of our food... A smear of soup on a man's beard looks disgusting, though there is of course nothing disgusting in the soup itself. I presume that this follows from the strong association in our minds between the sight of food, however circumstanced,

---

1. I distinguish this from the claim that one sense is *paradigmatic*, as I suggest touch may be. Touch provides the model, the basic form, but that is not to say that other senses don't register disgust in their own right. We could, in principle, experience disgust and have no tactile sense at all, via smell, taste, and sight—yet those senses register disgust because of their touch-like features. It is not that only touch truly registers disgust and the other senses do so derivatively or by association; rather, the other senses embed contact-like elements. It is not too much to say that all senses approximate to the condition of touch— they all involve impingement and proximity. Probably touch was the first sense to evolve.

and the idea of eating it."[2] The English word "disgust" has the same root as "gustatory," so in its original meaning it is synonymous with "unpleasant to taste." Thus, the soup in the beard strikes us as disgusting because we would find it disagreeable to taste the food thus bespattered. And the same would be true, for Darwin, in the case of other disgust objects: rotting flesh, internal organs, feces, snot, bugs, warts—these are all things we are reluctant to put in our mouths, chew, and swallow. We are disgusted by a thing perceived, then, just when we think of ingesting it and know it to be either toxic or nasty tasting; so visual disgust, say, depends upon gustatory disgust. A disgusting object is simply one that we would reject as food, whether this rejection is mediated by taste itself or some other sense that does duty for taste. A poisonous substance will thus be the most disgusting thing of all, while anything nutritious (and taken to be so) will be exempt from disgust. Natural selection has installed disgust in us, according to this theory, as a protective device, to ward off toxic foodstuffs.[3] Thus, we regard fresh-cooked meat as wholesome, but are disgusted by rotten contaminated meat. And we regard vegetables as acceptable, but not the feces that result from their digestion. Disgust is geared to edibility, nourishment, and health.

As a theory of the original meaning of the English word "disgust," this is unexceptionable, since the word is defined spe-

2. Darwin, pp. 256–257. Darwin's theory is discussed by Miller, chap. 1, Menninghaus, pp. 183–184, and Rozin et al, pp. 637–638. The idea that disgust arises from the sense of taste is not unique to Darwin: Rozin rejects it, as a general account of disgust as it now exists, but is more sympathetic to the idea that disgust had an evolutionary origin in food rejection. That may be true, though the emotion is now quite far removed from its biological origin.

3. Darwin's beard example ill suits his own general theory, because the beard does not make the food toxic exactly—just as food chewed by someone else is not converted into a poison. So that cannot be the *reason* the food in the beard is found disgusting. What Darwin is searching for, obviously, is a neat adaptationist explanation of disgust—which looks unlikely.

cifically by reference to taste and what is palatable or unpalatable. But the word now has a much more capacious meaning, and it is *this* meaning that we are trying to capture. The German word "ekel" is not defined by reference to taste at all, and German writers have accordingly not followed the model of Darwin in restricting the concept to taste.[4] That is fortunate because the theory faces some obvious counterexamples. It is not a necessary condition for something to found disgusting that it be, or be believed to be, in any way toxic or non-nourishing: many animals that we find disgusting are not regarded as toxic or lacking in nutritional value—rats and bats, slugs and insects—and many a child jibs at eating fat, though she has no wish to maintain that fat is toxic or low in calories. Would you no longer find yourself disgusted by rotting corpses if you learned that they make a tasty and healthy meal? Blood is found repellent but is not nutritionally deficient, not to mention fresh raw heart and kidney. For many items, it is not that we find them disgusting because we reject them as food, but rather that we reject them as food because we antecedently find them disgusting— judgments of nutritional value play no role here. Nutritious human feces, if such there could be, would not be rendered acceptable just by that fact (imagine if some clever scientist found a way to recycle shit as food, without changing its *Sosein*). Nor is it sufficient for an object to be found disgusting that it be toxic or nutritionally lacking. That would make disgusting most of the inanimate world, to start with, since most inorganic things are not edible—metals, for instance. A foul or bitter taste in the mouth causes food rejection, but not necessarily emotional disgust, as with certain chemicals. Bad tasting is not the

4. See Menninghaus, chap. 1. He complains that English-speaking writers on disgust, for example Miller, ignore the rich contributions of German-speaking writers on the topic—evidently justly. His own work displays an astounding breadth of scholarship, as well as keen theoretical insight.

same as disgust producing. Thus being toxic or non-nutritious is neither necessary nor sufficient for being disgusting. In certain cases, disgust tracks toxicity, but in general the relation is far too loose to build a comprehensive theory around. Even if disgust began as a protective response to bad food, way back in evolutionary history, it has long since lost exclusive contact with that primitive biological imperative. And let it be noted also that the absence of disgust from animals and infants gives the lie to any attempt to ground adult human disgust on a general requirement to protect the organism from bad food—since animals and infants obviously share this need. They spit things out well enough without feeling the emotion of disgust. Finding something to taste bad, or to cause an upset stomach, or even malnutrition, has nothing essentially to do with the emotion of disgust. The only solid connection here is that if we find something disgusting, we don't want it to touch our mouth or ingest it—not because it won't nourish us, but simply because we don't want that kind of contact with what disgusts us.[5] Great man though he was, Darwin was off on the wrong foot here. And one general lesson to derive from this failure is that it is unlikely that we will find any simple biological purpose that disgust serves: that is, it is not a simple adaptation—any more than our aesthetic sense in general is. Disgust is more sophisticated and subtle than that.

(b) The Foul-Odor Theory. One of the problems with the taste-toxicity theory is that many disgusting objects are found to be so when not actually in the mouth of the subject and when there is no intention to consume them; then it is necessary to

---

5. Darwin's bearded man offends us primarily because we find hair in the mouth offensive—soup in the hair is like hair in the soup. Oral incorporation of other people's hair is generally found repellent, especially when mixed with food: but this is not because we think hair is poisonous (we wouldn't like harmless fingernails and food together either). There are reasons for not wanting things to have contact with the mouth that have nothing to do with simple toxicity.

posit that we are *subjunctively* disgusted—if the object *were* in our mouth, then we *would* find it distasteful. Linking disgust to smell overcomes this kind of objection, since smell takes in much more of the surrounding world than taste (you can smell things you are not currently tasting). And certainly, the olfactory sense is one that registers the disgusting stimulus with remarkable intensity—with indecent intimacy, one might say.[6] Is the disgusting, then, simply that which smells bad? Two of our basic cases confirm this theory—the putrescent and the fecal—and the characteristic stink is surely a large part of the sensory basis of disgust in these cases. Would rotting flesh and fresh excrement seem so revolting if they were sweet-smelling? Would the gorge rise at their presence if it weren't for the evil odor? Is the mere sight of them sufficient, with the olfactory aspect totally eliminated, even by memory and association? What if feces smelt like chocolate and corpses like roses? These questions have force, and might prompt the idea that disgust and foul smells are bound inextricably together—that the nose is the primary organ of disgust registration.

But again there are problems of necessity and sufficiency. Many examples show that things can be found disgusting that do not offend the nostrils. Wounds and bodily malformations of many kinds do not smell bad, if at all—warts, for instance. Nor do internal organs give off much of an odor. Most bodily secretions have little to no olfactory effect (ear wax, semen), and certainly do not depend on such an effect for their disgust potency. Animals that revolt us don't smell very different from animals that we enjoy, and some smell hardly at all yet still strike many as utterly abhorrent (e.g., snakes). Sagging old flesh smells

6. Kolnai stresses smell, describing it as "the true place of origin of disgust" (p. 50). He writes: "through the organ of smell small parts of the alien object become incorporated into the subject, which makes an intimate grasping of the alien object [*Sosein*] possible. It is in the *intimacy* made possible by the sense of smell that there is rooted its primary significance for disgust" (p. 50). Note that the notion of intimacy here brings in tactile contact.

exactly like young firm flesh. Dirt can be odorless, while being visually offensive, as well as sticky to the touch. So: many things are found disgusting that are guilty of no olfactory infraction.[7] As to sufficiency, there are many bad-smelling things that are not reacted to with disgust: mustard gas and chlorine have an unpleasant smell, for example, but do not provoke disgust. Such smells signal a potentially dangerous substance and so prompt retreat from the source, but this defensive reaction is not a case of disgust—any more than nasty tastes always evoke the emotion of disgust. Fear may well be produced by such smells, but that is a very different matter, as we have seen. Associated evil odors may characterize certain core cases of disgust, but they don't constitute the *essence* of the category—however important they may be to the disgusting aspect of those core cases. In fact, I believe that corpses and feces *would* still be found disgusting, though maybe less so, if the smell factor were eliminated; indeed, I incline to the view that the bad smell we experience in these cases is a *product* of an independently established disgust reaction. In other words, we find these things to smell bad because we *already* find the source of the associated odors disgusting: the same phenomenal smell from another source would not have an identical repellent power for us (though it is hard to see this because we are so accustomed to the association). In a possible world in which roses gave off the scent produced in the actual world by feces, the people would not be revolted by roses as we are by feces: knowledge of the nature of the source affects the affective response (more on this later). It is a mistake to try to *reduce* the emotion of disgust to

---

7. Would complete loss of the sense of smell (with no olfactory memory either) remove disgust from feces? That seems highly doubtful: touching and tasting them would remain off-limits. I think myself that the disgust produced by the smell of feces largely derives from the simultaneous apprehension, by perception and memory, of their tactile and visual qualities; smell concentrates or funnels these other modalities. The senses interact in a single moment of disgust consciousness.

its sensory trigger, as if the trigger can do all the work of producing the emotion; in fact, the emotion arises from the way the trigger is interpreted—and this can involve general principles not contained in the trigger, but brought to it. Corpses and feces smell bad to us, at least in part, because of what those smells *mean* to us—because of what corpses and feces *are* (or so I shall maintain). In short: a person could be capable of disgust and not have a nose at all, so long as she thought about the world in a certain way and could perceive it by means of other sense modalities. This is why animals don't feel disgust—the lack of cognitive substructure—despite their generally superior sense of smell (I would bet that feces smell a lot *stronger* to a dog than to us, despite the notorious canine tolerance of such odors). Smell can indeed be a rich source of disgust, but it is not what disgust consists in. In fact, a case can be made that the disgust aspect of disgust-inducing smells owes a lot to the *tactile* dimension of smell: the actual physical presence of molecules from the smelly object *in* the nose, and the phenomenological sense of immediate contact with the foul object—as if the object were coating you, enveloping you, entering you, holding you in its noxious embrace. Bad smells repel us so because the source seems to be acting magically at a distance *on* us—reaching out to touch us with its abhorrent being. By virtue of their penetrating odor, feces, say, seem to grow tentacles that intrude upon our bodily space, leaving a foul residue on our person. To smell something is to be touched by it, literally and metaphorically. Smell offends because of its affinity with touch.[8]

8. That is, contact and contamination go together. The worst smell is the smell of the noxious substance *on* you, as when you step in dog shit. The nose is telling you that contact has occurred and contamination must follow. The closer the object the more offensive its smell becomes, because the threat of contact has increased. Touch is probably the most basic sense biologically, because the contact of objects with the organism is so important to its survival; the other senses warn of potential contacts. The body's boundaries accordingly carry huge psychological weight.

(c) The Animal-Heritage Theory. We tend to think of ourselves as special: as superior, distinguished, unique, with a dash of the divine running through our silken veins. We stand proudly above nature, with the other animals arrayed beneath us. Nor is this grand self-conception—this species narcissism—without foundation or warrant. For we do possess language, science, art, philosophy, and a moral sense. Among evolved beings we are, in some respects, definitely a cut above. In some traditions, this biological distinction is described as the possession of a *soul*, which other animals are said to lack. We are supposed to have been created by God, himself a perfect being, with none of the marks of the animal, at least in the core of our identity. Or, in another tradition, we have created God, as a projection of *our* special being—godly being what we are, or aspire to be, in our essence. We are not merely biological; indeed, in our inner being we are not biological at all. Yet when we contemplate our existence in its entirety we cannot altogether escape our animal nature: we too must die, and rot; we must eat, digest, and excrete; we cannot reproduce without recourse to the messy process of copulation. The body is a locus of disgust, a gruesome biological engine. Maybe we are not so special after all? Acknowledging the facts of our bodily identity, we feel brought down a peg or two, demoted in the grand scheme of things. Feces are not so grand, and yet we live by means of their production; without them we are nothing. This thought can be hard to bear. We want the focus to be on our godlike side, but our biological side keeps asserting itself. We squirm at our own mode of being, as if we are worms (and actually food for worms in the end). We have no trouble accepting that other animals are temporary packages of squelchy fragile tissue, subject to the deep laws of organic existence, but we feel ourselves inwardly to transcend such base material. It is sobering and lowering to recognize that we are not so different from them after all. Anything that presses this point home will occasion discomfort, as our vaunted quasi-divinity dissolves into the mess of organic reality. And we are reminded of it continually, just by our own experience of our bodies. We strive for ontological distance from our animal bodies, for spiritual transcendence, but we must accept that everything we are depends on them.[9]

It is then a natural thought that the disgusting is what drives home our biological roots. To be confronted by our own feces and other aspects of our organic being is to have our nose rubbed in the repellent facts of our real nature as animals like other animals. We are special, but not special enough—not sufficiently transcendent. The prime objects of disgust are simply those things that remind us of our kinship with the broader biological world. To be disgusted at the human body is just to acknowledge the disagreeable truth about our own nature— that we are dirty animals too. Put in terms of evolution, disgust objects assert our evolutionary continuity with the more ancient animal world—the heritage we carry with us of where we came from (and where we are going). Disgust is our response to that part of our nature that demotes us from our supposed position of godlike stature—a part we can neither deny nor escape. Even our loftiest thoughts, our most profound moral insights, depend in the end on the energy we derive from masticated food, once that commodity has undergone the gruesome process of digestion, ending in the expulsion of foul-smelling waste products. Shit, shockingly, is the sine qua non of the soul. That thought occasions a kind of scandalized repugnance. Disgust is the emotion we feel when we are forced to confront our animal nature— our immersion in the biological world inhabited by rats and worms, digestion and death. We are disgusted by the world of worms because we see that we live in that world too, and the fact

---

9. This will be the main theme of Part Two; I merely touch on it here.

does not sit well with us. Indeed, the central core of the body—what the whole contraption relies upon—is itself a wormlike entity: the alimentary canal, beginning at the mouth and ending at the anus, is like a worm coiled through our body, mindlessly converting living things into dung. It is a blind, consuming, voracious tube. That primordial worm, stretched through every animal body, is surrounded by other soulless organs and tissues, scarcely less repellent (with the repulsive brain, seat of all our pretensions, perched ghoulishly at the top): but structurally and functionally it is still a worm. The intestines *look* like a big squashed worm. We feel disgust at ourselves because knowledge of our biological nature drives home our immanence in the world of wriggling, damp, organisms—that world we pride ourselves on standing above. A real god would feel no such emotion, being wholly removed from the organic universe; but we are condemned to live in two worlds—the world of the transcendent soul and the world of the digesting body. We are a disgusted species because we are a *species*.

An analysis of disgust along these lines has been proposed by Paul Rozin, the psychologist who has done the most to bring the topic of disgust to scientific respectability. He writes:

> Anything that reminds us that we are animals elicits disgust. An examination of the seven domains of disgust elicitors we have identified thus far suggests that disgust serves to "humanize" our animal bodies. Humans must eat, excrete, and have sex, just like animals. Each culture prescribes the proper way to perform these actions—by, for example, placing most animals off limits as potential foods, and all animals and most people as off limits as potential sexual partners. People who ignore these prescriptions are reviled as disgusting and animal-like. Furthermore, we humans are like animals in having fragile body envelopes that, when breached, reveal blood and soft viscera that display our commonalities with animals. Human bodies, like animal bodies, die. Envelope violations and death are disgusting because they

are uncomfortable reminders of our animal vulnerability. Finally, hygienic rules govern the proper use and maintenance of the human body, and the failure to meet these culturally defined standards places a person below the level of humans. Animals are (often inappropriately) seen as dirty and inattentive to hygiene. Insofar as humans behave like animals, the distinction between humans and animals is blurred, and we see ourselves as lowered, debased, and (perhaps most critically) mortal.[10]

This is well put and I detect some glimmers of truth in these remarks, but the theory as it stands is open to telling objections, as follows.

First: is it true that anything that reminds us of our kinship with animals is found to be disgusting? If that were true, literally, then Darwin's *The Descent of Man* would be deemed a disgusting work, since it insists strenuously on our affinity with animals. So, not *all* reminders of our animal nature are objects of disgust. Second: why should our kinship with animals per se provoke disgust? Not all animals are found to be disgusting; some are regarded as cute and cuddly. The suggestion appears to be that we think of animals as inferior to us. But why should mere kinship with something deemed inferior to us occasion disgust at ourselves? We feel kinship with human children, whom we regard as our inferiors, but no resulting sense of disgust pervades our contemplation of them or rebounds back on our own self-conception. And what if you are of the opinion that animals are *not* inferior to us—that, on the contrary, we are (in many ways) inferior to them? Then being reminded of our kinship with them will elicit something more like pride than disgust. Third: not every trait of animals is found to be disgusting, just as not every

10. Rozin, "Disgust," p. 642. He cites Becker's *The Denial of Death* as a source. There is no reference to the seminal Kolnai, however.

trait of humans is—fur and feathers are not disgusting, or swift agile movement, or maternal love. If we think of our hair as similar to the feathers or fur of an animal, there is no reason on that account to feel disgust at ourselves. Only certain traits of animals are considered disgusting, but then we must have some other criterion of the disgusting than simple similarity to the traits of animals. Perhaps we find particular traits of animals disgusting because they resemble the traits in ourselves we *antecedently* find disgusting—so Rozin has put the cart before the horse.[11] We find organic processes disgusting no matter who or what possesses them; it is not that they are disgusting *because* animals have them. Suppose there were no (other) animals—we are alone on the planet and always have been. Then we could not make an invidious comparison between humans and animals, revolting at our affinities with such lowly creatures. Would we in such a situation feel no disgust about our own bodies? I think not. Besides, if we regard animals as inferior to us, then that makes us superior to them; so why doesn't the comparison make us feel better about ourselves? After all, we have a kinship of sorts to many things that we deem inferior to ourselves, such as doorknobs and grass, since we are all physical objects: but no disgust results from appreciating that kinship—just a sense of our own elevation. The kinship only generates disgust if we *already* find the thing in question disgusting: but then why do we find animals disgusting to begin with? It can hardly be that we do so because we sense a kinship between them and still lower things! Fourth: we really don't need animals to convince us that we die—we know that well enough by observing our own species. Death may play a role in

---

11. Menninghaus critically discusses Rozin's theory (pp. 223–225), making some of the points I make in the text—notably, the point that we find ourselves more disgusting than we find other animals.

accounting for disgust (see below), but awareness of animal death is not essential to appreciating that role. Finally, we like to keep some animals as pets, stroking and pampering them: *they* are not disgusting to us. Why should we not select these animals as the ones to which we are most akin? Then we won't find anything repellent about ourselves, according to that favorable comparison. The animal-heritage theory needs a reason to select the disgusting animals, but then we need to be given a criterion of the disgusting that is independent of merely being animal. If mere similarity to animals were the crux, I would find my view of myself as having catlike agility and the cunning of a fox a reason for self-disgust—which I certainly don't. And taking myself to have evolved from animals, with many of their traits still in me, is not by itself any ground for disgust at myself—it entirely depends on the traits. What if I reject the whole theory of evolution, supposing my species to have been directly created by God? Do I then abolish all reactions of disgust to my bodily nature? Hardly. What is true here is that I find aspects of my organic nature disgusting, as I do those of other animals, but the *reason* for that disgust is not that we *share* such a nature—the traits are disgusting quite independently of any such sharing. It may be true that my organic being drags me down, ontologically, mocking my intellectual and other pretensions, but this has nothing to do with my animal heritage. I would not find myself less disgusting if I became convinced that I evolved from an intellectually *superior* species, since my organic nature would still be an affront to my self-conception as a godlike entity. Interspecies comparisons have nothing to do with it. It is not that we find certain traits of animals disgusting *and then* transfer this disgust to ourselves because of a felt kinship; we feel the self-disgust anyway. In point of fact, we generally find our own organic nature *more* disgusting than that of other species, as the case of feces pungently demonstrates. I am not disgusted at myself qua animal, but qua human being.[12]

(d) The Life-Process Theory. Living organisms are what we find disgusting, even if they are recently deceased. What are their chief characteristics? There are basically two: food incorporation and offspring production. Both are rich in disgust materials, especially when we consider the machinery that makes them possible—the digestive and reproductive systems. Here it is natural to speak of an organism's "plumbing," because the anatomy that is responsible is a mass of pipes and pumps, conveyers of fluids and semi-solids—not just the intestines but the veins and arteries, and the tubes and channels of reproduction. This organic plumbing, unlike the (empty!) metal pipes of the plumbing trade, is a prime locus of human disgust. The fundamental life processes proceed through this articulation of soft and slippery pumping pipes. Should we then seek the essence of disgust in the life processes that constitute our plumbing? Is it life itself—at its raw organic foundation—that elicits our disgust? Even in death the life force pulsates and gurgles, as dead flesh is made food for bacteria and worms, resulting in the most disgusting thing of all: the rotting corpse. Putrefaction is a living process. Is it then the very processes of life that excite our disgust? William Ian Miller endorses a view like this in his excellent book *The Anatomy of Disgust* (it could

---

12. I suspect the initial plausibility of Rozin's position depends upon an equivocation in the use of the word "animal": there is the neutral use where we merely refer to other species, and there is the loaded use when we speak of "the animal in us," intending disapprobation. The latter connotes disreputable urges, organic functioning, and the non-psychological part of humanity; but the former has no such negative connotation and includes traits of animals that occasion no disgust (such as their movement and psychological traits). When we use "animal" in the latter way, we in effect point toward the part of ourselves that occasions disgust: but then the theory becomes uninformative—saying merely that we are disgusted by what disgusts us.

have been called *The Disgust of Anatomy*). Here is what he says:

> What disgusts, startlingly, is the capacity for life, and not just because life implies its correlative death and decay: for it is decay that seems to engender life. Images of decay imperceptibly slide into images of fertility and out again. Death thus horrifies and disgusts not just because it smells revoltingly bad, but because it is not an end to the process of living but part of a cycle of eternal recurrence. The having lived and the living unite to make up the organic world of generative rot—rank, smelling, and upsetting to the touch. The gooey mud, the scummy pond are life soup, fecundity itself: slimy, slippery, wiggling, teeming animal life generating spontaneously from putrefying vegetation.[13]

Life soup—a nice image: so the disgusting is the bubbling, reeking, living soup that surrounds us? Miller's words are not perhaps as analytically precise as one would wish, and no attempt is made by him to show that his "theory" can provide necessary and sufficient conditions. But I take it we know what he is driving at: the soupy processes that make life possible excite our disgust quite dependably—the soft and soggy tissues of the body, the numerous trickles and spurts of our bodily fluids. Then there is the rapid assault of the ravenous living on the dead, so that they too can digest and reproduce. Life goes forward by dint of these organic processes—the filthy plumbing of the body, with its symptoms and by-products. And these life processes are coolly oblivious to our hot wills and fervent ideals: they proceed, for the most part, automatically, performing their gruesome work behind the scenes, quietly, methodically. They are, in effect, independent agents, assertive of their rights and determined to complete their tasks (just consider the pressing

13. Miller, pp. 40–41.

bowels and their unblushing imperatives). Nor do they cringe and hide, sparing us their grotesque operation: we are made rudely aware of them whenever the need is great. The stomach will rumble, the fart will escape; the mother's water will break, and the glistening baby will be ejected. Who has the power here—the body or the mind? The body, of course, because we are biological organisms first and foremost, subject to biological laws; and anyway there can be no mind without body. The sheer force of life processes constantly astounds. Life processes and feelings of disgust thus seem intimately joined.[14]

Again, these reflections strike a plangent chord. The disgusting is indeed limited to the organic, and paradigms of the disgusting pertain to what I have designated our physiological plumbing. But again, the theory seems too undiscriminating about *what* aspects of life are deemed disgusting. Not *everything* about living organisms disgusts: the mind is not disgusting, after all, and it too is a life process, part of the biological world; nor is movement—running, leaping, swimming, flying—found disgusting. So what makes certain life processes disgusting and others not? We need an independent criterion of the disgusting to answer that question, since the concept of life itself is too broad to capture the range of objects that disgust us. Talk of soup and plumbing is all well and good, but these are metaphors, in need of literal interpretation. Additionally, the concept of life seems too *positive* a concept to provide what we seek—a basis for a strongly aversive emotion. Isn't life good, or just neutral? But disgust objects are bad in some way. Don't we celebrate life, not deplore it? If life processes are indeed disgusting (some of them at least), then we need to bring these processes under some other concept than *life*, which fails to

14. We can be more specific: what chiefly disgusts are the *generative* life processes—particularly digestion and reproduction, with their organs and fluids (and including the generation of bacterial life by the corpse).

deliver the negative punch we seek. It simply cannot be that a rotting corpse or a mound of excrement is found disgusting because it makes us *think of life*. What if we think of life in the form of a field of swaying flowers or a flock of pretty birds? Life processes may often be disgusting, but they are not disgusting qua life—that is not what *makes* them disgusting. And isn't life, in fact, the last thing we think about in the presence of these stimuli? Don't we think rather of...death? Miller subsumes death under life, by noting that death is an occasion for new life, but the primary fact here is death—a highly negative fact, one might say. When we are confronted by the disgusting processes of life, such as digestion or decay, what they may suggest to our mind is not the throbbing reality of life, but the grim static reality of death. We bring these processes under the concept *death*, conceiving them in that negative context. This is the theory to be considered in the next section. For now, let me conclude with the observation that life and the living are marked both with disgust *and* with its lack. Human culture—art, science, philosophy, morals—are aspects of life, as is the mind that generates these things: but no one thinks these things are disgusting. There is more to life than soup: it isn't *all* gurgling pipes and rank liquids with chunks in them.[15]

(e) The Death Theory. A linkage between disgust and death is a common refrain in writings on disgust. Ernest Becker's trenchant work *The Denial of Death* repeatedly juxtaposes

---

15. One of the things that influences Miller is the fecundity of life, its excessive, uncontrolled bounty. What occasions his disgust, it seems, is life's want of economy and fastidiousness. This is why he finds swarming insects disgusting. But I don't find much to resonate with here: thousands of penguins huddled together give me no jolt of disgust; nor do fields of grass or extensive forests. Excess disgusts only when it is an excess of the already disgusting (as I observed in chapter 1). Also: small bits of things can be quite disgusting, independently of any hint of excess or lack of restraint. There seems to be an element of Puritan strictness in Miller's disgust reactions (as also in Kolnai): *surplus* is automatically frowned upon.

revulsion at our human body with the fact that we know we must die; the fear of death, he contends, lurks behind out tendency to feel disgust.[16] The fear of death runs deep in the human psyche, a nagging constant of adult consciousness, and with it we feel disgust at the body we know must die. We are disgusted at the body because it is the agent of our death, and we fear death above all else; accordingly, what reminds us of our inevitable death is experienced as disgusting. The body has death written into it, owing to its finite and vulnerable biological nature, and this unwelcome message sends spasms of disgust through our anxious consciousness. Disgust is our desperate response to the jabbing fact of mortality. And this is not just death at some distant fixed time, but as a possibility at any moment—unpredictably, catastrophically—as the body reveals its standing fragility. We are born to die and ever at risk of death, and we are revolted by that fact. Nausea is our response to finitude. We are disgusted at the machinery that makes death inevitable. Our fear of death is directed to its biological vehicle—the body—in the form of disgust.[17]

16. Becker writes: "man is a worm and food for worms. This is the paradox: he is out of nature and hopelessly in it; he is dual, up in the stars and yet housed in a heart-pumping, breath-gasping body that once belonged to a fish and still carries the gill-marks to prove it. His body is a material fleshy casing that is alien to him in many ways—the strangest and most repugnant way being that it aches and bleeds and will decay and die. Man is literally split in two: he has an awareness of his own splendid uniqueness in that he sticks out of nature with a towering majesty, and yet he goes back into the ground a few feet in order blindly and dumbly to rot and disappear forever" (p. 26). Later, explicitly linking death and disgust, he says: "The anus and its incomprehensible, repugnant product represents not only physical determinism and boundness, but the fate as well of all that is physical: decay and death" (p. 31).

17. The internal organs disgust because they vividly advertise our total dependence on things that might gum up and malfunction at any moment and are bound in the end to succumb to time and entropy—they *guarantee* our death. Hence the horror of the visibly beating heart that may stop beating at any moment and must constantly pump viscous blood in order for us to be alive and conscious at all.

This line of thought is confirmed by a highly salient fact about disgust: its paradigmatic object is the rotting corpse. What could remind us of death more forcefully than the sight, smell, and touch of a dead body going the way of all flesh? In this putrefying entity we see that all along we have been clinging to life by a thread—that once the protective mechanisms of the body are shut down we are quickly made food for the lowest of creatures. With the immune system gone, we are literally eaten from the inside out by the bacteria that naturally inhabit our bodies, patiently biding their time. In a very real sense, the body is fending off death at every moment. This is a highly disagreeable thought. It is impossible to evade the reality of death, as we strive to do, if you are brought face to face with it in the form of a cadaver. The cadaver brings a rush of unwelcome reality, and disgust surges. Thus, the cadaver is found to be disgusting because it is the emblem of death, not because it is the scene of new life. We are strongly averse to death, and disgust encapsulates our aversion. We want the dead thing out of sight and mind so that we can return to our habitual denial of death.

The death theory also appears to score a second major victory in the form of feces and the digestive process. For what is digestion but an agent of death? We eat living tissue, plant and animal, and this can't happen without killing the living things we eat. A turd is, in effect, the corpse of the organism we earlier consumed.[18] We cannot live without killing, and the evidence of it is present every day of our lives. Digestion is a death factory. We feel disgust at this process of destruction, with the final product a pungent reminder of the death that preceded it. Shit signifies the death necessary to life.

Wounds also slide smoothly into place, because a wound, especially a severe, flesh-cleaving one, is a harbinger of death. Before modern medicine, anything but a superficial wound

18. Hence the aptly named article by Leo Bersani: "Is the Rectum a Grave?"

was almost certain to lead to death, courtesy of infection. And the blood loss associated with an open wound is also likely to result in death. Wounds disgust us, then, because they are conditions of the organism that precede and cause death. If the wound is severe enough to involve the release of internal organs, as with evisceration, then the level of disgust will be correspondingly high, since such wounds lead quickly and inevitably to death. Thus our three core categories of disgust object—putrefying corpses, feces, and bodily wounds—all seem to lend themselves to treatment by the death theory. In the terms of phenomenology: the intentionality of disgust-consciousness includes in its field the objective correlate of death—death in the form of a present exemplar of it (the corpse), death as having occurred in the past (feces), and death as it might occur in the future (wounds). In feelings of disgust, death is all around, overtly and covertly implicated. Disgust is a mode of consciousness that carries us affectively toward the contemplation of death.[19]

Further confirmation of the theory comes from the fact that animals feel neither disgust nor death anxiety. That is, they are not haunted their whole lives by the consciousness that they will die; they are spared that human torment. And at the same time they appear insusceptible to disgust. The two go together, suggesting that the *reason* they lack disgust is that they also lack the fear of death. They simply don't apprehend themselves as mortal, so nothing can remind them of their mortality; in particular, knowledge of their body does not carry with it awareness of the inevitability of death. They never think: "I am an organism and must therefore die—damn this wretched body!" They just don't conceive themselves in

---

19. So the child will begin to feel disgust just when thoughts of the inevitability of death begin to crowd his or her consciousness. This could be empirically investigated.

such terms. Death for them is not an *issue*, a source of dread
and resentment—so they do not react to the awareness of its
reality with the aversive emotion of disgust. In this sense, they
are not averse to their own given nature, as we humans tragi-
cally are. They do not regard their manner of being as a death-
to-be, with the body as death's complicit enabler. Their
consciousness does not incorporate this sickening recognition. Animal consciousness is not a death consciousness, as
ours is, miserably so.

The general cognitive principle that brings disgust in its
wake is then, according to this theory, the thought that death is
our fate, as well as that of all living things. We subsume the perceived world under this conceptual schema, bringing objects
into relation with the death concept. Things are interpreted as
falling in the shadow of death—or rather, within its bright,
stinging light. Our awareness of death is like our awareness of
the sun: it is hard to gaze at directly, because it hurts the eyes so,
but it is always present, always casting its remorseless, burning
light. This awareness, according to the death theory, is what
produces the emotion of disgust. We avoid contact with the
disgusting object because we want to avoid the reality of death.
If we can destroy it or hide it away, then we can keep death
from intruding too insistently on our troubled awareness.
Avoiding the touch of disgust objects is one of our stratagems
for denying death—for distancing it. Disgust is thus an episte-
mological project—the avoidance of information we would
rather not hear about. Accordingly, disgusting objects are
shrouded in secrecy, kept private, not talked about—all in
order to shield ourselves from the unmentionable and repellent fact of death. In disgust, we strive for ignorance of the
object; we don't want ongoing acquaintance with it. Death, too,
is a subject that we prefer to keep in the shadows, smothered in
taboo and secrecy. Disgust is death speaking to us, a little too
plainly, a little too tactlessly. We are a disgust species because

we are an awareness-of-death species. When we encounter a corpse our whole mortal condition is laid bare: it is *I* lying there, rotting and dissolving. We see our fate in the object and disgust envelops us.

The death theory has, I think, the awful ring of truth to it—and indeed, for a while I thought it was correct. The horror integral to disgust is just the horror of death, seen obliquely. But it faces an awkward problem: the *skeleton* (also the cryogenically preserved body). Bones are a problem because they too remind us forcefully of death, *yet we don't find them disgusting.* Standing over a putrefying corpse is one thing, but proximity to a skeleton is quite another. The bones are not *rotten*, and this is what disgusts us about the fleshy corpse. The skeleton is lifeless, like the cadaver, and is an equally powerful emblem of death, but there is a marked difference in disgust value. Therefore disgust cannot simply be a function of the recognition of death.[20] For much the same reason dried (or powdered) feces are nowhere as revolting as wet fresh ones, yet both betoken the death that preceded them. Nor are scars and bruises generally as disturbing as fresh open wounds, yet they also indicate bodily damage and vulnerability. It is not death *as such* that provokes disgust, but the specific character of the death-implying stimulus. But we have yet to say what this specific character consists in. Once more our theory, though promising, seems to cast the net too wide, entailing that certain things ought to be found disgusting when they are not. Death may be a necessary condition of disgust, but it is not a sufficient condition. Perhaps the skeleton counterexample should not surprise us, because other reminders of the reality of death—such as verbal reports—also carry no tinge of disgust. The stimulus has to have a certain character, a specific *Sosein*; a mere propositional content refer-

---

20. Kolnai notes the non-disgusting character of the skeleton, but he also includes the mummified corpse, which seems to me not so clear: see p. 53.

ring to death will not suffice for disgust to set in.[21] The question, then, is what the missing ingredient might be—which takes us to the next and final theory.

(f) The Death-in-Life Theory. We have just seen that it is not sufficient to excite disgust that an object or event should convey information about death. The case of a verbal report of death is already enough to demonstrate this: if I say, "People die all the time," I do not thereby stir up disgust in you. Why? Because my saying this (or writing it) is just an acoustic signal (a mark on paper) and such things do not produce disgust. The skeleton also conveys information about death—it tells us that a person or animal has died—and it does so in an extremely incontrovertible manner: the skeleton is part of the body of someone once living, and no one (in normal conditions) can survive the removal of their skeleton. (Future medical science might make complete skeletal replacement possible, for cases of bone disease, but not at the moment). But why does this part of the body fail to excite disgust, at least once the bones are "clean" and the marrow removed? (Or maybe I should say "much disgust," since we are not entirely comfortable with the touch of a skeleton.) It is surely because bones don't strike us as *organic* in the way the rest of the body does—the muscles, the internal organs, the various fluids and semi-solids. Bones seem to belong with the world of inanimate materials—with, in particular, the world of *rocks* (they are composed largely of calcium, after all). Fossilized bones simply are rock, and they don't strike us as morphologically very different from the original. Bones are hard, dense, unbending, breakable, non-putrefying, and odorless—quite unlike the soft tissues of the body. Thus the body

21. Also, death which takes the form of an instantaneous conversion to smoke and ashes, as in some science fiction, seems to eliminate disgust, since the ashy residue occasions little disgust (at least of the kind depicted in the science fiction I am thinking of).

divides into two compartments: the bony frame and the fleshy covering, and these are differently processed in our thought and feeling. When bones are replaced with metal rods and the like, there is no deep ontological shift, but the same is not true of an artificial heart or leg, if these replacements are inorganic. If a person's biological bones were completely replaced with metal or plastic "bones," the eventually resulting skeleton would not cause disgust in an onlooker; but the case is not so different from actual bones, because we don't make much of a distinction between these materials. The *Sosein* of bone is pretty much identical to that of a suitable inorganic replacement. The skeleton is more like a machine than the rest of the body, a collection of articulated hard parts: thus it clanks and rattles. The skeleton does not strike us as living tissue (though from a scientific standpoint it is—it grows, etc.).[22] Somewhat the same thing can be said about cryogenic preservation, though here the flesh survives the transformation: the warm squishy organic parts have made the transition to *ice*, which is solid, lifeless, unbending, and so on. To freeze something is to suspend the life processes within it, to render it (temporarily at least) inanimate: iced flesh is quite unlike the putrefying kind. The transformation to ice subtracts from the disgust value of the object, by altering its ontological category. (It is an interesting question whether the freezing of excrement can also negate its disgustingness—and it does seem that some disgust subtraction would occur in such a case.)

These reflections suggest the amendment to the simple death theory that we need: what is disgusting is death *as pre-*

---

22. Skeletons strike us as more eerie than disgusting—odd remnants of life that seem removed from life in their physical composition. Holding a (clean) skull in one's hands is a very different matter from holding a freshly severed head, or partly decayed head: the latter might start to talk, but not so the former. In the skull, we see the lifeless infrastructure of the body, not its familiar soft and fleshy reality.

sented in the form of living tissue. It is death in the context of life that disgusts—the death or dying of the living. Not death *tout court*, but death in the *midst* of life, surrounded by it. Or again, it is the living *becoming* dead, making that dreadful transition (or the dead becoming living, as with zombies, vampires, and so on). Disgust occurs in that ambiguous territory between life and death, when both conditions are present in some form: it is not life per se or death per se that disgusts, but their uneasy juxtaposition. The disgusting is "death-life" and "life-death"—neither one nor the other, but both. What disgusts is the *interpenetration* of life and death, the incongruous joining of the two. In the frolicking lamb, say, we have a pure case of life, so no disgust accrues; and in the bare white bones of an elephant's skeleton, we have an adamant affirmation of death, which also declines to disgust. But in the decaying corpse of a human being we have that intermediate zone of the recently-living-but-now-deceased that is also home to a riot of posthumous life in the form of organic agents of decay and dissolution. Not pure life or pure death, but an uneasy, almost paradoxical, combination or crosscurrent of the two. It is the *incongruity* of the combination that is the focus of our response, as if two great opposites have mysteriously joined forces. We want to keep these opposites apart, where they belong, but they insist on intermingling, generating a paradoxical (and sickening) mode of being.[23] Disgust occupies a borderline space, a region of uncertainty and ambivalence, where life and death meet and merge. In the corpse, death is incontrovertibly present, yet volatile life has not been totally expelled from its *Sosein*; in the skeleton, by contrast, death is there in all its stark permanence,

---

23. There is a normative element here: these two things—life and death—*ought* to be separate and apart, yet they insist on converging. They *should* be mutually exclusive, not mutually dependent. Nature is going *wrong* here: it is breaking the *rules*. Nature is not conforming to our human expectations of how things *rightly* should be.

with no hint of the living to qualify it. The eyes of the corpse may suddenly open, we feel, but the eyes of a skeleton never can (and dead eyes are a condensed focus of disgust). The flesh of the dead body is still relevant to the ongoing processes of life, though in a grisly, perverse way, but the skeleton has been cast out into the world of rocks and chemicals, with life just a distant memory. We might say that the proper object of disgust is really a process, rather than an object or condition: it is the *process* of putrefaction that excites our disgust, as it shifts an object from prior life to manifest death by an application of life (in the form of devouring bacteria). In all disgust objects, a process of transition seems essential, where the two poles of the transition are life and death (soon I will go through our list of disgust elicitors in order to test the theory in detail).

The writer who articulates this position most powerfully is Aurel Kolnai in *On Disgust*, though an anticipation of it can be found in the nineteenth-century German aesthetician Karl Rosenkranz, and possibly others.[24] I shall quote Kolnai at length:

> The prototypical object of disgust is, as already intimated, the range of phenomena associated with putrefaction. This includes corruption of living bodies, decomposition, dissolution, the odor of corpses, in general the transition of the living into the state of death. Not however this state itself, since the nonorganic is, in contrast, not at all experienced as disgusting. Not even a skeleton or a mummified corpse—for what is "gruesome" is not "disgusting." The mark of a disgusting object is found quite specifically in the process of putrescence, and in

---

24. On Rosenkranz, see Menninghaus, pp. 132–133. Rozencranz sums up by saying: "The appearance of life in what is in itself dead is the infinitely revolting within the disgusting." p. 132 The core of disgust, for this writer, as for Kolnai, is putrefaction; he therefore notes that the inorganic cannot be disgusting, except by analogy.

its carrier. There exists an image of putrefaction as an optical-tactile-olfactory formation which is, though complicated, still such as to possess structural unity. Between, say, rotten meat and rotten fruit there is after all a similarity of coloration, not to speak of other common features such as softening. In general we repeat once more that something dead is never disgusting in its *mere non-functioning*, for then even fresh meat would be disgusting, which is definitely not the case. Rather, substantial decomposition is necessary, which must at least seem to put itself forward as a continuing process, almost as if it were after all just another manifestation of life. Already here we encounter the relation of disgust to what is positively vital, to what is animated. And indeed there is associated with the extinction of life in putrefaction a certain—quite remarkable—augmentation of life: a heightened announcement of the fact that life *is there*. Evidence of this is provided by the reinforced smell that accompanies putrefaction, the often glaring change of colors, the putrefied "sheen," the whole phenomenon of turbulence characteristic of putrefaction. But not every pathologically intensified activity is disgusting: neither the ravings of a lunatic, nor the agony of the dying are so. It is not the living being as a whole that in dying becomes disgusting, but much more the body, in its parts: its "flesh," for example. Thus it is not similarity to death in any sense that is disgusting, and neither is it the approach of the moment of death—but rather the terminating section of life *in death*.[25]

In this powerful and suggestive passage we find the essential idea of the disgusting as a process that intermingles life and death; neither pole suffices to define it. I am not sure that Kolnai is right to declare fresh meat and mummified corpses definitely not disgusting, rather than just less disgusting than their putrescent cousins—in fact, the mixture of life and death

25. Kolnai, pp. 53–54.

in these cases would seem to qualify them—but I think he is right to stress the paradigmatic status of putrefaction, and to see in this process the template for other disgusting phenomena. Disgust has one foot in the vital and living and the other in the dead and dying: not the dead *or* the living, but the "living dead." Disgust proceeds from an oxymoron, a kind of collision or clash of categories. Indeed, it results from the friction between two of the categories most central to our conceptual scheme as self-conscious animals, and hence encodes our "existential predicament": Life and Death. When these resounding categories refuse to stay separate, but merge together, disgust floods in. Not that *any* two major categories will induce disgust if they threaten to coalesce—say, the abstract and the concrete: it must be specifically the categories of Life and Death. We fear and shun death and we embrace and celebrate life, but when the two come together, or are hard to tell apart, our reaction is to turn away in disgust—as if we wish to remain ignorant of the fact of interpenetration. We feel positive about the life that throbs even within putrefying flesh, but the heavy weight of negative affect concerning death robs that positive feeling of its usual value: we are torn, conflicted, confused. We don't know whether to laugh or cry—to marvel or to wince. The astonishing force of life impresses us, but the terrible inevitability of death dampens and depresses. Putrefaction, as disgust paradigm, transparently combines both: the vital and the nullifying. As we will see shortly, this structural antinomy repeats itself with respect to other disgust objects.

One more piece needs to be added to the picture sketched by Kolnai and developed here: it concerns the precise understanding of the notions of life and death that are operative in the complex of reactions that constitute disgust. Is it simply the notions of life and death that might apply to a plant that are in play, or is it something richer and more interesting?

Surely the latter: it is the notions of life and death *as they apply to a conscious being.* In the case of humans and many animals, life is the life of a perceiving, knowing, feeling subject—sentience in the broadest sense; and the death of such a subject is the death of a sentient being. My life, say, consists not just of biological processes inside a living body, such as might occur in an insentient worm, but of psychological processes inside a conscious self—indeed, that is the part of my life that really matters to me. Death, for me, is the end of that subjective self, not merely the end of a functioning organism. So when life and death come together, and are apprehended as paradoxically unified, we see consciousness and its termination brought together. In the rotting corpse, we see something that once housed a conscious being and no longer does—and it is as if the consciousness still obscurely resides within the body awaiting its final dissolution. The consciously living is still somehow hovering around the organically dead, and the dead impinges on the living: this is a moment of deep metaphysical transition—consciousness turning to mindless, disorganized matter.[26] Similarly, in feces we can see the death of living things, some of them sentient, which have ended up as food; but as well, we see the life processes *of a sentient being* at work. The conscious life of the food animal is obscurely present in the feces of the predator—after all, it has been consumed along with the organic tissue—but we can also see the imprint of the conscious life that has done the consuming. Conscious animal digests conscious animal: shit is the visible sign of that absorption. The strange vitality of shit, phenomenologically

---

26. I don't of course mean that the corpse *is* semi-conscious; I mean that we can't help seeing the marks of conscious life within it. This is why we dread any twitching or exhalation—the jaw dropping open is a guaranteed shocker. We close the eyelids to simulate sleep because the open eyes give such a strong impression of conscious life. The passage to death should be marked and unmistakable, not ambiguous and reversible (as with the risen dead).

speaking, reflects its embedding in the world of sentience. Our attendant thoughts of life and death here contain ideas of the presently conscious and of the no-longer conscious. And even if the life that combines with death is of the non-conscious kind—plant or bacterial life—there is still a conceptual connection to consciousness, because we think of life primarily in terms of sentient life. The microorganisms that are consuming the dead body may not be sentient beings, but they are on a continuum with forms of life that are so sentient; and the horrible vitality they exhibit is *as if* conscious will were at work in them. The plants that are eaten are at the bottom end of a scale that includes conscious mammals, such as humans, at the other end. Life, for us, is paradigmatically conscious life, and death is paradigmatically the termination of consciousness (of the conscious self); so when we contemplate a life-death nexus, we are reminded of the paradigm cases. Accordingly, our appalled awareness of these life-death juxtapositions is shot through with ideas of the conscious and the once conscious—and of their peculiar relations to the world of biological entities. The corpse was once a sentient being existing by courtesy of a biological entity, and the decay we witness is the activity of tiny living organisms that suggest sentience at a primitive level (a fortiori for maggots and worms). Thus the puzzle of the biological incarnation of consciousness—and the tragic nature of that incarnation—lie at the heart of our disgust reactions—because consciousness and its termination are conceptually present in the life-death pairings that prompt disgust. The emotion therefore has a complex, implicit conceptual substructure, tying together such grand oppositions as Life and Death, Sentience and Insentience. The borderline of life and death is what produces disgust, according to the death-in-life theory, but this borderline is closely bound up with ideas of consciousness and its annihilation—as well as with the tragic and perplexing dependence of consciousness on biological matter. It is a kind of metaphysical emotion, spanning the divide between (roughly) mind and matter. The disgust objects are no doubt themselves material, but these objects are brought under psychological concepts—and this shapes the contours of the emotion.[27]

27. This implies that there is no disgust without possession of the concept of mind—which explains children's late acquisition of disgust. Similarly, there is no guilt without possession of the concepts of right and wrong, so children won't feel guilt proper till they grasp elementary moral concepts.

5

Handling the Cases

I HOPE MY READERS sense a strong element of truth in the death-in-life theory. My task now is to survey the class of disgusting things to see how well that theory can deal with the data. Some of this work is obvious enough, but some requires a little ingenuity. I propose to move at a brisk pace, assuming the reader can fill in the gaps.

(1) The rotting corpse is the easy case and has already been amply covered. It is instructive to note our different responses to the slow dissolution of the body by microorganisms and its consumption by means of fire: between putrefaction and cremation. The organically corrupted tissue is at the zenith of disgust, but the residual ashes of cremation scarcely merit a disgust response at all—they are dry and powdery, more mineral than animal. There is no life in the ashes, nor is consumption by fire an organic process; but it is a very different matter with putrescent flesh, in which life is still beating its insistent rhythm. The whole process of digestion, excretion, and reproduction still goes on within the decaying tissues, whether by bacteria or worms and flies—while within the ashes no organic life stirs. Diseases of the flesh, such as leprosy, obey the same law: alien life is corrupting the flesh of the host organism, visibly and horribly. There is something living actively at work in causing the flesh to lose its usual integrity,

not a mere loss of form as a result of physical forces. More-over, contagiousness demonstrates a vital organic force—a spreading of invisible and inimical disease life from one victim to another. Disease is a form of life—it is one life form pitted against another—but fire is not. Corruption of the flesh is not the same as its destruction.

The theory bears on the ambivalence I earlier noted: that we are both repelled by the disgusting and yet oddly attracted to it. There are two distinct points to be made here. First, we have a similar ambivalence toward death itself: yes, it is feared and avoided, but it also has, or can have, a certain appeal, as a release from mortal life with its slings and arrows. Hamlet notoriously sees both sides of the question clearly, and he dithers: we are certainly attached to life, but we are also irritated and disillusioned by it. Death has its dark appeal. If the disgusting is generated (in part) by our attitudes to death, then it will inherit that ambivalence: the spectacle of death in the shape of a corpse can produce aversive and attractive attitudes, precisely because we have aversive and attractive attitudes toward death itself (though the former attitude is typically much stronger). Second, if disgust is a consequence of a life-in-death nexus, then a further ambivalence will be created, since life attracts and death repels. Imagine if pretty flowers regularly grew from the body of the recently departed, as the nutrients of the body are exploited by this generally attractive life form: we would probably still be repelled by the spectacle, but we would also marvel at life's ingenuity and at the gorgeousness of its result in the present anomalous case. Such "death flowers" would excite sharply different emotions in us, causing pronounced ambivalence. (The same ambivalence would arise if healthy human babies grew from decaying flesh.) Thus, the secondary tonality of attraction that clings to the basic aversion of disgust has an explanation in the death-in-life theory: death has its appealing side, and life-in-death has the appeal of life. However, the major theme of feared death naturally dominates.[1]

What about the self-other asymmetry of disgust that I earlier identified? Introducing death suggests the following line of thought, which is perhaps as obscure as the emotions for which it tries to account. We have a clearer conception of the death of others than we have of our own death. We can witness their death, with the remaining body and so on, but we cannot witness our own death or observe the body that remains. There is an asymmetry in our conception of death: our own death is conjectural, not immediately given to us, while the death of others is a datum. As we live, we experience the death of others, but we do not experience our own death—certainly not till it occurs, and possibly not even then.[2] Now, when we are repelled by the (living) body of the other, we think of *his* death, which we grasp quite clearly; but when we observe our own body, noting its disgust quotient, while not being *as* repelled by it, we think of our death—of which we have merely an obscure conception. The asymmetry of clarity about death, from the first- and third-person point of view, thus correlates with our differential disgust reactions with respect to ourselves and other people. In short, we find ourselves less disgusting because our own death is not so real to us—as if it is something we can't quite believe in. And, indeed, we can never be acquainted with it as we can the death of others. It is simply easier to view the other under the aspect of death than to view oneself under that

---

1. We are also *curious* about death, as we are about corpses, feces, and other disgusting objects. Death attracts us epistemologically (that "undiscovered country"). We already know a lot about life, having lived it, but death is a dark secret.

2. This is the old point that we cannot experience the event of death because we do not persist through it. Of course, if by death we just mean leaving the body behind, then consciousness can persist through death in *that* sense: but this is not death in the sense of being an *end* to consciousness.

aspect, so we don't find our own body so redolent of death—and hence have a weaker disgust response toward it.[3]

I have spoken of life's grim end, but what of its gross beginning? The body mutates to nothing in death, but the process of gestation is one in which nothing mutates to life. We are dead before we are alive, as we will be dead after we are alive. Gestation is mainly hidden, of course, owing to the opacity of the female's body, but we get hints of it at various points. And nothing about it is especially lovely: the cramped and coiled fetus swamped in fluid; the wormlike umbilical cord; the grisly birth process with its blood and placenta; the dilated uterus, sometimes ripped and bleeding; the pain and wailing.[4] The onset of life is almost as bathed in disgust signals as its termination—though, of course, the process itself has a far happier outcome. The initial transition to life mirrors the final transition to death—high-water points of disgust in the life of the organism. The fetus is not yet an autonomous living being, more like a bloated internal organ than a fully functioning creature, quite unable to survive outside the mother's body. It is an almost-life, at risk of extinction, poised between nothingness and existence, an intermediate entity: in it we see a precarious quasi-life, a fragile upsurge from the emptiness that precedes it. So the birth process excites mixed emotions in us: the promise of a future life, but also a disturbing proximity to the void, as well as reminding us

3. This asymmetry couples with the one I mentioned in note 10 of chapter 3, "The Architecture of Disgust," namely that I find my body more extraneous to my sense of my own identity than I find other people's bodies in relation to their identity. Thus, I experience the death of others *and* I regard them as more deeply identified with the disgusting body.

4. Menninghaus quotes a poem of Barthold Brockes, which begins: "The Filthiness of Birth, the Grave's Decay and Dung, Thus a Lifetime full of Needs ends like it's begun. Tell me: what is a Man? In Seed he is but Slime, In Mother's Womb a Clot, a Curd in milky Whey, An unperfected flesh" (p. 88). And, as has often been remarked, we are born, literally, between feces and urine (or their conduits). It is a good thing that newborns have no sense of disgust!

of our ultimate dependence on the body's biological plumbing. Accordingly, it provokes a strange confluence of joy and revulsion. And during birth there is always the terrifying possibility of death, for baby and mother, which imbues it with a potency all its own—an arena of potential death that is the very font of life. Here life and death appear together in multiple interlocked terms, and we feel the pressure of their proximity. Disgust hovers like an unwelcome guest over the maternity room, as well as hope and joy. Once the infant (and the mother) survives the death-saturated trauma of gestation and birth, with the baby no longer just a belly-swelling parasite, disgust decently retreats, to be replaced by the emotions proper to pulsating life (but then there is uncontrolled excretion to contend with). As the corpse is a repulsive token of life's ambiguous end, so the fetus and newborn are semi-repulsive tokens of life's fraught beginning. Gestation and putrescence are phases in the life of the organic body, marking the rise from nothing and the fall into nothing. If babies smelt like dead bodies, and dead bodies smelt like babies, things would not be so very different for us: we have to tolerate a measure of disgust at both stages. The death-in-life theory accommodates our emotions with respect to each phase of life.

(2) How do the waste products of the body conform themselves to the death-in-life theory? It is hard to imagine a disgust object more charged with life and death than feces. The death part we have covered: the digestive process takes living things as input and delivers dead things as output. As has been well said, the rectum is a grave.[5] The digestive system takes recognizably living beings—plants and animals—and mashes them mercilessly to a brown pulp, reeking and foul. The turd is a rancid

---

5. See note 18 in chapter 4, "Theories of Disgust" for the reference. But is the grave also a rectum, with corpses featuring as large turds? They do eventually become the excrement of worms and such. We can interpret each disgust object in the light of the other.

corpse, even more debased than your regular rotting specimen. But there is life here too—at least functionally speaking. For the digestive process is the very foundation of all animal life: the extraction of nutrients from the carcasses of other living things—the vital act of energy transfer. Digestion is a living process, preceded by other living processes—hunting, gathering, food preparation, and ingestion. Feces may be dead, but they are the foundation of life—life breathes in them. They take life, but they also give it. That foul odor is the smell of life as well as death. I have no wish to romanticize the turd, but in it we see (and smell) the by-product of the essential life process. Thus life and death exist co-presently in feces, and disgust is the upshot. The turd cannot move or grow, like the dead thing it is, but its status as organic material is unquestionable—which is why, as manure, it can aid other life, and can be re-ingested by certain species as nourishment. In the cartoon *South Park*, feces have been known to walk and talk: that is metaphorically quite an apt expression of their status as living things.[6]

What of other bodily products? They too belong to the functioning organism, aiding the processes of life—mucus, blood (including menstrual), earwax, and urine. Notice that these things do not disgust while performing their function inside the body; it is when leaking from the body that they take on a different aspect. The reason, I suggest, is that once they leave the body they enter the sphere of death: they are no longer integral to life,

---

6. Inside the body, fecal matter is arguably a living substance, like blood and mucus—it is *part* of the functioning organism. It dies only when released from the anus. Fecal particles do literally make up the entire organism, including the brain. We cannot dissociate ourselves from shit. Our vitality comes from it. We seldom, if ever, set eyes on the digestive substance as it exists between the stomach and the colon, but it must be intermediate in consistency between vomit and excrement—and hence aesthetically worse than either. That vile stuff is the very core of our life fuel, the sine qua non of our most profound thoughts and feelings, our most lovely creative products. Deep philosophical thoughts are ultimately shit-based.

but merely expendable waste, soon to desiccate, deteriorate, and provide food for lowly life forms. They are moving from life to death before our eyes (this is particularly true of escaping blood).[7] They are a microcosm of the death of the whole organism, a foreshadowing: erstwhile vital substance is slipping and trickling into oblivion, mere food for worms and their ilk. Blood in circulation is one thing, but blood flowing freely from a wound is another matter—passing from life-essence to messy, useless deadness. Flowing blood is life leaking away. Puddles of blood are pictures of mortality (death isn't much of an artist). Mucus too performs its vital organic function inside the body, but once it escapes from the body it strikes us as disturbingly *de trop*. Semen, the very crucible of life, suffers a drastic demotion to pointless sticky daub once it is spilled on the ground, only to be consumed there by unfussy insects or whatever. Such secretions are caught up in a life-to-death transition, a migration from living body to entropic world, and as such excite our revulsion. Incontinence hits us particularly hard, because here the transition is systematic and uncontrollable, a steady leaking of bodily life-substances into the inanimate world (I am speaking here of incontinence of the nose as much as of the bowels and urethra). Imagine your response if every bodily orifice began to discharge its contents uncontrollably!

Tears pose a theoretical challenge: they leak from the body yet occasion no disgust. Two points can be made to deflect the challenge. First, it is not the function of tears to perform vital work inside the body; it is their function to be released outside. Tears do not lose their biological utility by being expelled from the eyes—they gain it. Second, tears have powerful associations to emotions

---

7. I observe that bodily waste is at its most appalling when in the very act of leaving the body's interior—as with the dangling turd, the running nose, and spurting blood. The residue left on the ground is not so violently disgusting and declines in disgustingness as time passes. The closer to breathing life the material is the worse it seems.

that do not disgust us at all—such as grief and loss, as well as joy and relief. It would be hard to react to tears with disgust while sympathizing with the emotions from which they spring. Their watery character also helps, since water is a disgust-free inorganic material. But notice that tears, or streaming eyes, can elicit disgust in certain circumstances, depending upon their etiology. The chronically watery eye—a kind of incontinence of the tear ducts—will produce a modicum of disgust; and the diseased eye, releasing viscous fluids as a symptom, will definitely move us in the disgust direction. Even the tear of grief or joy will earn our mild revulsion if left too long upon the cheek, becoming sticky and icky. Tears, I am inclined to say, are the exception that proves the rule: they are a very special case. Sweat belongs in the same general area as tears, because its function is also to leak from the body, and it is physically watery, associated with worthy labor, and less tolerated the longer it is permitted to linger. Sweat is like breath—a purposive expulsion from the body's interior with a low-profile *Sosein*. Sweating, breathing, and crying are accordingly nothing like bleeding, urinating, and drooling.[8]

Here is an interesting thought experiment. Suppose you lived in a world in which stuff chemically identical to our mucus, earwax, and blood occupied a very different role from the role they occupy in the actual world: the mucus stuff oozes from trees like sap, the earwax stuff occurs in the core of an apple, and the blood stuff flows in the rivers and oceans. In this possible world, let me add, these substances have never occurred in noses or ears or bodies, so that you, as an inhabitant of this world, have no thought of them doing so. Suppose, too, that the "mucus" and the "earwax" substances have demonstrated nutritional properties in the imagined world and can be easily incorporated into enticing recipes; maybe they even protect against certain diseases. The "blood" stuff, for its part, offers

8. Other writers have said much the same about tears: see Miller, p. 90.

excellent opportunities for swimming and surfing, and can be drunk as a hearty beverage, especially when cooled and spiced. Now, do you think that in that possible world you would be disgusted by these substances, just as you are in the actual world? I suspect you would not. And the reason is that their actual disgust value depends on their place in the life-in-death nexus, which has been abrogated in the imagined world. These substances are only disgusting *in context*. Perhaps even feces could be stripped of their repulsive character by altering their place in the natural world—say, by imagining them as a form of health-giving mud, having no relation to the digestive process. Once their significance as emblems of life and death has been thought away (admittedly, not an easy task), they might strike us as relatively harmless. (This is all assuming, of course, that nothing chemically *similar* to them also emanates from the human body in the possible world in question: in that world our blood is like orange juice, our feces like chocolate pudding, our earwax like butter). The local perceptual features of the substances in question take on a disgust value because of the way they fit into the biological order, but the two can be conceptually separated—and when they are so detached, the human disgust response may become decoupled from them. Of course, this is a difficult thought experiment to be clear about, since, given our actual experience, the associations in question are deeply entrenched; still, the question is worth pondering and intuitions can shift surprisingly. As a point of reference, ask yourself about the disgust value of ripe cheese: it is minimal for most of us, but imagine that the same stuff oozed from a human orifice—would you want to eat it then?[9]

---

9. Let's have a label for the type of theory I am developing: we could call it the "contextual" theory of disgust, because it emphasizes how the disgust stimulus must be embedded in a wider biological context involving life and death. The label has of course been used for several other doctrines, but it is not inapt, and we philosophers like a label to pin on our theories.

(3) The body also sports disgusting formations on its surface, as enumerated earlier. Let us confine ourselves to wounds, warts, hair, and sagging flesh as representative examples. In the gaping wound, two points are evident: that it is a potential harbinger of death, and that it is a condition of a living body. As the blood flows, or the wound suppurates, the living tissue affirms its biological identity, but death lurks ominously in the wings, winking conspiratorially. In the wound, we see the corpse foreshadowed, but we also see the vital animal. It is not like seeing the snapped bone of a skeleton, where death is pure and unqualified; no sign of life is visible there. In the flesh wound, by contrast, the living body is still asserting itself—the processes of life are still active. Disgust, then, is the natural upshot. The extreme case is the exposed and beating heart: here the wound is grievous, the prospect of death imminent, but the evidence of pulsing life is unmistakable. This is a wound that juxtaposes life and death particularly starkly, and it excites our emotions accordingly.[10]

Warts fall into the category of alien growths, along with tumors and the like. They indicate virulent life, gone to excess. Cancer, after all, is the unchecked growth of cells, as if the life force has lost all control and sense. There can be too much vital augmentation of the flesh. Such growths and tumors are pathological, sometimes leading to death. Warts generally stay within tolerable bounds of proliferation, but in rare cases the growth can become massive and smothering, with the affected body part barely recognizable beneath the warty profusion—and a strong access of disgust follows. In principle, at least, one could die of such an affliction, if only by suicide. Alien parasitic life

---

10. Perhaps the most gruesome imaginable death involves parading the victim's heart or entrails before his still-living eyes, so that his last moments of consciousness are filled with self-disgust. Extreme horror movies sometimes exploit this kind of imagery.

can produce death in the host, and certainly sickness. The skin protects the interior of the body from outside intrusion, but it too can become the site of alien life forms. The sight and touch of things growing on one's body, when these are not proper parts of the body, is an occasion for disgust, the reason being that life is here coupled with death in a paradoxical superposition. To be killed by cancer is to die from the excessive life generated by one's body—and cancer tumors strike us as particularly abhorrent.[11]

Hair follows the same general pattern. Hair grows, but it is inherently dead. It lacks the warmth and texture of flesh, like toenails and fingernails. Confined to the head we tolerate it, though it can easily turn disgusting if it becomes greasy or unkempt. But anywhere else on the body it creates a zone of disgust if present to excess: the bushy eyebrows, the bristling nostrils, the apelike back, the hairy legs, the curly efflorescence of the pubic area. Hair must be strictly controlled, not just allowed to follow the wild dictates of nature. Just consider your response to waking up one day to find that your leg hair is now two inches long and that your pubic hair has sprouted to the size of beehive! Hair can quickly come to seem like an alien growth itself, with an uncanny dead-alive quality. In adolescence, when hair growth encroaches on new territories, it is common to feel some self-revulsion, until custom dims the novelty. Suddenly, it seems, you have been overtaken by an alien life form, as the hair sprouts and bristles, and hair management becomes a daily concern. It is notable to what degree people these days seek to remove the

11. In the same category we find bodies bloated by disease or by post-mortem processes; this seems more revolting than withering. Obesity is also a form of excessive life, in the shape of surplus adipose tissue—which, after all, stores essential energy. To be covered all over by an alien growth certainly excites strong disgust. This is life out of control, and contributing to death. To literally burst from overeating is also a case of a life process leading to a gruesome death (as in the old Monty Python film *The Meaning of Life*).

hair that adorns their body; it begins to seem paradoxical that they don't have the same attitude toward the hair on their head.[12] It is not that this "reminds us of our animal nature" (whatever quite that may mean); it is rather that rampant hair is reminiscent of an alien infestation—as well as possessing an ambiguous nature as semi-alive. Imagine if straw grew from your armpits instead of hair: it too would disturb by dint of its living deadness, as well as seeming like life grafted on from elsewhere. In science fiction, future people are often depicted as totally hairless, as if to suggest that when civilization progresses hair will be a thing of the past—the body will become purified of all disgust elements. In utopia, we are all smooth and hairless. On the other hand, cavemen are always depicted as primitive and hairy, with questionable personal hygiene. It is as if body hair is equated with *dirt*, with hints of disease and parasitism thrown in. And a shudder is produced by the information that hair still grows for a short while after death. We are not happy with body hair, except within strict limits, and its death-in-life associations are apparent. If body hair really were an alien life form, some sort of parasite, with untoward consequences for health, we would surely be strongly repulsed by it. What if it turned out that this is really so?

Sagging flesh fits the theory neatly: it is a sign of poor health or age, that is, proximity to death. But it is flesh after all, living tissue. When flesh sags we witness the fall of the body from youth and vitality to age and decrepitude; what was once the locus of blooming life is now an area of looming extinction. Folds and wrinkles have the same meaning. Thus, the body of the old woman is often regarded as the disgust object par excel-

12. Some people do: they shave their heads completely. Very short hair may reflect the same distaste for flowing locks. Beards go in and out of fashion, but most men prefer to be clean-shaven or at least not shaggy. The "clean look" always has its smooth appeal. We must never appear *overtaken* by our hair, as if infested by it.

lence, with the breasts (cruelly) the prime area of revulsion. The breasts were once the site of life and fertility, but now they suggest only the march of time toward inevitable extinction. I daresay the testicles and penis of the old man have much the same quality—the buttocks too. When flesh ages, it has the inescapable mark of death upon it, yet it is still the flesh of a living conscious individual.[13] A signifier of life changes its polarity to become a signifier of death, but it still exists (though precariously) on the side of life. We might conceptualize it as a state of pre-putrescence—early-stage decay of the body. Disgust is the natural response to this life-to-death transition. (I am not of course saying any of this is fair, or that we should not try to moderate our responses, only that it is the way things are, intelligibly so.)

None of this has anything to do with normality and abnormality. Being abnormally muscular or slim does not provoke disgust, as I noted earlier, and some of the disgust objects just cited are perfectly normal. Death is normal, after all. Our disgust reactions do not track normality and abnormality, but the incongruous conjunction of life and death.

(4) The internal organs occasion little, if any, disgust while safely enclosed within the body (we don't perceive them there, after all), but if they become exposed disgust sets in with a vengeance. While they are within and covered they perform their proper functions; they are part of the life process. But once they are brought into the harsh light of day, they cease to perform those life-giving functions, and death becomes imminent, or actually present. Wounds are the normal cause of such

13. The flesh of the *very* old is in a class of its own: thin translucent skin, veins bulging, discolored, mottled, inelastic, loose, flabby—the corpse looks already to have taken up residence. We accordingly feel a kind of terrible tenderness toward such aged individuals. In them, we see death impinging on life, overlapping with it, yet heroically held at bay. Such a person is indeed often described as "having one foot in the grave."

exposure, and the exposure itself threatens the integrity of the organ. Evisceration is the extreme case. Thus disgust correlates with a breakdown of functioning, which correlates with death. Yet these are vital organs, referred to as such; so we have again that combination of life and death in the exposed or removed organ. The orifices, though not designed to expose the internal organs, can threaten to do so, and in pathological cases actually do (prolapsed, etc.). It is natural, then, that they too should attract their share of disgust, as potential avenues of revolting release. Suppose the navel were an orifice of some description, capable of widening to an inch or so, and that so dilated it could reveal the intestines or even let them protrude; then, I fancy, we would regard it with a good deal more trepidation than we do now and would contrive to keep it decently covered—especially if there were medical conditions in which the intestines might actually peep out. There is a disturbing contingency about the safe coverage of the internal organs; the sack in which they are enclosed might, we fear, suffer a breach, with the contents spilling forth. Only a thin membrane prevents the organically functioning interior from moving to the death-signifying exterior—from vital-to-life to inimical-to-life. The easily torn skin is what separates life from death. Disgust finds a rich vein to resonate to in that unfortunate fact.

The sexual organs are a special case, being, as it were, *between* the inside and the outside. This is most clearly true of the female organs, but the testicles too have an inner-outer duality, both because of their capacity for retraction and descent and because they are a containing sack (they contain what surely *belongs* on the inside). Whence the disgust these organs can so easily provoke? The answer is not far to seek, though it is somewhat different in the two cases. The penis is tumor-like in its appearance, a kind of grotesque floppy growth dangling between the legs (hardly necessary as a means of urination); indeed, the word "tumescent," meaning "swelling," has the same root as "tumor." As if that were not enough, the penis also has a suppurating side—notably in the form of semen. The tumor expels its pus-like fluid. Then there is the smelly urine it continually leaks. It also has a will of its own, animated by its own whims and projects; it is disturbingly like an alien life form attached to the body. The testicles only add to the gruesome picture: wrinkled, hairy, and loosely hanging—incapable of voluntary movement, yet occasionally mobile. Thus the male genitals eloquently connote both life and death: the life of an animate organ, essential for the reproduction of life; but also the hint of death in the tumor-like appearance and olfactory characteristics. It can also be the remote cause of death-inducing conditions, such as pregnancy and sexually transmitted diseases. It has a dagger-like ability to stab, by aggressively entering the body of another. It can lead its owner to acts of violence, such as rape. Loss of sexual potency, on the other hand, is a forerunner to old age and death ("erectile dysfunction" is an early indicator of general bodily dysfunction—it is the death of the penis). Life and death coexist in complex and subtle ways in the penis and testicles, telling a story of triumph and tragedy.[14]

The vagina has a somewhat different interpretation, being most saliently a wound-like formation, a rip or fissure in the body's outer smoothness (sometimes referred to with the words "gash" and "slit"). It thus symbolically partakes of the properties of all wounds. But it is also a literal locus of life generation, not merely a mimetic threat to life. To complicate matters further, it

---

14. There is also the point that the penis in a flaccid state appears quite lifeless, not being equipped with muscle; but it can spring startlingly to life when an erection takes hold—only to return before long to a state of lifelessness. It rises from the grave, as it were, and then lapses back into it. The hair and veins of the penis also work obliquely to connote life and death. It can get dirty and smelly easily, a microcosm of the living body as a whole. And it is the locus of a strong sensation, viz. orgasm, which is integral to life. The penis seems to pack a lot of symbolic life and death content into a relatively small organ.

also bleeds, where this bleeding is not a threat to life, as one might naively suppose, but a necessary condition of it (given mammalian physiology). The vagina presents itself as a bleeding wound that is nevertheless the sine qua non of life—a paradoxical configuration. Again, a dense matrix of life and death connotations attends the vagina. Put it together with the penis and the density increases: the tumor and the wound, one thrusting and stabbing inside the other, potentially a source of death, yet contriving to body forth as the foundation of life. Here, life seems to make use of death, appropriating it, silencing it. A tumor and a wound are violently combined in a vital act to produce a fresh life, itself redolent of death.[15]

The body is constitutionally a perilous zone, never far away from death, yet brimming with life. To have life *is* to be close to death. Whatever is living can quickly be made dead. When we contemplate life, therefore, we cannot help but think of death. The living is what can die, and death is the inevitable fate of the living. The two concepts are bound inextricably together. Disgust feeds upon this fundamental existential fact.

(5) There is no difficulty about extending the above points beyond the human body to other animal bodies, but that is not yet to address our disgust reactions to other species *as such*: rats, bats, vultures, snakes, worms, insects, spiders, etc. I think there are two categories to consider here: (a) animals that are closely associated with human death and human filth, and (b) animals that themselves resemble death in some fashion. We should note that disgust reactions are quite variable with respect to animal species, depending on how the animal is con-

---

15. I am aware that I am accentuating the grotesquely anatomical side of sex here, ignoring its more appealing aspects. Let me then simply add—for the record, as it were—that it can also be the expression of love, and entirely enjoyable. In combining those opposite extremes lies its peculiar charm. The incongruity is also what makes sex fundamentally indescribable. It simply makes no sense. It is unintelligible. Sex is a kind of baffling non sequitur.

ceived by the disgusted subject. I myself don't have much in the way of disgust reactions to animal species, but I know that many people do; it is therefore necessary to delve into the psychology of those who profess such disgust, however cursorily. Rats are commonly associated with human waste, that is, garbage, and they are held to be denizens of the graveyard, as well as the sewer. They can also in fact carry deadly diseases. Yet they are a vigorous and indomitable life form, all twitch and scurry. Disgust comes naturally in their case, and fits the schema so far sketched: aggressive life enmeshed in death and decay.[16] Bats are stereotypically believed to feed on blood, human if available, and some species of bat really do. They also dwell in dank caves and sleep vampire-like during the day. Their look is vaguely fecal. Again, the explanation of our disgust here is clear. Vultures receive the same treatment, in view of their marked penchant for rotting flesh. Worms come in many different varieties: some are outright parasites, the Guinea worm being perhaps the nastiest, while others merely dine on dead flesh (for the rest it is guilt by physical resemblance). The parasitic worms cause ill health and even death, sucking our life into theirs. The non-parasitic worms show a bit too much fondness for the decaying flesh of other species. Both are uncomfortably close to death, while asserting their own life claims (the mosquito is in a similar position). The ant troubles us far less, because it does not seek to profit from human death or filth, save accidentally. Note that these species do not set out simply to kill us, like a simple predator; they insinuate themselves into the disgusting corners of the human

16. The rat's tail is found particularly repellent by some people: long, pinkish, and (relatively) hairless—quite wormlike. The whole rat seems unnaturally fearless, like a driven insect, and with a disturbing liveliness to its movements. It insists on leaving its dark glistening droppings all over the place. The rat strikes us as comprehensively filthy. It represents life at its most driven and ruthless, tolerant of muck and death and everything vile. Rat's tail soup, anyone?

animal—the rotting corpse, the bodily interior, the blood, the feces, the garbage. They thus possess a kind of borrowed disgustingness, which a predatory cat does not possess (so lions don't disgust us). A fly that consumes our fecal matter excites special abhorrence, a fortiori if it insists on settling on our food afterward. Such species are found to be disgusting because they traffic in the independently disgusting.[17] They are types of life that connote death, directly or indirectly.

But the second category cannot be explained in this way, since not all insects, say, do traffic in the disgusting (though some do, such as cockroaches and dung beetles). I suggest that something different is going on in these cases: the insect itself is perceived as lying *between* life and death. The insect is animated, twitchy, quick, but it is also curiously machinelike—with its hard exterior, its coolness to the touch, and its mechanical behavior. Tiny robots don't disgust, because they are not organic, and insects are in some ways close to tiny robots; yet they are not simply robots, because they are organisms after all, with squishy insides to prove it, as well as ravenous appetites. Insects impress us as a kind of intermediate quasi-life: they move and proliferate like living things, but the soft fleshiness of the higher animal is not their physical mode of being. They seem mindless and heartless, like battery-driven toys, but there is no denying their place on the tree of life. Insects strike us as borderline animal life. They exist one rung up from lifelessness. They are not dead exactly, like zombies, but they also do not attain to life of the fullness exemplified by the higher species (fish are one

17. There is a type of beetle that lives off the excrement of bats: the stuff piles up in the bats' cave and the beetles loiter at the bottom feeding on it. This is a perfect disgust configuration: bats (possibly blood-sucking), insects, and rampant coprophagia. Moreover, there can be millions of these beetles in one cave, scuttling and scoffing, one crawling on top of the other, up to their little ears in bat shit. (I wonder what happens to the beetle excrement—bacteria food, I presume.)

rung up again). They are the living dead—and therein lies their peculiar disgustingness.[18]

Snakes and reptiles are another case again. Their cold-bloodedness argues for a reduction to the lifeless (at least from the perspective of the warm-blooded), but that does not do them justice—reptiles can be quite nippy on their feet and show many of the standard signs of more "advanced" life. In general, the standard-issue reptile is only marginally disgusting to most of us—no more so than most other species. The snake, however, is another story. I feel no strong revulsion to snakes, but plenty of people do: so what is the rationale for their repugnance? There is first, and prosaically, the matter of the venom—as if death lurks very close to the surface of a snake. But other animals are deemed equally dangerous and excite no disgust. The Freudian suggestion, endlessly reiterated, is that the snake is like the penis and inherits its psychic meaning. But lots of things are like the penis, morphologically speaking, and yet don't excite disgust (shoehorns and magic wands, say). Proximity to the filthy earth may play a role, what with slithering on their belly and so on. Then, too, they have a wormy look to them. If I were to grant myself Freudian license in speculation, I might be tempted to find in the *Sosein* of the snake, not the penis, but the *turd*: the snake is an uncannily animated turd, slimy in appearance, glistening, tapered at both ends, thick in the middle, often dun-colored, possibly poisonous. The snake is accordingly not a phallic symbol, but a fecal symbol. But I will refrain from

---

18. The fact that they are so small serves to hide from us their more vital features, so that it is easier to think of them as tiny machines or mobile specks of dirt. They have often been supposed to arise by spontaneous generation from mucky mounds, as if they are small balls of semi-organic matter. In swarms or nests, the impression of aliveness is magnified, which makes them appear closer to life collectively, and yet still tiny inanimate things individually. They thus have a kind of ambiguous intermediate status, neither of one category nor the other.

assenting fully to this speculative suggestion, charming though it is. The snake's special disgustingness for some people must, I fear, remain somewhat of a mystery. Perhaps it stems, at least in part, from the mistaken idea that the typical sheen of a snake's scales is an indication of sliminess, where the oily substance is emitted from within. Or perhaps mild disgust is confusedly amplified by strong fear. What should be noted in all these cases is that we are dealing with a kind of peripheral or reduced disgust, so that the diagnosis in terms of death-in-life will become correspondingly tenuous and glancing.

(6) Plants sometimes disgust us—how does the death-in-life theory handle that case? Decaying plant matter can cause disgust, especially in food: this seems a special case of putrescence, though notably milder than in the case of flesh. The life of microorganisms mixes with the death of the plant. No new issue arises here—though the prospect of ingestion is not normally at play in the case of the rotting corpse (except when the animal carcass is one we planned to eat). It is not the mere deadness of the plant that offends, as with dried grass, but the evidence of encroaching life within this death. However, there is still the case of the disgusting healthy plant—seaweed, some fungi, a slimy seed or pit perhaps. Here, I think, we have a simple case of analogy, with sliminess being the operative quality: some plants can be slimy just like a slimy organism or organism part. And slime is the mark of the dank and decaying, as well as of the worm and the slug. This is why the disgust is minimal here—it rests merely upon analogy. It is doubtful that slime would be found disgusting in plants if it were not already found disgusting in animals. Nor is an animal disgusting simply because it is slimy; rather, slime is disgusting because certain animals exhibit it—worms, in particular.[19] Thus slime in plants can

---

19. What is slime exactly? The *OED* gives: "an unpleasantly moist, soft, and slippery substance." Notice the weight carried here by "unpleasantly": we don't describe a moisturized face as slimy, yet it is moist, soft, and slippery;

easily be overcome as a source of disgust, as when we learn to eat seaweed and fungus after some initial reluctance: the quality itself is not robustly disgusting, and is not found to be so in all cultures. The only plants that might be reliably disgusting would be those that flourished in a sepulchral setting—graveyard plants. To my knowledge, there are no such cemetery-specific plants, but if there were a type of toadstool, say, that grew only over graves, somehow absorbing the putrescent bodily tissues beneath, then we might have a strong candidate for a disgusting plant. But note that its disgustingness would be entirely derivative, not intrinsic. It is hard to see how a healthy form of plant life *could* be intrinsically disgusting, though it might be feared (if poisonous or predatory). Botanical disgust is a decidedly marginal phenomenon.

(7) Dirt can carry disease. All animals therefore have a means for cleaning themselves. Dirt also deters sexual partners and social relations generally. Dirt smells. Dirt is depressing. Dirt is everywhere. Dirt is unavoidable. In these truisms we see the reason that dirt is found to be disgusting. An animal that eats is bound to get dirty in the process, or one that defecates, or mates, or just hangs about in the world. You can't live in this fallen world without filth clinging to you. But filth is unhealthy and unsightly, and must be removed. The corpse cannot remove

---

nor is all lubrication thought of as slimy. So it is not the sensory features as such that count; there has to be an additional sense of unpleasantness. But what does that derive from? Not from the sensory features themselves, evidently. I suggest it derives from the *context* of the sensory features—what has those features and that thing's particular significance for us. Thus a slug or worm is described as slimy because it is unpleasantly slippery and moist—but the unpleasantness derives from its being the kind of creature it is. I am suggesting that the relevant context here includes the death-in-life meaning of the slug or worm. The very same tactile feel might not be found unpleasant (i.e., disgusting) in another context. We describe soft and slippery qualities as *slimy* when they are embedded in a context that warrants disgust and not otherwise.

dirt from itself, nor does dirt have any meaning for it any more. Living things, by contrast, must clean themselves of dirt or risk becoming a corpse or a hermit. The dying animal is often a dirty animal, and pitiful for so being. So excessive dirtiness is interpreted as death-related; dirty flesh is akin to dead flesh. But the dirt that an animal accumulates is part of its life as an organism— its path through the grimy world. Dirt is thus a sign both of life and of death. Accordingly, it disgusts. And if the dirt takes the form of feces or urine or other bodily excretions, then so much the worse, since they embody the death-in-life principle themselves. In a dirty tramp, say, we see clearly the amount of dirt that living entails (in our own case too), but we also know that too much dirt threatens life. We can't live without it, but it can be the death of us. Dirt is the universe's way of reminding us of what we are—mortal life forms. The gods have no need to wash: dirt does not attach itself to them during life, and they do not turn to dirt in death. We, on the other hand, exist in a universe of dirt, as organic beings, and dirt is what we are destined to become—mere dust beneath the feet. For us, to be is to be soiled, in life and death.[20]

(8) Many people find certain sexual practices disgusting (which is to be distinguished from finding them immoral): for example, interspecies sex, anal sex, and masturbation. Procreative intercourse is deemed (relatively) non-disgusting. Why the difference? What set of attitudes renders one innocuous and the other repellent? I trust I am saying nothing revelatory when I observe that in the intercourse case, children can result, while in the other cases, no children can result. It is the difference between fertility and sterility. If all sex were of the non-procreative

20. What is the kind of dirt we are most anxious to avoid and wash off? Feces, certainly, but also the residue left by touching dead animals—specifically, meat. This is clearly death-involving—indeed, typically slaughter-involving. I am sure that undertakers wash their hands a lot—or always wear protective gloves. We don't want the smell and stickiness of death on our fingers.

variety, then the species would soon die out, obviously. Species death would result from exclusively "deviant" sex. Thus in such sex, extinction can be clearly discerned—the end of human life, in fact. The consequences of exclusively non-procreative sex are comparable to those of a nuclear holocaust, that is, species annihilation. Yet we don't find nuclear annihilation disgusting exactly (except morally); nuclear weapons are not disgust objects—they are not even animate. A talent for mass death is not itself a (physically) disgusting trait. But the annihilation of the human species by exclusively non-procreative sex is different from species extinction by nuclear war, in that the means of extinction are highly life-involving in the former case. That is, there is still a lot of thrusting of organic body parts into other organic body parts, or at least the intentional manipulation of body parts resulting in ejaculation and the like. The "deviant" sex is just as vital and organic as the "non-deviant" sex; it is just that its outcome (if practiced exclusively) is a vast extinction. So, again, we see shadows of the death-in-life pattern recurring. If your focus in sex is the production of life, then the non-procreative kind will seem like a recipe for death, and then disgust will be set to make its entrance. There must exist a strong taboo against excessive emphasis on non-procreative sex, because of its catastrophic consequences if widely adopted; and if engaging in such sex is felt to be a powerful temptation, then an emotion like disgust is needed to deter us from it. After all, procreative sex has the prima facie undesirable result that babies are born that must be taken care of—and all for that fleeting pleasure. If we could detach the two, then we could have the pleasure without the responsibility—and wouldn't that be nice? (Contraception detaches the two, but it has not had time to configure the deep emotional dynamics of human beings by means of natural selection.) The force of this argument needs to be counterbalanced by a strong disinclination to engage in sexual practices that sever the tie between pleasure and procreation—which is where disgust comes to the rescue. The appeal of homosexuality is apparent, from a certain point of view, but its results for species survival are prohibitive; so disgust is deployed to negate the appeal, at least for the majority. Without such disgust, and given the evident appeal, people in general might resort to homosexuality as a substitute for heterosexual sex—and then where would we be? The same point applies to oral and anal sex: the momentary pleasure is there without the accompanying responsibility for children, so a taboo is essential to keep people centered on the penis-vagina variety of sex. In any event, the association between "deviant" sex and species death is clear enough, so we have the materials to explain how disgust accrues. I daresay, too, that if it weren't for pleasure and the biological imperative of procreation our natural sense of disgust would discourage even heterosexual intercourse. There is always an undertow of disgust in any kind of sexual practice, since sex always brings us into contact with things we generally prefer to shun. Perhaps the question should really be why we are not more disgusted at heterosexual intercourse than we are, given our general bodily queasiness; and the answer must be the pleasure that we derive from it, as well as the biologically based desire for offspring. Certainly, we find little that is aesthetically appealing in the sexual congress *of* other species (as distinct from *with* other species). As for non-procreative sexual practices in other species, these strike us as distinctly not on—quite revolting, really.[21]

Of course, the danger of species extinction is minimal, at least so far in history, because relatively few people wish to engage exclusively in non-procreative sex—that is, the kind that does not involve depositing sperm inside the vagina. If the

---

21. Homosexuality is apparently fairly common in other species, as is masturbation in some—but I have yet to hear that oral and anal sex have caught on in the animal kingdom. Nor have lesbian threesomes and "facials." I suspect our disgust at such animal antics, if they were to occur, would be quite strong.

balance ever changes, for one reason or another, then we will have to think again. As things are, a general, though not universal, disgust at "deviant" sex suffices to keep the specter of species extinction at bay. No doubt such disgust has diminished over time, as sexual tolerance has increased, and it is an interesting question how far this process can go without undermining the basis of human survival. What if oral sex became all the rage, displacing intercourse entirely? Maybe one day we will come to regret the steady loss of disgust at non-procreative sex.[22]

(9) The last category is moral (including intellectual) disgust. As I remarked earlier, this is arguably an extended and possibly metaphorical application of the concept of disgust, so that it would be a mistake to try to assimilate it too closely to core non-moral applications (has anyone actually vomited in response to a perceived immorality?). So I won't say much about the topic, noting simply that there is a vague analogy between core cases of disgust and moral disgust: namely, in the notion of mental hygiene or orderliness or being governed by rules. Sloppy writing, say, is disorderly and lacking in rules; it is chaotic and formless. We do speak of "messy" writing, even of "putrid prose"; we may even refer to dull writing as "dead on the page." On occasion a lousy (!) piece of writing evokes the ultimate condemnation: "That's shit!" A person may undergo "psychological decay," as their intellectual capacities deteriorate. In these locutions we see hints of the death theme in reactions of disgust. An immoral person may be described as "dissolute," and the evil character is often depicted as cadaverous. Of course, the ultimate in disgustingly immoral acts is murder—an act

22. Technology may contribute, as it already has in the form of pornography and "sex toys." Holograms, dolls, and robots might eventually come to absorb a sizeable proportion of human sexuality. And if the ideology of sex changes, because of worries about overpopulation and so on, people might start to feel more inclined to non-procreative sex. Population shrinkage would be the obvious result.

with death as its purpose and outcome. So reverberations of death surround and shape our expressions of moral disgust. We can conclude, then, that moral disgust incorporates many of the same themes that characterize the non-moral kind, though tenuously and figuratively.

I conclude from this survey that the death-in-life theory makes intelligible sense of the data of disgust. We see the common thread running through the domain of disgusting things—their principle of cohesion. The core cases exhibit the principle clearly, while the other cases shade off to a penumbra. The grouping is not arbitrary or wildly disjunctive, but reflects a single conceptual structure, with variations and extensions. To be disgusting is to meet certain well-defined conditions. Thus we have arrived at an *analysis* of the concept of disgust; or again, we have discovered the *essence* of disgusting things. We now know what it is that *makes* something disgusting.[23]

---

23. This reflects my general meta-philosophical position: see *Truth by Analysis*. The concept of disgust is not a family resemblance concept or a primitive, indefinable concept; it is a complex concept with nontrivial necessary and sufficient conditions. One lesson here is that great variety in the extension of a concept does not entail that it lacks an analysis and must be a case of family resemblance; the correct analysis may have to be pitched at a sufficiently high level of abstractness that it can incorporate the variety we observe.

6

The Function of Disgust

IT IS BY NO means clear what the biological function of disgust might be. As I noted earlier, the Darwinian taste-toxicity theory runs into obvious trouble: disgust cannot be viewed simply as a protection against the ingestion of unhealthy substances. This is connected to the obscure origin of disgust in the human species: how can we speculate about the origin of disgust if we don't know what its purpose is? Only if we know its function can be know *why* it arises. What kind of adaptation is it? Is it perhaps a by-product of some other direct adaptation? Nor should we expect that its function, assuming it has one, is anything simple— as fear has the simple function of motivating the animal to avoid danger. Disgust might play a more complex role in the overall human psychological and biological economy. In this section I propose to make some exploratory remarks, nothing more, about this very difficult question.

We can note, to begin with, that disgust is antithetical to desire or appetite. If I am disgusted by something, then I have no desire or appetite for it (I am putting aside issues of ambivalence here). If a certain potential foodstuff disgusts me, then I will not want to eat it; nor will I seek contact with flesh I find disgusting. So disgust functions to curb or delimit desire. Satiety also functions in that way: my appetite for food diminishes the more satiated I am, to the point of disappearance. But the emotion of disgust is not to be identified with mere feelings of satiety—as it might be, a sensation of fullness in my stomach. That would be neither nor sufficient for disgust. Still, there might be a clue here about the function of disgust, because it is at least *one* way to curb desire, among others. In the case of animals, that way does not exist, since they do not feel disgust; feelings of satiety do the job for animals. Is there some way in which desire differs between humans and animals that might bear on the presence of disgust in the former but not in the latter? Why should we humans need disgust in addition to sensations of satiety in order to curb our desires? And why should we feel disgust toward things that are actually quite nourishing and not at all toxic?

The answer, I suggest, lies in the *scope* of human desire as compared with animal desire. Human desire is apt to have unlimited scope: it is excessive, greedy, uncontrolled. We want everything and we want it now. We always want the best, the biggest, the most expensive, the most sought after, the most desirable, the most depraved. We are greedy for food, sex, fame, money, real estate, violence, and even moral distinction. We never seem to know when we have had enough. We have a tendency to overindulge, bite off more than we can chew, take it to an extreme. Once one appetite has been temporarily satisfied we move restlessly on to another. We are never content with what we have. Partly this is because we think obsessively about the future: we are anxious about what tomorrow may bring, so we try to consume as much as possible today. Maybe food will be short in the future, so let's eat a lot now and horde as much as we can. Maybe sex will be unavailable next week, so we should indulge ourselves as much as possible today. What adds to this is that we are not limited to thoughts of the finite: we can conceive of endless supplies of the things we desire—and no finite number of these will ever exhaust what we can conceive of. Our desires become essentially infinite, unquenchable; we always want more, and more, and more again. Thus we are given to excess, neediness, and manic consumption. We would consume the whole universe if we could! This leads us to a generalized promiscuity in our desires: we can get more of what we want if we are undiscriminating about the objects of our wants. This obviously applies to sex, but it also holds for food. We are omnivorous and capable of eating a great variety of types of food, and human sexuality is notoriously flexible and open-ended. We don't just want more of the same: we crave variety, novelty, and adventure. We will try anything, go to any lengths, and we will never give up. We yearn, and strive, and yearn again, and strive some more. We never stop the mad dance of desire. We know no limits. We are lost in the swirling vortex of our rampant wishes.

But, of course, this appetitive excess is only one part of our nature. On the other side, we have a tendency to curb our excesses, to be moderate, prudent, and safe. Our desires may be infinite, but we also realize that giving in to them can be bad—prudentially, morally. You may want to stuff yourself full of rich food till you can hardly walk, but you will pay the price later. You may want to get as drunk as a lord, but the thought of that hangover will curb your enthusiasm (sometimes at least). So we walk a tightrope between excess and moderation. We are forever holding ourselves back, reining ourselves in. The intensity of wayward desire calls for a muscular will. This suggests a hypothesis: disgust came about as a means of curbing our excesses. Disgust is the strong force needed to counterbalance our excessive tendencies: it keeps us on the rails when we strain to break the bonds of all decent restraint. Disgust therefore exists because of a prior tendency in our make-up, namely, boundless excess. Without disgust, excess would get the better of us. In the simplest case, disgust exists, not to prevent us eating poisonous food, but to prevent us eating too much *good* food. The food is fine; it is our exaggerated desires that threaten disaster. We want more than is good for us, more than we can handle. Our excessive desires push us hard in a certain direction, and then disgust steps in to restrain these desires. Disgust arose in the species because excessive desire had already arisen and led to unhappy results; we could not contain ourselves by will alone, so the genes (or culture) invented an emotional mechanism to contain us. Disgust arose to combat human greed—promiscuous, boundless, and heedless. Once it had arisen it could proceed to diversify and mutate, taking in new objects by analogy or association; but the original disgust objects (according to this hypothesis) were objects that we were unhealthily greedy about.[1]

Evidence for the hypothesis can be found in a simple and striking fact: we can feel disgust for things that we normally desire—once we have had our fill of them. Even the most delicious food may revolt us if we are already bloated with it. The twentieth oyster may be found repulsive while the first nineteen went down a treat; it may even cause vomiting. Sex may strike us as the most desirable thing in the world, but after we have had enough of it attraction may turn to repulsion. If we have indulged to excess, disgust is apt to set in, and given our exces-

---

1. As a general point, not all adaptations are to the animal's environment, physical or social; some may be adaptations to the animal itself, even to its particular psychological structure. If a trait of an animal is antithetical to that animal's survival, then an adaptation to that trait could conceivably evolve—as a way of coping with the trait in question (supposing that it cannot be directly eliminated). This is what I am suggesting in the case of human desire: its excessiveness is threatening to the animal's well-being, but it cannot be simply eliminated, so a new psychological trait arises to contain it—and that trait is disgust at what the animal so excessively desires. That is, disgust is an adaptation to a psychological trait of the human animal. Those animals with the adaptation do better than those without it, so it becomes widespread. A species can undergo change to cope with itself as much it can undergo change to cope with the environment. There can be adaptations to adaptations (and so on indefinitely). We might indeed say that the animal's nature is *part* of the environment to which it must adapt.

sive desires we often do indulge to excess. It is not that the desired object is toxic or unhealthy in itself; it is our extremity of desire that is unwholesome and unhealthy. If it were not for disgust, we might act on our excessive desires till we exploded or wore ourselves to a frazzle.[2] Surfeit itself can be experienced as disgusting, as when food is too rich or the plate too full or the courses too many. Very sweet food is often found disgusting, or very fatty food. Both sweetness and fattiness are excellent sources of nutritive value, but too much of a good thing can be a bad thing. Greed is wanting too much of a good thing; disgust is the aversive reaction that curbs greed. Disgust saves us from ourselves, with all our wild grabbing and grasping.

But how does the excess theory of the origin and function of disgust apply to our paradigm cases—corpses and feces? Here we must think our way back into prehistory, into primitive human society. And we must be prepared to be bold. Sexual desire and hunger are basic motivational states, and obviously very powerful. Humans want lots of sex and lots of food—and both commodities can be in short supply. In such circumstances, excessive human desire starts to spill over: we start wanting to have sex with more things than fertile human adults, and we will eat anything that seems edible. You can see where I heading with this: early humans started desiring sex with dead bodies and wanting to eat feces. Or maybe it was not shortage that prompted our pre-disgust ancestors but simple greed: they just wanted more and more, with variations and permutations, and weren't too particular about how they got it. At this point in human evo-

---

2. Note that feelings of satiety are not always enough to stop us: we often keep going in the face of such feelings—as with "stuffing ourselves." This is where disgust can add its powerful force to curb desire: we develop a terrible revulsion to something we have hitherto strongly desired. You don't just feel full and stop eating; you positively don't want the food near you any longer—you push the plate away and can't even stand the smell of it. This is what animals don't seem to feel about food they have just gorged themselves on—not that they do that very often.

lution, then, we are to imagine rampant, untrammeled, indiscriminate desire, with no disgust response in place: free-flowing desire beyond biological necessity, beyond reason, beyond sanity. The early humans were thus tempted to necrophilia and coprophagia (maybe also desiring to eat decayed human flesh), and we may suppose that they gave in to those temptations. The result may not be simple ill health: the objects desired may not be toxic or otherwise dangerous (some animals, after all, do eat feces, their own or those of other species—they contain some worthwhile nutrients). Still, the desires in question are excessive and (not to put too fine a point on it) mad—they are not conducive to psychological wellbeing, stability, and so on. They need to be curbed, possibly because of their psychopathological effects. Remember that our early humans resemble us in many respects: they have morality, an aesthetic sense, communal ways of flourishing, self-respect, and self-loathing. Giving in to their excessive desires, in the form of sex with dead bodies and eating shit, does not sit well with other aspects of their nature. They feel conflicted, confused, disturbed, unhinged—yet still driven. Incestuous necrophilia and coprophagia, in particular, produce tempestuous feelings of emotional turmoil in their sordid souls. They feel madness coming on (and isn't giving in to every passing desire a clear sign of madness?). Or maybe just too much time and energy gets used up in the pursuit of these things, when other more beneficial options could be pursued—alive people, nuts and berries.[3] The essential point is that the desires are

---

3. These may be less exciting options, but they are psychologically safer. And here we come upon another characteristic of human desire—the lust for excitement. We seek novelty, strangeness, and risk. It is not enough to get what we want; we have to feel excited about it. This can fuel a taste for transgression—for the breaking of codes and prohibitions—and necrophilia, for example, is certainly a case of that. Disgust, then, can operate to curb desires that serve the cause of lust for excitement. Again, it is doubtful that animals are "sensation seekers" in the way we are. They are wholesome creatures, but we humans—not so much.

excessive and contraindicated by other aspects of their nature; it is just not good for you to have such crazy desires and to yield to them. That certainly seems true of many human desires: they are hyperbolic, subversive, unbalancing (consider the current desire for fame and celebrity at any cost, even imprisonment). And if satiety and good judgment won't stop them in their tracks, then something blunter and more potent will be needed. Here is where disgust comes in: if we are strongly repelled by something, we will not desire it. So the genes (or social conditioning) step in to curb the excessive desires that threaten to overwhelm the psyche: we become disgusted by something we would otherwise be tempted to eat or fornicate with—in the present case, feces and corpses. Our "default condition" is overweening, indiscriminate desire: but this is not good for us or other people, so disgust arises to dampen our excesses. Disgust prevents us from following our unruly inclinations, our anarchic appetites. Animals don't experience disgust because their appetites are more sensible, finite, and practical. But human appetites can be stupid, infinite, and imprudent—so we need something to inhibit their wilder manifestations. Our appetites, left to their own devices, can lead to madness, breakdown, and social anarchy; therefore, they must be controlled by a suitably powerful countervailing force. Disgust is an adaptation evolved to deal with an aspect of human psychology, namely our runaway desires. Compulsion and obsession are part of the human emotional landscape, often to the extreme detriment of the individual; and we can readily imagine these traits leading to necrophilia and coprophagia unless powerful aversive dispositions are put in place. Human desires, unlike animal desires, are prone to such deformations and exaggerations; disgust is nature's way of trying to rein them in. Then, once disgust has a hold in the mind, it can take off and assume other objects and roles; but the hypothesis we are considering is that in the beginning disgust operated to bring appetitive excess to heel. If our desires had all along been sensible, limited, and sane, then we would have discounted corpses and feces as objects of erotic and gustatory desire, focusing instead on live people and ordinary food materials. But human desire is wild and infinite in scope, never contented, forever in search of novelty and challenge.[4] We are a constitutionally curious and innovative species, always ready to try something new, unwilling to remain on the well-trodden path, and our desires reflect this curiosity (animals just plod on in the same old way). Often, our desires are perverse and rebellious, impatient with rules, regulations, and old habits. Without an inbuilt countervailing force they will lead us to do almost anything, however bizarre and irrational.[5] Disgust is that force. Disgust is the human psyche policing itself, putting up self-imposed barriers.

Why human desire should be so anarchic as to *need* policing is another question. It must have something to do with the human imagination and intellect, our grasp of the future, of possibility, of mortality; animals don't have any of that, so their desires remain pragmatic and grounded. Our desires are far more flexible and free—but also more inflated and unhinged.

4. This would explain the deep ambivalence to the disgust object that I mentioned earlier: we were *first* attracted to corpses and feces and only *later* turned against them. Disgust was applied to an antecedent attraction as a device of self-control. But disgust is sufficiently aversive to counteract the underlying attraction in the modern mind, so it has gone into a kind of remission. The attraction is now but a dim memory of our species past, when it was conceivably the dominant psychological force.

5. Have I rediscovered the id, the ego, and the superego? In a sense, I have—but not the sexual id, ego, and superego envisaged by Freud. What I take over from Freud (and many others) is the idea of a primal reservoir of desire that needs taming in some way—the id. As for the relation between disgust and the superego, it would obviously be wrong to identify the disgust faculty with the moral sense as inculcated by society, as Freud conceived the superego. Furthermore, I don't see primal desire as brute and instinctual, like the desire of animals; on the contrary, I see it as distinguishing humans from animals and as arising from specifically human traits, such as intellect, language, and imagination. However, the *structural* relations between desire and disgust mirror those Freud envisaged between the id and the superego.

The very freedom of the human mind, abetted by imagination and an awareness of possibility, enables us to form desires of kinds undreamt of by other animals. What animal wants to become a billionaire, or a rock star, or a serial killer? But humans can desire anything conceivable, no matter how extreme and bizarre. That is part of what makes us distinctively human, for good and ill. Disgust is unique to us because of this kind of amplified and ramped up desire—or so I am (tentatively) suggesting. This theory is, of course, highly speculative: I put it forward as worth considering because I know of no other theory of the origin and function of disgust that seems to me even remotely plausible. This theory, at least, locates disgust in something recognizably and distinctively human, and it links disgust to a psychological phenomenon that is as extreme as disgust itself. In a sense, what we are really disgusted at is ourselves—for our pathology of desire. Disgust is indeed a defensive reaction, but the defense is against our own reckless and dangerous psyche.[6]

I want to end this part of the book with a reminder of the power and pungency of the emotion of disgust. It cuts deep into the psyche, and is capable of lingering and festering. I once saw a homeless hippy in Berkeley, California, begging for money; as I glanced over at him, scruffy and grimy, a tremendous grey bogey literally *swayed* from his nose, like a gooey worm. I almost

6. Do we have any other self-defensive reactions formally like disgust? The obvious suggestion would be guilt: we feel guilt in order to curb our tendencies toward morally bad actions. In the rough old days, we just performed the bad actions, acting on our anarchic desires; but this became a liability, mainly because of the reactions of others, so we evolved guilt as a way of suppressing the immoral desires. A less obvious candidate might be our tendency to forget our dreams, given their frequently disturbing content: our ancestors used to dream and vividly remember their dreams; but this became intolerable, so the species evolved a mechanism to *dis*remember them. In general, humans have a psyche that *needs* inbuilt controls—unlike other animals. The enemy lies within the gates.

threw up on the spot. I couldn't eat without being nauseatingly reminded of the sight for several days; and even now, many years later, the memory can assault my stomach. The visual image is like a stab to the guts. Then there are Jonathan Swift's famous lines about his beloved: "No wonder how I lost my Wits; Oh! Caelia, Caelia, Caelia shits!" Disgust can lead to derangement, even insanity; this is why despots use it to "break the spirit." Hell is surely a place of unending disgust, as well as pain. Disgust hits us hard and refuses to leave us alone. It is a very distinctive feeling, deeply unpleasant (though not exactly painful). It resonates in the psyche, tormenting and irrepressible. When we want to feel it least we sometimes feel it most (say at a funeral), and it is difficult to suppress the behavioral symptoms. It is a searing emotion, one that penetrates to every corner of the self. It is close to despair in its unstoppable power. It slices like a knife. It makes us its helpless victim. In the next part of the book, I want to enquire more deeply into how disgust figures in our conception of ourselves—what it tells us about human nature. It might tell us something as disquieting as the emotion itself.

PART TWO

DISGUST AND THE HUMAN

CONDITION

7

Our Dual Nature

DESCARTES DIVIDES THE HUMAN person into two parts, corresponding to mind and body. The essence of mind is thought. The essence of body is extension. Mind is exempt from the reach of mechanism, but body is subject to mechanism. This means that the human body is classified along with other extended bodies—such as machines and purely inanimate things in general. Physics can treat all extended bodies equally. When we think of our bodies as extended we think of them as belonging with other bodies, mechanical or geological or astronomical. Mechanism has long since lapsed as a theory of the physical world, but still the tendency has been to conceive the human body as continuous with other "physical" bodies. From one point of view, this is not wrong, but it serves to obscure an important fact about the human body, so far as our affective relation to it is concerned—namely that it is an organic, biological system, and hence an object of disgust. There is nothing disgusting about machines and mountains and stars, but the human body—like organic systems generally—has the talent to disgust. We do *not* think of ourselves as "the ghost in the machine"—not only because we don't think of ourselves as "ghostly" (immaterial, incorporeal), but also because we don't think of our human body as a "machine," if that means similar to a human artifact such as a car or a robot. Our attitude toward machines and organic bodies is quite different. Descartes' picture omits this crucial difference, and so fails to record the very special relationship we have with our bodies.[1] The simple point is that we are disgusted by our bodily nature—not as a merely extended thing, but as an organic thing (a thing with "plumbing"). Descartes' philosophy elides the anus. His view of the body is drily antiseptic and abstract. The extendedness of the body is not an emotional issue for us as intelligent conscious beings, but the disgustingness of the body is. We might say that the body exhibits a certain dualism itself—between its non-disgusting properties, such as extension and movement, on the one hand, and its disgusting properties, such as digestion and bloodiness, on the other. If we are to understand our feelings about ourselves—our affective *Umwelt*—then the latter are crucial.

Descartes' dualism represents a reification of an undeniable duality. One aspect of our nature attracts such labels as "soul," "spirit," "self," "mind," "personhood," and "consciousness." When we think of ourselves in this way, collateral concepts and categories are brought to bear: we are described as "symbolic," "normative," "rational," "self-conscious," "free," "cultural," "reflective," and "transcendent." On this side belong our ethical and aesthetic senses, as well as our intellectual powers and linguistic abilities. We value this side of ourselves, even comparing the human being to divine beings; in self-congratulatory mode, we think of ourselves as "godlike" and make invidious comparisons between humans and other animals. But we must also acknowledge another side that excites far less admiration: the side relating to the body. This side we characterize with such locutions as

---

1. I don't think Descartes was blind to the distinction: he was suggesting that contrary to appearances, the body works *as if* it were a machine (by law-governed contact causation, etc.). The opposite impulse regards nature in general as an organism, which Aristotle's natural teleology was apt to do. I am not here disagreeing with Descartes about the mechanistic thesis, merely noting that it is phenomenologically misleading: the organic and inorganic *strike* us quite differently.

"organic," "animal," "creaturely," "biological," "law-governed," "decomposable," "finite," "abject," and "ghastly." Attitudes here can range from the outright hostile to the mildly critical. Irresistibly, this side of our nature is experienced as "lower"— not something to celebrate or boast about, still less to liken to the godlike. On the one hand, then, we have a *heroic* nature, while on the other we have a nature that is...well, less than heroic (*sub-heroic* maybe).[2] And these two natures exist side by side, in uneasy juxtaposition: the godlike and the (shall we say) animal-like. The former invites esteem, but the latter is mired in disgust—because the organic body is apt to elicit revulsion. One part of us is disgusted by the other part—the "good" part by the "bad" part. To be more concrete: he who has a soul also has an anus—he who thinks also shits. And there cannot be the former without the latter: the "fine" part of our nature is dependent upon the "gross" part, the "higher" on the "lower." We cannot cast off our gross nature, like an old skin, because without it we can have no existence at all; no cosmetic surgery can remove the disgustingness from our identity. Moreover, the gross continually *confronts* the fine with its inescapable reality: we are tied to it epistemologically, as well as ontologically. We are disgusting and we know it, know it in our marrow—yet we feel ourselves to be much more than that, and to exist essentially outside of it. There is, we insist, a pocket of our being that is free of all disgust—the part we call the "self" or the "soul" (the "person" seems to incorporate too much of the body). Indeed, we might be supposed to have concocted the idea of the soul precisely in order to carve out a section of our being that is not touched by the disgusting, a kind of pure kernel. We are admittedly saturated with gross

---

2. I borrow the concept of the heroic from Becker: see chapters one and eleven. The general idea is that we want to stand out, to assert our specialness in nature, yet we are encumbered by a body that qualifies or diminishes the heroic stature we crave. The inner hero is clothed in the body of an anti-hero.

materials in our bodily nature, yet we feel that there is something in us that transcends those materials: so we contrive a notion of "soul" that is stipulated to be innocent of all disgust elements—to stand quite outside the organic realm, akin to the divine.[3] The concept of the divine itself seems specially designed to avoid the grossness of biological nature, and we reserve a place for ourselves in that charmed sphere by identifying a divine ingredient in our nature. The soul is that divine part of the human being that has no tincture of disgust clinging to it—and so cannot be identified with anything like a heart or a brain, still less with the entire biological organism. At any rate, the human animal presents itself to itself as an amalgam of the disgusting and the heroic (as I have styled it). We experience ourselves as occupying both realms simultaneously and inextricably.

At one moment, the human being repels himself; at another he excites his own adulation. We esteem ourselves for our "spiritual" side, and yet we despise ourselves for our foul and filthy side. Thus, our nature as human beings can be described as paradoxical, incongruous, dissonant, disjointed, disjunctive, divided, contradictory, hybrid, mismatched, and ambiguous. We are a synthesis of opposites, a compound of disparate elements. Our emotional reaction to ourselves reflects this incongruity: love and hate, attraction and repulsion, narcissism and despair.[4] Divine poetic utterance issues from the transcendent soul—while at the same time a pungent fart escapes the anus, like a mocking

---

3. The soul is that part of ourselves that never needs to be scrubbed, because it is clean by nature. Accordingly, it can be beautiful through and through, which the body never can be. In art (religious art, in particular) the body merely symbolizes the soul, which is art's essential concern. The body is merely the grotesque mask the soul is condemned to wear during its mortal existence.

4. We can't just happily combine a positive attitude to the thing which is our soul with a negative attitude to the thing which is our body, as if they had nothing to do with each other: for we are *persons*—entities with both sets of attributes. It is *I* who is both great and squalid. Hence I must combine contrary attributes in a single entity. Put differently, the body is *mine*.

demon of the digestive system. The two sides of our nature are fused, yet each pulls in its own direction, wagging a finger at the other. Our fine side deplores our gross side, while our gross side seems intent on dragging down our fine side. We are caught in the middle. Animals and infants feel no such ambivalence about their nature, because disgust is foreign to them: the duality in question has no hold over their thoughts and feelings. The gods also suffer no such qualms, because there is nothing about them *to* disgust, not having an organic nature. Only mature human beings, of all the creatures of the natural (and supernatural) world, feel this awkward split, this wretched dissonance. We are, as has been well said, the "god who shits," and we are only too well aware of our peculiar status.[5] In another image: we are the worm that philosophizes. Trapped in our natural grossness, we nevertheless aspire to great things—and even achieve them. We feel greatness glowing within ourselves, yet at the same time we are flooded with the sordidness of our nature as mere organisms. We exist as a kind of ontological oxymoron.[6]

Consciousness itself encourages the sense of a divided nature. Ontologically, consciousness is not the *kind* of thing that can disgust the senses. It would be a category mistake to attribute (physical) disgustingness to consciousness—to thoughts, sensations, feelings, and acts of will. Consciousness strikes us as transcending the organic, as existing outside of

---

5. The phrase occurs in Becker, p. 58. Then again we are described as "gods with anuses" on p. 51.

6. The conflict is perhaps more apparent from a third-person perspective than from a first-person perspective, because of the diminished disgust we feel for ourselves. In the case of others, we acutely sense the clash between love and admiration, on the one hand, and repulsion and disgust, on the other. No matter how heroic we find another person, no matter how much they distinguish themselves, they are still subject to the awful democracy of the disgusting body. There is not a person on earth who could not make you retch, no matter how great and beautiful of soul.

it.[7] From the inside, it gives us the *illusion* that we are not constitutionally disgusting. If we knew only facts about our own conscious mind, and nothing about the human body, then we could never deduce that we are also a gross bag of biological tissue. This is why we are perpetually *surprised* by our gross nature, taken aback by it, as we are not by our rational symbolic nature. Simply by being a center of consciousness, who would ever guess that he or she is (also) a perishable envelope of ghastly goo with leaking holes in it? We feel a proper pride in the achievements of the human mind, which seem to belong so intimately to us, but this is coupled with dismay about the squelchy organism we also turn out to be, which seems to exist at one remove from our essence. Consciousness appears to us as a non-disgusting zone of reality, but then we discover that we are also enmeshed in another zone consisting of gross biological material. A priori we know ourselves to be pure and clean in our conscious core, but a posteriori we find that we also wallow in filth.[8] The self-assured nobleman (or woman) discovers that he (or she) has humble and detestable roots. There is grime beneath the surface sheen of the conscious mind, but consciousness

7. I do not mean to take a stand against "materialism" here. If the identity theory is true, then states of consciousness *are* states of a disgusting internal organ. I am speaking of how consciousness naively strikes us, and how its appearance shapes our self-conception. Certainly, we don't *introspect* our conscious states *as* revolting brain states—quite the opposite, in fact.

8. That is, we have immediate knowledge of our non-disgusting consciousness by way of acquaintance, but we have inferential knowledge of our disgusting bodily nature. It could have *turned out* that we are not disgusting, because the nature of the body is not a given, as the nature of the mind is; the body is something we discover. Thus we are apt to think of our disgustingness as contingent, while our nature as non-disgusting conscious selves is necessary. It is epistemically possible that we are gods, so to speak, given only introspective awareness—though that may not be metaphysically possible (for familiar Kripkean reasons). That is basically what I hold: we are necessarily not gods, metaphysically, but it is epistemically possible (from the inside) that we are gods (if not terribly spectacular ones).

itself is not grimy. Given that we are essentially conscious beings, then, as well as biological entities, we are existentially condemned to experience ourselves as, *both* clean and unclean, superlative and sordid. The very nature of consciousness introduces the split in our being that I am highlighting. In an insentient worm there is no such split, because such a being is nothing but biological tissue; sentient organisms, by contrast, contain a privileged sector, where their minds are located. Self-reflective beings, such as ourselves, recognize that their minds are (in this sense) pure, but then they must also acknowledge that their bodies are vile, and that acknowledgment comes as an existential shock—a trauma from which no recovery is possible. It is a stunning discovery—and not a welcome one—that pure rarified consciousness, in all its glory and variety, has its basis in that pulpy sponge-like growth we call the *brain*. That is not at all what we would have expected viewing the conscious mind purely from the inside.[9] The organic brain is the *last* thing we would have expected to form the basis of the mind. And the shock here is not just metaphysical; it is also aesthetic—for the brain is just so revolting to the senses. It resembles nothing so much as a mound of dung! From the inside, consciousness gives a quite different account of itself, thus engendering a kind of illusion about the kind of beings we are. Our inherent duality only becomes apparent when we assume the outside perceptual point of view and take in the body and its base anatomy. The conscious mind presents itself as a very different kind of "internal organ" from the heart, the lungs, and the kidneys.

---

9. Part of the fascination of neuroscience is surely the sense of wonder that conscious life depends upon such an unprepossessing organ as the brain. It just seems so *surprising*. It is nothing like discovering that the circulation of the blood depends upon the heart. The brain-mind connection can never be boring, because it seems like a natural miracle. How astonishing that the emotion of joy depends upon neural excitations in the amygdala! That grotty little collection of cells is responsible for my entire emotional well-being.

Negative emotions thus coexist with positive ones in unresolved confusion and profusion. We cringe at our bodily nature, becoming self-critical, self-loathing, ashamed, and beset by anxiety about the betrayals the body may visit on us. Much effort is expended to conceal, to minimize, and to protect. It seems like an insult or a joke or a tragedy—or all three. Who would play such a trick on us? Yet, on the other side, there is pride, self-worship, and grandiosity. The human condition is to be subject to these contrary emotions, pulled in both directions—a Divided Self. Are we magnificent or are we wretched? The only answer seems to be: *both*. If only we could become united beings—all body or all spirit—then we could relax in our undivided nature. But that is out of the question. We may strive to transcend our biological being by accentuating our finer side—by art, by religion, by science—but it remains stubbornly in place, and is the basis of all transcendence. No amount of heroism, no feats of creativity, no contact with the divine, can ever free us from the necessity to produce, with monotonous regularity, pound after pound, and ton upon ton, of stinking, revolting *shit*. No matter how much we may admire or love another human being, we can never free ourselves of revulsion at what they are or can easily become. Jonathan Swift could not even reconcile himself to Caelia's shocking (but routine) bathroom acts—and that was before he even considered the question of her possible future incontinence. Sartre maintained that we are condemned to consciousness of our own freedom, which we try desperately to escape; I am saying that we are condemned to consciousness of our own filth, which we also want badly to escape. Disgust is a highly disagreeable emotion, and its prime object is ourselves: that is not a predicament to which we can ever become happily reconciled. We may try to evade it, we may become numb to it, we may simply resolve to live with it—but we can never regard it with equanimity, as just one more fact about the human species (like the fact that we walk on two legs).

Every day we are confronted by species self-disgust, directed toward ourselves or other people, and every day it jabs and twists in our sensitive consciousness.[10]

And there is a further, immensely disquieting, fact: our very survival as a self or soul *depends* upon the body we find so problematic. It is not just the fact that we die that disturbs us, but that our death is in the hands of a gross and alien mass of tissues. If the bowels cease to perform their gruesome work, it's lights out for the transcendent soul that frets about its proximity to the organic body; we *need* the thing from which we so alienated. The soul may despise the squelchy organs of the body, as if there were undesirable neighbors, and would never accept any claim of deep kinship between itself and them, yet its very existence depends upon those despised organs—their pumping and squirting. It is a little too much like having to accept that all one's finer feelings and achievements depend upon the activities of a nest of vile worms. This seems like an insult to one's dignity—being forced to feed and tend to a bunch of wriggling worms, on pain of ceasing to exist (and remember that the digestive tract *is* a kind of worm). Would things be much worse if we really were symbiotically dependent on a species of worm for our survival? We are embedded in the repugnant, unable to survive without it. It isn't very godlike, is it? The body strikes us, in this mood, as a foul prison we cannot escape. Only death can release us from the disgusting, but life is saturated in it. This

---

10. Perhaps I should clarify my earlier point that consciousness is not itself disgusting: for how can that be so, if consciousness is regularly confronted by disgusting objects? The answer is that the *objects* of consciousness can be disgusting without consciousness itself being disgusting (of course, consciousness also has a great many non-disgusting objects, where the question doesn't even arise). This is shown in the fact that there cannot be higher order disgust consciousness: we cannot be (physically) disgusted by disgust itself. I am disgusted by feces themselves, not by my disgusted consciousness of them. I am not doubly disgusted—by feces *and* by my disgust at them.

seems both unfair and incomprehensible: unfair, because an affront to our finer nature; and incomprehensible, because a senseless contingency—nature out of joint. And it is all because of our incongruous duality, our anomalous species ontology. We suffer from "Swift's syndrome": an intense poetic revulsion at the privy.

Let us consider the matter diachronically, in an effort to gain further insight into it. Organic bodies evolved on planet earth long before anything like a self-reflective conscious self did—many millions of years before, in fact. The design of these bodies was clearly not arrived at by consultation with such self-reflective (and aesthetically sensitive) beings. Above the level of plant life, the basic architecture is a tube-like structure that takes in nourishment at one end and expels waste products at the other—a worm, in short. Different body structures developed around this wormlike tube, to enable mobility and so on, but all animals are structured as organs and tissues surrounding a central digestive tract, humans included. For millions of years, no one batted an eyelid: the various species of animal felt no repugnance at the design Nature had laid down (and what other design possibilities did Nature have?). The dinosaurs led a blissfully disgust-free existence, idyllic in its way. But then, very late in the day, after eons of animal evolution, a species evolved that regarded organic matter rather differently—a queasy, weak-stomached, and hypersensitive species—and this species found the constitution of the animal body to be an object of distaste and disdain. In certain circumstances, this troubled species (*Homo disgustus*) would even vomit when the body underwent one of its routine performances. Thus was born the first and only self-loathing species on the planet: the species whose members found biological reality itself to be emotionally and aesthetically abhorrent. And, to see it from their point of view, this was not really all that surprising, since they, after all, were beings endowed with an aesthetic sense and the basic design of the animal body had never been vetted by anyone possessing such a sense.[11] Certain sensibilities had newly evolved in this refined species, but the body that housed them had not been devised with these sensibilities in mind; a clash inevitably resulted. The basic body design was an inflexible biological given that had stood the test of evolutionary time, but that is not to say that a creature with a fine sense of the beautiful and the ugly would find the design to its liking (or one burdened with an awareness and terror of death). Natural Selection woke up one day to discover that it had attached a refined mind to a vile body.[12] Oops! Up until that point, the members of the various species had all been indifferent philistines, not giving a fig about filth and phlegm. But it was too late now, because the body design was what it was and the squeamish refined minds could see things in no other way. Once culture got seriously under way, the disgust factor only deepened, but the bodies didn't change—it was like it or lump it. The members of the refined species chafed and dreamed of other purer bodies, even making small steps toward their creation—which only made their predicament worse. But the die was cast.

Was there a way out? Theoretically, yes; at least there was the thought of a way out—in the form of *metamorphosis*. The unprepossessing caterpillar, itself a type of worm, could change into the beautiful butterfly, so Nature had allowed for dramatic

11. I see an anti-Creationist argument taking shape here: why would an intelligent designer create a species so at odds with itself? He must have known how we would regard our bodies, yet he went ahead anyway. That doesn't seem very intelligent—more like a stupid mistake. Natural selection can make stupid mistakes of this kind, because it is not directed by intelligence and foresight—but surely not an omniscient god. This is a more general version of the well-known argument that an intelligent benevolent god would never place the anus so close to the vagina or make the penis spill both semen and urine.

12. Eventually, Evelyn Waugh came along to write a novel called *Vile Bodies*, as if in protest against our natural lot: highbrow taste passing judgment on biological crudity.

bodily transformations from the (relatively) disgusting to the (relatively) beautiful. In principle, then, the psychological novelties coeval with the origin of Man (for that was the disgusted species' name) could have been accompanied by suitable physical transformations: the body could have evolved to be more congenial to the mind tied to it. This conceptual possibility occasioned a good deal of resentment and fretting in the mind of Man, because clearly Nature had been too lazy or ill willed to arrange it; it left Man the task of simply (as they say) sucking it up. They just had to live with it, no matter how confused and miserable it left them. Of course, the practical problems about arranging such a metamorphosis were much larger than our fretful species supposed, and there was no precedent for it in their biological line. But they were also an impatient and thoughtless species in many ways, so there was no use arguing with them.[13] Also, the case of the butterfly was less simple than they made it seem, because if you examined the butterfly closely, it was by no means as lovely as legend had it, especially once you looked past the gossamer wings at the sticklike abdomen and its squishy content. In fact, the very idea of a disgust-free animal body was really a fantasy, cooked up by a species that refused to accept that digestion was a simple fact of biological existence (that English writer, Mr. Swift, seemed particularly dense on the point—what did he *expect* of his beloved Caelia?). It wasn't at all clear that Nature (or Anyone Else) could have done much to improve the disgust-value of the human body, given the basic parameters of life; once the perceptual and emotional apparatus of disgust is in place,

---

13. Don't people spend half their lives wishing their bodies were different? Slimmer, smoother, and less smelly; taller and stronger; of a different sex; of a different species; made of different materials—the full spectrum of human corporeal discontent. Animals have no such transformative fantasies. Dissatisfaction with our given body seems part of the human condition: we are filled with revisionary dreams of one kind or another, more or less extreme.

organic life is bound to activate it. Still, the abstract notion of metamorphosis haunted Man's imagination and made him strain at the bit of his biological heritage. He couldn't stop thinking about a better class of body. And there was no denying the point that there had been no consultation in the matter (you were to be given sweaty armpits, like it or not). The more those minds progressed, the more sensitive they became, and the more the body seemed to lag behind, mocking the pretensions of the minds that subsisted within them. In an evolutionary instant, Man was demanding toilet facilities and privacy and soap and water and air fresheners, while the anus and its adjuncts went on plying their ancient trade, unmoved. At a very late stage of his evolution Man developed ever more ingenious ways to improve, as he saw it, the manners of his body, even devising (we peer into the distant future now) a system for removing, by a kind of selective teletransportation, waste matter from the digestive process before it ever reached the large intestine—thus eliminating the need for defecation, and with it the anus (the waste just evaporated from inside the body, to be recycled as building materials).[14] But there were many millenniums before this handy piece of technology was developed (in the year 3010 by Apple-GE), and so the usual handwringing continued for a very long time—besides, there was still a lot else about the body that didn't sit well with Man. Man felt abused and victimized, full of self-pity—as if he were

14. Kant has a delightful creation myth in which the "digested residue [of certain fruits] vanished through an imperceptible evaporation": quoted in Menninghaus, p. 57. Kant speaks of the residue as being "sweated out." This was our state before the anus existed, he supposes, which preceded the fall. My piece of science fiction is about the future disappearance of the anus as a result of technology—but Kant and I have the same basic picture. The thought is that human life would be better if shitting were eliminated in favor of something cleaner and less visible. (Let me record my pleasure at finding that Kant also had a side interest in the profound topic of defecation.)

the hapless target of a cosmic joke in exceptionally poor taste.[15]

I am trying, queasy reader, to cut through the numbing effect of custom—to make the familiar unfamiliar. Just because something is an inescapable fact of life—almost as old as life itself—doesn't mean that it has no power to disturb and shock. In fact, the nerve of disgust seems to stay sharp and focused, not to dull and weaken with the passage of time, even with respect to our own excessively familiar bodies. But it isn't so easy to grasp afresh what a strange predicament we find ourselves in. We are the only natural (or unnatural) creature to be repelled by its own nature! Let me then try another way to bring the scent more pressingly to our nostrils. Suppose you were housed from birth in something like the Matrix: crucially, you have no information about what kind of body you possess—though you have experience of a virtual world. You never see, touch, smell, or taste your body—though you have perceptions of other types of body from dawn till dusk. Naturally, you develop certain affective reactions to the bodies you experience: some bodies disgust you more than others, and you form opinions about what kind of body you would like to possess. Suppose you come to the view that a human body would be the best choice (odd, I know, but let us proceed with the story). Then one day, by some heroic revolution, you are released from the Matrix and

15. Suppose that life on earth *had* been created by a form of supreme intelligence, divine or extraterrestrial, from among a menu of possible choices, some more aesthetically acceptable than what we observe all around us. Wouldn't we then feel pretty annoyed and cheated about how things are? Wouldn't we feel justified in complaining to the creator about the design he or she had picked? After all, other more palatable choices had been available, and yet were apparently passed over. It seems cruel, or negligent, or a nasty practical joke. The truth, of course, is that the design arose by biological accident, not by foresight and intelligence, so there is, alas, no one to complain to. Our divided nature is not part of nature's *plan*, but a kind of weird accident. But being an accident does not prevent it from being formative.

delivered into reality—to be confronted by your actual body. You find that you possess, not the desired human form, but the body of a *worm*: six feet long, mottled, multi-pedal, slimy, wriggling, and foul smelling. I suggest that you would feel horribly upset and surprised: you never imagined you could be *that* revolting, given the elevation of your thoughts, your keen ethical sense, your high-brow taste in art. The reality would seem like an enormous affront to your self-conception, your personal dignity, and your peace of mind. *I am not a worm!* The perceived incongruity between your fine inner self and your ghastly bodily incarnation would grate and grind; you would long for the life of corporeal ignorance you enjoyed in the Matrix. A godlike mind should *not* have a wormlike body, with the vertiginous ontological dependence that that implies.

But if being a worm would be found so shocking and lowering, then why wouldn't being a *human* be found similarly disagreeable? What if in the Matrix you fancied the idea of having a tiger's body, or a body made wholly of light, or precious metals and gems? You have never anticipated that you might turn out to have a human body, and indeed you have developed some distaste for such bodies in the Matrix (some nasty accidents, horrible diseases). You are finally liberated and find you actually have the body of a tubby middle-aged man with a flatulence problem. Remember, you have never experienced yourself as possessing such a body in the Matrix, so you have no prior habituation to it. Wouldn't that be almost as bad as finding you are a worm? Wouldn't an intelligent, sensitive worm, though hardly in love with its body, respond to the human body as more disgusting than its own—simply because it was more *used* to the worm body? Maybe we humans are much more disgusting, objectively, than we think, dulled as we are by familiarity. Maybe intelligent, sensitive tigers would rank worms and human beings as about equal on the disgust scale, right near the bottom—with itself the least disgusting animal, and elephants and reptiles somewhere in between (sounds about right to me). We are an ungainly creature ("a poor, bare, forked animal," as Lear observes), with our disproportionate arms and legs, our oddly distributed patches of hair, our wrinkled and folded skin, our small writhing mouths, our weak teeth, our abnormally smelly feces, our unreliable orifices, our violent and messy birth process. It is not as if the human body is some huge biological prize, given out only to the best and the brightest; in many ways, it looks like an experiment that may or may not work out in the long run (the unsteady upright posture, the pressure on the spine, the massively swollen head). We have become accustomed to it, to be sure, but that doesn't mean it wouldn't be as bad a result in the lottery of the Matrix as the worm body. The body of pure light would have been so much nicer, because it isn't organic at all, or we might have preferred one of those shining metallic robot bodies we have seen strutting about so confidently in the virtual world. Anything but the dirty, slab-footed, stiff-backed, tottering, loose-skinned, podgy, partially bald, multiply leaking baggage they call a "human"! My point, human reader, is that from the perspective of the inner self—our psychological or "spiritual" side—it is jarring that we are *any* kind of organic being, human included. The human soul would jib at biological nature no matter what type of body we ended up with.[16]

What if you really were a divine being? What if you were, in fact, the Son of God, and well aware of it? Jesus of Nazareth is held by some to be just such a divine being. Let us entertain the hypothesis. Jesus grasps his own divine identity clearly, and he also comprehends the nature of God more fully than ordinary folk; his manifest divinity throbs unmistakably within him. Yet

---

16. As Becker remarks, we are "out of nature and hopelessly in it" (p. 26). We always feel some distance between ourselves and nature, as if nature is just not up to our high standards; yet we are also products of nature. We are nature at odds with itself—uniquely so. Our nature is to be both inside and outside nature, and to feel the tension.

he must also endure the bodily trials of mortal creatures: the defecation, the flatulence, the erections and ejaculations, the adolescent pimples and sprouting body hair, the runny nose, the sweaty groin. Jesus is, literally, a "god who shits." Wouldn't this strike him as simply ludicrous, a kind of malevolent joke—a bizarre and abominable affront? More than that, wouldn't it produce in his consciousness a deep sense of schism and paradox? True, he knows it is the price he must pay to move among us, but it must also strike him as an intolerable demotion, an ontological slap in the face. And the disciples must feel it too, as they live with and worship their divine savior—who must clean his anus just like them. Of course, such unnerving thoughts are deemed by some to be tasteless at best and blasphemous at worst—and I am sure there are theologies that exempt Jesus from the contamination of the disgusting—but this very fact attests that a clash of attributes is being envisaged here. It is simply not in the *nature* of the godlike to shit. Jesus could not regard this fact about himself with equanimity. His greatest sacrifice for us was freely to adopt the mantle of the disgusting—without constantly averting his eyes and holding his nose. The elevated cannot also be the base; the fine cannot merge with the coarse. Jesus is a radically split being.[17]

The same tension recurs with respect to mortals promoted to the ranks of the semi-divine: monarchs, movie stars, and Great Thinkers. As every loyal subject knows, Her Majesty the Queen of England, Elizabeth II, is physically incapable of farting,

17. If you hopefully believe that the soul can happily co-exist with shit, then ask yourself how you feel about the proposition that the soul is *made* of shit. Surely *that* sounds intolerable. Yet it is not so far from the truth, since the body's nutrients all come from digestive material, and the soul needs nutrients too. Further, the person is *made* of the body, partly at least, and the body is an object of disgust. We can't dissociate ourselves from the disgusting body by contriving some sort of dualism in which body and mind have no commerce with each other—as if they are strangers passing in the night. The soul cannot deny its dealings with shit.

try as she may. Marilyn Monroe never had a menstrual period or bad breath. Immanuel Kant never picked his nose or wiped his arse. Once idolized, such individuals are imaginatively placed beyond the sphere of the disgusting; they have become purified and cleansed. The esteem in which they are held precludes recognition of their mortal filthiness. Angels don't have anuses. And, in as much as we ourselves approximate to such superior beings, we too experience our bodies as alien encumbrances, betrayals of our dignity and pride.[18] The disgusting is felt as an anomaly in our being. It just shouldn't *be* there.

A crude image suggests itself: the refined aristocrat, with his exquisite manners, his fine silks, perfumed, spotless, an aesthete, gracious in everything he does—with a filthy uncouth peasant strapped to his back, belching, farting, and shitting. The aristocrat can never remove his attached peasant, yearn for separation as he may; nor can he ever become accustomed to the latter's disgusting ways: they are locked inextricably (and inexcusably) together. The aristocrat looks down his nose at his attached peasant, resents him, regarding him with scorn and derision: look how he spoils the splendid appearance of his manifest superior! If it weren't for him, the aristocrat would cut a dashing figure, accepted into all the best circles; but the vile peasant is here to stay—an embarrassment and a burden. If only he could be kept hidden, like some terrible family secret, but that is not feasible— he insists on revealing himself, sometimes at the worst of times. Here is the sparkling aristocrat, discoursing on the fine paintings

---

18. Imagine farting loudly while lecturing on philosophy. That would be highly embarrassing. Why? Because the image of the philosopher is so far removed from the reality of the digestive body: that reality has been temporarily bracketed as the depths of philosophy are plumbed, only to erupt jarringly. The audience is subject to existential shock—an ontological category-crossing has occurred. The philosopher was all soaring abstract intellect and now his creaturely nature has leapt from the shadows. This is why we think of the body as *betraying* us—letting out a terrible secret. The organic body should quietly hide itself away, not rudely announce its presence.

in his art collection, his eyes lit with inspiration, the picture of elegance—and suddenly the peasant lets out a loud belch, destroying the effect entirely. The trouble, my fellow humans, is that *we* are both aristocrat and peasant rolled into one—so we can't even pin the grossness on someone else. *Our* peasant is proximate to the point of identity. It is not merely that we are condemned to be always touching the untouchable; we *are* the untouchable. It is like the old fairy tale of the prince imprisoned inside the frog: the haughty and handsome young royal finds himself stuck inside the body of a slimy, warty, lowly reptile. He longs for release, but only a miracle can work such magic; he must languish for years inside the repellent alien mass. Its essential nature is quite other than his, yet it functions as his de facto body. The final release, as the princess kisses the frog, offers the prospect of escape from the loathed body, as a body more proper to a prince is substituted—a de jure body (but *that* body too has its orifices and secretions and all the rest). The implicit lesson here is that our body type is contingently ours, relative to our minds, and it is all too froglike. The aristocrat and the peasant, the prince and the frog, the human soul and the human body: the same basic theme recurs.

Animals, as observed, don't feel this way. A frog is quite content to be a frog. A tiger has no problem with its felinity. There is no sense of alienation, no dream of release. Animals have no conception of God and no aspiration to emulate him. They have minds, to be sure, but these minds do not foster a brooding sense of resentment at the organic. Animals are free of the affliction of nonnegotiable disgust, toward themselves or others. They feel no incongruity in their nature, no aesthetic or ontological split. Defecation is just one fact of life like any other; the anus is not a locus of embarrassment and taboo. For many animals, indeed, the anus is a focus of interest and pleasure, as are its products (we tend to find this utterly incomprehensible and obscurely blame the animal). Nor is there any ambivalence about the sex organs.

Animals do not segregate themselves uneasily into two parts, venerating the one and deploring the other. There is no "existential anxiety" about their animal condition, nothing to fret and puzzle over. Nor is there any need to conceal their animal nature from each other, for fear of giving offence and courting rejection. Social life is not hedged about with fraught prohibitions designed to protect others from one's less pleasing aspects. The affective life of animals is thus quite different from ours, which is saturated with disgust and its accompanying anxieties and strategies. Animal consciousness is not a filth consciousness (it is apt to be more a fear consciousness).[19]

It is customary to express one's conception of the human condition by telling a creation story that dramatizes its key elements—especially the trials and troubles of human life. In that spirit, then, I now offer my own creation story, designed to give narrative shape to the abstract picture I am presenting. It goes like this. In the beginning, we were disembodied spirits, dwelling happily in the Garden of Eden. We could communicate with each other, enjoy the sights and sounds of nature, listen to music, engage in intellectual enquiry, gossip, and tell jokes. Life was sweet, no question. We were also immortal, naturally, and so had no fear of death or disease. God had made us this way, with our happiness at the forefront of his beneficent mind. Many centuries had gone by in this calm and civilized manner, with no hint of discontent with our lot. We felt that God had done well by us.

---

19. I am not saying that no other species *could* be like us, or that other existing species may not evolve in our direction, or even that no other species on earth has the beginnings of disgust consciousness (maybe some primates do). My point is just to distinguish one kind of species consciousness from another, whether other animals might attain to the disgust kind or not. In fact, the consensus is that other animals don't feel disgust, but that is not crucial to my position. There might even be a species somewhere with greater disgust consciousness than our own, both because of its bodily nature and its psychological sensitivities: we are surely not the most disgusted species conceivable. Some poor creatures in a remote galaxy may have an even harder time with themselves than we do. Tranquility of spirit in naturally evolved beings is not uppermost in nature's mind.

Then one day a rabbit came into the garden and began nibbling on a plant. (It was rumored that God had sent the rabbit to us for our amusement.) We observed the rabbit nibbling, noticing the way fragments of the plant came off in its mouth, followed by chewing and swallowing, as parts of the plant disappeared inside the rabbit's body. If the rabbit were left undisturbed for long enough, the whole plant would certainly be consumed. For some reason, this spectacle troubled us: emotions arose in our heart that we had never felt before. We felt a mixture of envy, resentment, vanity, hurt pride, and powerlessness. This little furry beast could do something we could not do! It could *consume*. Being pure spirits, we could do no such thing. We could not bite off a part of the material world and take it inside us for our own pleasure and benefit. A rebellious spirit arose in us—as if we had been short-changed, deprived of our natural rights. How could God have given the rabbit an ability he had denied to us? And it wasn't as if the rabbit were anything special—it was just a mindless nibbler, not a Self-Reflective Thinker and Rational Being. We began to wail and cry out to God: "Oh, great God, why hast thou given unto the lowly rabbit the power to Consume, while leaving us, thy Chosen Ones, without the means of taking the World into our Being and mashing it up?"—words to that effect. We wanted what *he* was having. After a few days of this ranting, God got back to us, explaining patiently that the rabbit belonged to another order of being entirely, and not one to envy. But we would not be fobbed off so easily, ratcheting up our rhetoric, and even turning quite nasty with respect to God's intentions, character, and dress sense. He grew impatient, informing us sternly that he could easily make us of the same stuff as the rabbit, but that there would be a price to pay. We could retain our intellectual and aesthetic faculties—that was not the problem—but we would have to be given a mouth, a digestive tract, and an anus. *Whatever*, we replied, not thinking too hard. We would also need sex organs, he added, because now we would need to reproduce, and this would require certain insertions and deposits—the exact nature of which he declined to dilate upon. That sounded fine, we said. Oh, and one more thing: we would have to become mortal, because that came with the rabbit territory. We hesitated for a moment, but by now we were so hell-bent on rectifying the injustice heretofore perpetrated on us that we agreed. The deal was struck, with God producing a contract from nowhere containing lots of fine print about who would be responsible for the final product, blah-blah-blah. Having signed it, God assured us that the next day we would awake to become little Consumers ourselves. It seemed like pure gain: we get to keep our souls as they were and we also have the bonus of a body that can Consume—a welcome ontological expansion.

And so it came to pass that, on the following day, as promised, we awoke with our spanking new bodies, though human not rabbit (God had been a bit vague about what kind of body we would be given). It was a funny sensation at first, sort of heavy and clumsy, but God had done the job well, and we couldn't wait to start Consuming. Ambling out into the sunlit Garden of Eden, we bit into our first chunks of the world—that red, round, sweet fruit was especially delectable. We salivated and masticated, peristalsis did its reflexive work, and the mashed fragments entered our eager new stomachs: we were Consumers at last! When the rabbit came to join us later in the day we regarded him with swelling pride, for we were bigger Consumers than he was: he no longer had something we didn't. All went smoothly for the first few hours, once you got used to operating the corporeal apparatus, though the sight of all that open-mouthed chomping made a few sensitive souls a touch queasy (the saliva mixing with the pulverized food, some dribbling down the chin). But then something completely unexpected happened: a strange pressure in the lower regions, uncomfortably close to the formations we now knew as "genitals," as if something inside wanted badly to get out into the open. The nakedness we had been enjoying suddenly seemed like not the best of ideas, as a peculiar premonition began to seize those most afflicted with the pressure—something highly untoward was about to transpire. Resist the pressure as one might, it steadily mounted, finally becoming overwhelming: and then—great gobs of stinking brown matter leapt from the lower parts of the new breed of Consumers. Some of it was solid, some of it very liquid—all of it smelt to high heaven. At the same time a grotesque symphony of farts and moans rent the air, accompanying the foul emanations that were now streaking down legs, forming steaming piles on the ground, and generally making a hell of a mess of things. The humans had never seen or imagined anything so vile—and it was oozing (in some cases *jetting*) from their own freshly minted bodies! Some of them, shocked and bewildered, felt another new sensation radiating from their middle portions, and before long streams of vomit were arcing from their gaping mouths. This new material rivaled the old one for its repulsive quality, and before long a chain reaction had set in, as the recently consumed food was collectively regurgitated in the form of a vile stew of food fragments and digestive bile. The vomit mingled with the excrement on the ground, polluting everything, reeking horribly. Oh, Lord! Who was going to clear it all up? No one wanted to go near the stuff, and yet it had settled where people needed to walk, sit, and talk. This was a steep price to pay for the privilege of being a Consumer!

And so the emotion of disgust was felt for the first time— and, lo, it was not good. Nor was this a one-time occurrence—a fecal singularity, if you will. It recurred approximately every twenty-four hours. Arrangements had to be made to accommodate it, life had to be organized around it, and *someone* had to clean the mess up. The concept of *dirt* was born, and *contamination*. We complained bitterly to God, of course, but he reminded us that he had warned us about the necessity for an anus—and what did we *think* was going to come out of it: gold, frankincense, and myrrh? As he explained, with frayed patience, you can't be a Consumer without also being an Excreter—that was just the way the world was, nothing he could do about it, sorry. Nor was that an end to the adjustments we had to make: the sex was messy too, the associated organs unprepossessing, the birth process grisly. Inside our bodies were assorted tubes and growths that turned the stomach (the stomach was one of them). The whole panoply of the disgusting was laid before us in short order, where only a few weeks before we had lived a disgust-free life. But still, nothing—*nothing*—quite prepared us for the first corpse. Death wasn't the center of the problem; indeed, such was the shock of the initial wave of disgust that some humans even welcomed it. It was the awful state of the dead body itself: within hours its inherent disgustingness doubled, tripled, quadrupled. It began to rot, subtly then riotously. At first nobody knew what to do—so they just left it where it fell and hoped things would improve tomorrow. *That* didn't work, so the problem grew worse with every passing day. After a couple of weeks, the scene was indescribable. Then someone had the bright idea of burying the rotting remains in the garden, out of sight and smell. A worker had to be recruited to do the job (or threatened into doing it), but nobody felt very comfortable about the plan—six feet under seemed too close for comfort for such a repulsive and contaminating entity. Again, life had to be structured around taking care of the problem, both practically and emotionally. There was much lamentation and gnashing of teeth, as well as bickering and name-calling. The social fabric unraveled.

It wasn't long before we trudged back to God with a petition, the sum and gist of which was: "Send us back to our previous disembodied state, please, oh merciful God!" But he was resolute, noting that the contract had stated quite clearly that the transformation was irrevocable, and we did sign it of our own Free Will. We were to live like this forever, unto our children and grandchildren, and unto their children and grandchildren, down through all eternity. With heavy hearts we returned to our lives as Consumers—two-legged bald rabbits—and tried to make the best of it. No regrets and all that. But the recollection of our previous disgust-free life haunted us down through the ages: somewhere in our species memory there lingered an apprehension of what life could be like without the body and its depth charge of disgust. This ancient memory showed itself in our mythology, in our dreams, and in our daily sense of the jarring and incongruous in our nature. The Age of Innocence never quite left our collective imagination—the fantasy of a life without the emotion of disgust. True, we would have to cease being Consumers (and Copulators)—and part of our fallen nature still reveled in that awesome power—but the price was so heavy that we could never quite surrender ourselves to our new condition. We wanted to exist solely and exclusively according to our finer nonorganic mode of being. The rabbit had tempted us, and we had succumbed, but the dream of a purer life never quite left us, and we always felt soiled in comparison. We felt ourselves lower and baser than we ought rightfully to be, as if dragged down by the dead weight of our organic constitution—immortals in the body of a worm. And our prelapsarian state still reverberates to this day in the unquiet recesses of our fallen souls. There are some zealots, indeed, who believe that the day will come when a Savior will arrive and return us to our ancient disembodied state, putting everything right with the world (the "anti-disgustarians").[20]

20. Kant's creation story, mentioned in note 14, is less extreme than mine (in paradise humans were embodied, in his version), but it has the same general upshot. Humans were banished from paradise to earth because they were tempted to eat a forbidden fruit, the digestive residue of which could not be "sweated out," requiring instead a fully functioning anus. The fall was from digestive innocence to digestive horror. The traditional Judeo-Christian story, on the other hand, strikes me as less realistic than my story. People do not, in general, have as strong an urge to *know* as they have to *consume*: they are quite content with ignorance, so long as they have a lot of stuff (inside and outside). Our greatest moral failing is surely not our curiosity, but our acquisitiveness—which is connected to envy, power seeking, status, and so on. Our fall from grace is thus better understood as prompted by acquisitiveness than by curiosity—not the tree of knowledge but the rabbit of consumption.

8

Repression and Disgust

IF DISGUST IS AN aversive emotion, and we feel disgust toward ourselves, then it follows that we are averse to ourselves. But we would rather not be averse to ourselves. It doesn't feel good to feel bad about yourself. When we don't feel good about a fact, we sometimes resort to certain psychological maneuvers to protect ourselves from the fact in question. We desire that something not be so that we know to be so, and we react by denying that fact to ourselves. This is the phenomenon of repression. I now want to claim that we are repressed about our disgustingness, and that this too is an essential part of the human condition.[1]

Two notions of repression must be carefully distinguished. One is the notion of repression we use when we speak of repressing a desire: we have a desire that we would rather not have, so we either attempt not to act on it or we strive somehow to weaken the desire itself. I desire a second martini, but believe I should control my alcohol intake, so I restrain myself from

---

1. The concept of repression has been so widely used (and abused) that it has become part of conventional wisdom that we are a repressed species. I think most of this is quite misguided, especially the Freudian concept of unconscious repression of sexual desires. I mean something quite different, as I go on to explain in the text. The point I want to make now is that I am treating the question of repression as not at all obvious, but as requiring serious argumentation. My thesis should not seem like a platitude. So try not to take the concept of repression as a given.

acting on my desire or I try to weaken it, say by reminding myself of the health hazards of excessive drinking. Repressing desires in this way may lead, according to Freud, to *sublimation*: the energy of the desire seeks some alternative outlet, good or bad. Freud believed, notoriously, that we repress our sexual desires in such a way as to lead to sublimation. This is *not* the notion of repression I am interested in here. I am interested in the notion that we use when we speak of repressing *knowledge* of some fact—as it might be, repressing my knowledge *that* I have certain sexual desires (say, toward my mother, in Freudian theory)—that is, motivated ignorance. These two notions of repression are quite distinct (I am not aware that Freud ever clearly distinguished them). We might call the first notion "appetitive repression" and the second "epistemic repression." To be clear, then, I am concerned here with epistemic repression: trying to shut out knowledge of a disagreeable fact. I could in principle undertake a project of epistemic repression with respect to knowledge of a taboo sexual desire without thereby undertaking any appetitive repression: I succeed in not knowing that I have the desire, but the desire is as strong as ever and is frequently acted upon—I just shield myself from knowledge that the desire exists and is operative. Equally, and more likely, I could undertake a project of appetitive repression without undertaking any project of epistemic repression: I manage to dampen down my desire, and not act on it, though I am still perfectly aware that I have the desire. The two notions are logically quite independent. My claim, then, is that we are epistemically repressed with respect to knowledge of our disgustingness: we try to shut out the knowledge we have of this fact about ourselves. The goal of the repressive project is entirely epistemic; it is not at all the same as trying to stifle disgusting desires or some such. Nor is it the project of trying to *become* less disgusting, say by enhanced personal hygiene or surgery. Nor is it the attempt to reduce the intensity of the *sensation* of disgust in response to a given range of stimuli. Rather, it aims to render our knowledge of our disgustingness unavailable or suppressed or inoperative. In other terminology, we try to prevent our implicit knowledge of our disgustingness from becoming conscious and explicit.[2]

I don't mean to invoke anything like the Freudian unconscious here. It is no part of my claim that the repression I am speaking of is itself unconscious or that it can succeed in rendering our knowledge of our disgustingness unconscious in anything like the Freudian sense (whatever quite that amounts to). I mean it in a far more commonsensical way, which I might illustrate as follows. Suppose the memory of a particular past incident gives me pain: I might, as we say, "try not to think about it" or "not dwell on it," banishing it from my thoughts whenever it involuntarily enters them. I can recall the incident if I choose to, so it is not unconscious in the Freudian sense, but I succeed in not letting it recur to torment me, and I develop strategies to get rid of it if it does (I choose to think instead of something pleasant). I might become quite good at controlling an unpleasant memory by these efforts. Or suppose I have a birthmark that I know causes other people to look at me strangely: I might make a point, over the years, of not harping on it, banishing it from my thoughts and so on, that is, repressing my knowledge of it—even though I know quite well that the birthmark is there. Perhaps I try to find a good side to it, convincing myself (maybe correctly) that it gives me interest and individuality. I have the knowledge, quite consciously, but I intentionally control its hold over me: I keep it mostly outside my current consciousness and I don't allow it to

---

2. It is hard to find good terminology here, because repression is rather paradoxical: it is the attempt not to know what one knows one knows. It is a kind of self-deception, in which one denies knowledge one knowingly has. For me, it is enough to establish that we intentionally avoid thinking about what we know quite well, which is not at all paradoxical. My claim is only the modest one that we are motivated not to dwell on knowledge we have.

dominate my thoughts. The important point, for my purposes here, is that there is such a project as repressing knowledge of a disagreeable fact that does not commit us to the full Freudian apparatus. Then my claim is that we repress our knowledge of our disgustingness in *that* kind of way: we undertake a project of motivated ignorance, or redirection of attention, or simply ignore the fact in question. If this is right, then we are not only disgusted beings, but we are also repressed beings in *virtue* of our disgustingness—that too is part of the human condition. In short, we know we are disgusting, but we try not to be too conscious of it; we try not to let the knowledge dominate our self-awareness. Speaking roughly and metaphorically, we try to prevent the knowledge from getting too much of a hold on us; we try and we succeed. That is, we successfully repress the knowledge.

The first point to make is that we are generally *silent* about the subject. We don't talk about it, or not much and only in special circumstances. It is not considered "polite" to do so (and that's why there is a problem of decorum about this book). At the doctor's office we may let loose, but generally we say nothing about our own or other people's disgusting traits. If we do talk about such things, then indirection, euphemism, and humor are brought in to soften the blow. We must certainly not talk about disgusting topics at the dinner table or as a romantic prelude. We must be discreet, hushed. However, it is possible to be silent about something while not censoring one's own inner thoughts about it. My evidence for thinking that we also repress our thoughts of the disgusting is that talking about it openly occasions internal discomfort and reluctance. We don't *want* to know—we prefer not to dwell on it. The knowledge is there in the background, but putting it into the foreground is experienced as offensive—it should be left in the mental shadows. Or, alternatively, discoursing on the disgusting can be experienced as a revelation or liberation—as if what was only implicitly suspected is now explicitly recognized—with a sense of relief that the repressive pressure has been released. We feel we have been avoiding the subject all along and now we can take the lid off, with the ensuing sense of incoming fresh air. If the repression is strong, however, offense is the more likely outcome, not a sense of enlightenment. In either case, we have evidence that something has been held down, epistemically speaking.[3] We recognize that we are disgusting, but this is uncomfortable knowledge, so we strive to keep it at the margins of awareness; bringing it to the center is then experienced as threatening—or possibly enlightening. Freud would say that we try to avoid knowledge of our true sexual desires; I am saying that we try to avoid knowledge of our reality as disgusting organic beings. This is knowledge we would prefer to be without, or at least knowledge that we don't want constantly before our minds. By contrast, there is no repression of our knowledge of our "spiritual" side, since this provokes no aversive emotion in us: we are quite happy to be constantly reminded of our intellectual gifts, our ethical sentiments, and our artistic sensibilities. We are motivated to repress only what disturbs us, but the "spiritual" part of our nature isn't disturbing at all—unlike the biological functions that constitute our bodies. If you have knowledge that disturbs you, then it makes sense to try to keep it away from full explicit consciousness.[4] That way you are not disturbed the whole time. You can rest easy.

3. This is the same kind of evidence we might have of other things recognized but not explicitly acknowledged: for example, an uncomfortable family situation that no one wants to talk about and that people only vaguely perceive. Habitual silence, or relief that someone is finally bringing the matter up, are signs that repression has been going on in such a case. There are surely many uncomfortable truths we try mentally to avoid.

4. The reason, obviously, is that explicit conscious knowledge is more closely linked to emotional responses: this is why we say that it "hurts to think about it." When the knowledge remains in the background, it does not to elicit emotions so readily. Why this should be, however, is not so obvious: why shouldn't focusing on the matter *reduce* its emotional fallout?

Nietzsche expresses the essential point with characteristic verve:

> The *aesthetically* insulting at work in the inner human without skin,—bloody masses, muck-bowels, viscera, all those sucking, pumping monstrosities—formless or ugly or grotesque, painful for the smell to boot. Hence *away with it in thought!* What still does emerge excites shame.... This body, *concealed* by the skin as if in *shame*...hence: there is disgust-exciting matter; the more ignorant humans are about their organism, the lesser can they distinguish between raw meat, rot, stink, maggots. To the extent he is not a *Gestalt*, the human being is disgusting to himself—he does everything to *not think about it*—The *pleasure* manifestly linked to this inner human being passes as *baser*: after-effect of the aesthetic judgment.[5]

Nietzsche is clearly of the opinion that (a) the human being is disgusting, (b) she knows she is disgusting, and (c) she does everything she can to flee from this knowledge. Away with it in thought! We repress what we cannot help knowing full well, because we are confronted by it constantly, and our emotions are shaped accordingly. We do everything to shield ourselves from our own perceived monstrosity.

Freud (influenced by Nietzsche) had hold of an important point when he described humans as a repressed species—we are rational cognitive agents who intentionally seek ignorance (in some areas). Animals know less than we do, but they do not *desire* to know less than they know; we humans sometimes *do* desire to know less than we know—because some of our knowledge is painful to us. Our consciousness is therefore a repressed consciousness—a consciousness aimed at itself in an act of epistemic negation. But I think Freud misidentified the true source of our

5. Quoted in Menninghaus, p. 81.

motivated ignorance: the knowledge we seek to suppress is knowledge of our organic nature, not of our incestuous sexual desires.[6] This effort can only ever be partially successful, given that we are confronted by evidence of our organic nature at all turns, but that doesn't stop us from striving to keep the knowledge as remote from the centre of our attention as possible. It is, quite simply, nothing to be proud of, but rather (as Nietzsche indicates) a source of existential shame. We are repressed beings because there is something about us that *merits* repression—and that it is perfectly rational to repress (like a painful memory).[7]

These reflections prompt a ticklish question: should we attempt to lift the repression I am referring to? In much twentieth-century thought repression is deemed to be ipso facto a bad thing: but this is by no means obvious, as the case of the painful memory shows. How beneficial would it *be* to be un-repressed about our disgusting nature? Maybe we just can't stand too much knowledge of our real nature: the human ego is fragile and vain, easily damaged by too much clarity about what we are as human beings. Depression, anxiety, and even insanity might be the outcome of a steady-eyed unflinching consciousness of our true nature (Kierkegaard thought as much).[8] How much good could

6. This is one of the main arguments of Becker's *The Denial of Death*, by which I have been much influenced. Becker is opposing standard psychoanalytic theory in which sex is the prime source of neurosis and repression.

7. In a similar way, we are repressed about how *selfish* we are: we overestimate our goodness and altruism. We lie to ourselves about our degree of virtue, for intelligible reasons. We protect ourselves from knowledge of our failings, though we may implicitly have such knowledge. We can do this simply by dwelling fondly on our good acts and trying to forget about our bad acts. No one wants to think of himself as a selfish bastard—or a disgusting tub of guts.

8. Becker strikingly says: "I believe that those who speculate that a full apprehension of man's condition would drive him insane are right, quite literally right." (p. 27) He then quotes Pascal: "Men are so necessarily mad that not to be mad would amount to another form of madness." More soberly, we have a need to repress our knowledge of our true nature, on pain of mental disturbance of one degree or another. Full self-knowledge is a perilous state.

it do us to remind ourselves every day of what a horrible heap of excrement we are? Better to dwell on our finer attributes and leave the rest in decent obscurity. On the other hand, we do already have a pretty firm appreciation of our organic being, so releasing repression can hardly be a case of letting the cat out of the bag. After all, I have not told you anything in this book about yourself that you didn't already know, at least implicitly. Perhaps the sensible answer is simply that some analytic clarity is desirable, but that we don't want to make an obsession out of trumpeting the truth about our disgusting selves the entire time. We don't want to get ourselves into state of constant brooding about how repulsive we are. Grudging acceptance maybe, or at least wincing recognition—but not obsessing about it to the point of paralysis. I suppose it might be maintained that we can tame the subject matter somewhat by analyzing it thoroughly and looking it straight in the eye—though I have not found that to be so myself. What I certainly reject is the idea that we can overcome our natural sense of disgust at ourselves, or convert it into something attractive instead of aversive. We can never convince ourselves that feces are fabulous or rotting corpses delightful. That way madness lies, in the form of coprophilia and necrophilia, which I do not regard as steps forward. Core disgust is something fixed and invariable, and there is nothing admirable or enlightened about denying its aversive quality. All we can do is squarely face the facts of disgust without becoming swamped by them, without letting them overwhelm us. And if they do threaten to overwhelm, then I don't think there is any real harm in a spot of repression now and then. Try to think of nicer things—because nice things are always nicer than nasty things.[9]

One further point about repression is worth mentioning. In Part One, I speculated about the origin and function of disgust, linking it to excessive human desire: disgust serves to dampen our

9. I here quote a well-known line from Kingsley Amis's *Lucky Jim*.

more egregious desires, or to prevent them from assuming perverse objects—as in necrophilia and coprophilia. In the present terminology, disgust acts as an appetitive repressor—a strong taming force. But epistemic repression of our known disgustingness has the opposite effect: by reducing the cognitive salience of disgust it works to counteract the appetitive repression caused by disgust. Thus excessive desires, tamped down by disgust, are given more freedom by the repression of disgust knowledge. Suppose person x desires object y in some way at time t (say, sexually or as something to eat), but that at some later time t', x becomes disgusted at y; then x will no longer desire y or will do so in an etiolated or ambivalent way. But now suppose that at some yet later time t'', x manages to repress the knowledge that he is disgusted by y; then x will no longer feel the same repugnance toward y—his awareness of y's disgustingness has undergone some sort of occlusion or eclipse. But that means that at some still later time t''', he can again feel free (or freer) to desire y, since his disgust has, so to speak, gone into remission—at least it is not as salient as it was before the work of repression was done. Thus epistemic repression can serve the interests of excessive desires. For instance, suppose you have a pressing desire to eat decayed food (as it might be, very ripe cheese): disgust may supervene to suppress this desire, making it seem like not such a good idea after all. But now, if you can repress your knowledge of the disgustingness of such "off" foodstuffs, say by directing your attention away from the bad smell and rotten appearance, the desire will find its fulfillment eased. Of course, such repression is a weak force compared to the strong force of disgust, since it is at best partial and equivocal, but it can at least diminish the inhibitive effect of disgust. Generally, the function of repression is simply to spare us the distressing burden of knowledge of our disgustingness, but as a side effect it seems to work to support unruly desires that disgust has inhibited. In other words, epistemic repression of disgust can in principle lead to the liberation of the desires against which disgust works. Suppose that such repression were far more powerful than it actually is, and suppose Freud was right that repression could render knowledge genuinely unconscious: then we could in principle completely eliminate our conscious knowledge that various objects are disgusting. In this way, we might render our knowledge of the disgustingness of corpses unconscious; consciously, we might even find corpses quite attractive. This might then lead to certain actions in regard to corpses that might reasonably be described as excessive. Any residual desire to have sexual relations with corpses might then have a clear psychological path to expression, since we no longer (consciously) believe corpses to be disgusting. Maybe we still find corpses disgusting *un*consciously, but that antipathy will now be countered by a conscious desire for the thing in question. Repression of this strong kind could then easily lead to a strengthening of excessive desires, by removing an obstacle to their existence and expression—namely, the disgust. Repression can accordingly function as an agent of *disinhibition* of desire—not, as in Freudian theory, as an inhibition. I don't think repression can in fact act in such a strong way (there is only so far that Nietzsche's *Away with it in thought!* can go), but I do think it can operate to weaken the psychic power of disgust—simply by not allowing it to dominate conscious thought. If so, disgust will have less power to deter excessive or perverse desire. Repression of this kind then acts as an adjunct, not to civilization, but to savagery, primitiveness, and ungoverned appetite—for it permits uncivilized desires greater freedom. It undoes the civilizing work of disgust, allowing the desires in question freer rein.[10]

---

10. In much the same way, if we repressed knowledge of our guilt, this would make bad acts more likely, because the inhibiting effect of guilt would be thereby reduced. If I didn't consciously and attentively dwell in guilt on the badness of my performing a certain act, then I might be more likely to do something similar again. Because guilt feels unpleasant, we have a motive for such repression, which will then serve the cause of morally bad desires. The same dynamic is at work here as in the disgust case.

What I find particularly interesting in this line of thought is the conflicted dynamic it finds in the operations of the psyche. Desires push us one way; disgust pushes back the other way; then repression gives a push to desire by weakening disgust. The counterfactuals bring the conflict out clearly: if it weren't for the disgust, we would act on the desires; and if it weren't for the repression, the disgust would overwhelm us. The repression prevents us from being overwhelmed by disgust, but in so doing it opens up a path for the desires that disgust inhibits. If it weren't for disgust, we would be overwhelmed by excessive desires; if it weren't for repression, we would be overwhelmed by disgust: but putting repression in place makes it *easier* for us to be overwhelmed by desires, because it weakens the dampening force of disgust. It all seems very precarious—as if we teeter on the psychic brink. If repression were stronger and more decisive, it might return us to the days of unruly desire, before disgust evolved to police such desire; luckily, it is weak compared to disgust, so we manage to maintain our veneer of civilization. It seems like a close call. The animal mind has no such precarious dynamic, simply because animal desires are not like human desires—greedy, lustful, perverted, unlimited, impractical, unbalanced, compulsive, curiosity-driven, imprudent, wild, and insane (just consider sadism and masochism). They therefore have no need of the curbing power of disgust, and hence no subsequent need to protect themselves from disturbing disgust knowledge. The desire-disgust-repression dynamic exists only for us, with all its discomfort and tension, and (if the excess theory of the function of disgust is right) it does so because of the pathologies of human desire. If we were more sensible in our desires, then we would have no need for inhibitory disgust, and thus we would have no need for disgust repression, with the cognitive dissonance and self-deception it produces. But to be more sensible in our desires, we would have to be very different kinds of being, probably lacking in both intellect and imagination. That would probably also require us to lack language: so it is the presence of language that leads us to be the kinds of egregiously desiring beings we are, and hence to the consequences of that quirk outlined above.[11] It seems to be a package deal: we get language, intellect, and imagination—but the price we pay is excessive desire, disgust, and repression. Of course, this is all tremendously speculative, but there is an appealing coherence to it: it links various aspects of the human psyche in intelligible ways. We are a species given to extremity of desire, prone to disgust, and burdened with repression, but also possessed of language, reason, and imagination—and these attributes turn out, remarkably, to be connected.

11. Full language mastery, not just of syntax and semantics, but also of communication skills, requires intelligence and imagination. Our ability to think modally—and hence imaginatively—is part of our understanding of sentence meaning, and we must have complex reflexive intentions to communicate properly, as Grice showed. According to my hypothesis, such sophisticated cognitive faculties interact with our desires to produce excessive desires, which then give rise to disgust, which then gives rise to repression. So language mastery is bound up with desire, disgust, and repression of disgust. To put it differently: the brain is an interconnected organ.

9

Thoughts of Death

I SHALL NOW INTERPOLATE some remarks about death and how we conceive of it. I have already commented on the close intertwining of the ideas of disgust and death: in disgust we see the imprint of death, and in death disgust finds one of its prime targets. The living body contains intimations of death and they disgust us; while in the dead body putrescence (itself a manifestation of life) ensures disgust in its own right. Disgust embeds glimpses or sightings of death, as it were, while death owns its special quotient of disgust. Also, the very survival of that prized entity, the Conscious Self, depends upon the integrity of an object steeped in disgust value, namely the animal body. But now I want to make a different kind of point about death and the conceptual framework in which it is embedded, which relates to the *modality* we attribute to death. I think that two apparently contrary thoughts come together when we contemplate our death: first, that death is inevitable, given the dependence of the self on the body; second, that death is contingent, given the intrinsic nature of the self. So, paradoxically, death—human death—is both necessary and contingent. It is necessary because the body is inherently vulnerable to disease, breakdown, and dissolution: we know enough about the biological world to know that organic bodies are not immortal (unlike electrons, say); we see them destroyed all the time, and their inner nature makes this fact intelligible. A simple loss of blood flow to the brain will cause death in frighteningly short order. The body is a soft and fragile vessel—so much is perfectly obvious to us. Even if medical science manages to sustain it for much longer than in the past, it is easy to think of methods by which it might be destroyed; not even the most extravagant science fiction can deliver a credible idea of a human body that is invulnerable to destruction.

But this fact about human cessation is evident only from the outside, by considering the de facto dependence of the self on the body. It is not evident from the inside by considering the self as it is presented to us in self-awareness. From the inside, the self seems not at all vulnerable to extinction: nothing about it, considered in itself, suggests the possibility of death. The self is not introspectively presented as a biological entity, subject to the dangers endemic to such entities, but as a psychological entity—an entity with thoughts and feelings (Descartes was right about this at least). From the internal perspective, then, it is epistemically possible that we are immortal: there is nothing in our knowledge of ourselves, as psychological entities, that is incompatible with the idea that we are immortal.[1] This is precisely why claims of human immortality, existing as a disembodied entity, are treated as real possibilities. The self is not the *kind* of thing that could suffer the severances and dissolutions that are proper to the body—not in its essential nature as given from the inside.[2] The self is not conceived as a spatial, divisible, and cellular thing, so it cannot suffer the fate of

1. I here invoke, again, the (Kripkean) idea that it might turn out (or might have turned out) that we are immortal (relative to our first-person knowledge of our minds), even though our mortality is a metaphysical necessity (in virtue of the dependence of the mind on the body). In other words, the subjective self does not contain its own mortality as an a priori entailment; it doesn't even make its mortality probable.

2. For my purposes, such claims need not be true, so long as they are regarded as true, since I am concerned with explaining our emotions, and here beliefs are what matter: it is what we *think* about the self that determines our feelings about the self.

spatial, divisible, and cellular things in general; it cannot be, literally, torn apart or cut into pieces. What about diseases? There are plenty of diseases that are fatal to the body, but there are no diseases *of the mind* that are fatal to the mind. Depression, mania, schizophrenia—none of these diseases is terminal. No mental disorder that we know of can literally cause the self to cease to be. So there is nothing we know about—from the inside—that could play the role vis-à-vis the mind that cancer and heart disease can play vis-à-vis the body. If we knew only mental facts about ourselves, with no knowledge of the body and its perils, then we would have no reason to believe that we are mortal; indeed, we would be justified in believing (however falsely) that we are immortal. Phenomenologially, our essence is to be immortal. Our knowledge of our mortality is grounded *solely* in our knowledge of the body and of the dependence of the mind on the body—not in our knowledge of the mind considered in its own right. From the internal perspective, it *might turn out* that we are immortal while, at the same time, given what we know of the biological world and our embedding within it, there is overwhelming evidence that we cannot live forever. We could say something even stronger: the mind gives the *impression* that it is not vulnerable to the kinds of forces that can destroy the body. Thus, the self naturally takes the self to be an imperishable entity. We know quite well what it would be for the mind to be immortal—to be freed from its dependence on the body—but we have no idea how the *body* could be immortal, given the kinds of accidents that can befall bodies (it can't be freed from dependence on itself). A disembodied mind could survive a nuclear explosion, since it is not part of the physical world, but not a physical body, no matter how medically enhanced. A disembodied mind is exempt from physical laws by definition, but not a physical object such as a human body.[3]

---

3. If Cartesian dualism were correct, then we would be immortal, so far as destructive physical forces are concerned. For how can you destroy with matter what is not

This is why it strikes us as contingent that we die. It is not a necessary truth about minds that they die, given their intrinsic nature as revealed from the inside. Death is not in any way written into the inner nature of minds, as we experience them. It is only when we step outside the mind and note its strange dependence on the body that we perceive the inevitability of death. Death of the self is extrinsically inevitable, but intrinsically contingent; our human finiteness is exogenous, not endogenous. The death of the self is inevitable, not because of what the self is in its inner being, but because of its de facto reliance on the body. Thus the two ways we have of thinking about the mind—first-person and third-person—generate different estimates of the modality attaching to death: contingent from the inside, necessary from the outside. Both estimates color our thinking about our death, leaving us confused and perplexed. On the one hand, we don't see why we *have* to die; on the other, we accept that death is forced upon us. What we should conclude, in my view, is that our first-person perspective creates an "illusion of contingency": it *appears* to us that the self is only contingently mortal, when we consider it purely internally, but that appearance must be corrected in the light of what we know of the self viewed from the outside, specifically its dependence on the perishable body. The underlying metaphysical modalities cannot be read off the mind as it introspectively appears to us, since this appearance ignores its dependence on the body. Still, that conclusion grates, because the *impression* of contingency is firmly rooted in the mind viewed purely from the inside. To repeat: the mind is vulnerable to no life-threatening ailments of its own (though it is, of course, vulnerable to diseases

---

made of matter (compare numbers)? But it is not in fact correct, so we can be so destroyed. However, immortality remains epistemically possible from the inside, and this gives rise to an illusion of real possibility. The modal situation is complicated and confusing, producing tangled emotions about death in us.

of the brain). The process of digestion, say, is vulnerable to afflictions that can adversely affect its functioning and lead to death, for example a blockage in an intestine. But the process of thinking, say, is not vulnerable to afflictions, of a psychological kind, that can adversely affect its functioning and lead to death. To be sure, thinking can be impeded by emotions or perceptual distractions or outright insanity—but such impediments never lead to death! We just don't know what it would *be* for a psychological event or process to lead to the death of a person (except, of course, through acts of suicide, which operate on the body). This is why we have no idea how a disembodied mind might be extinguished—and why disembodiment is generally taken to be a necessary condition of real immortality.[4]

I believe that in this clash of confusing modal intuitions we find the source of our *resentment* about death. For if death is only contingent, so far as the mind's inner essence is concerned, then why did God or Nature make it the case that we die (I am assuming here that we don't survive bodily death)? It is not as if the self, in its inherent being, and given the laws of nature, *had* to be mortal—as the body had to be. Aren't there possible worlds (quite close ones, in fact) in which selves like ours *are* immortal? We are mortal only because of the unfortunate dependence of mind on body, not because of what the self is intrinsically—so why not create a self that is not so dependent? I find it completely intelligible that *I* should go on forever, while conceding that my body is a finite and fragile thing that cannot

---

4. A disembodied mind cannot be run over or get cancer or be ripped apart. Perhaps only God could destroy it. It is necessary for immortality because bodies are necessarily subject to destructive forces, just by being collections of atoms if nothing else. In fact, it doesn't take much to disrupt the life-giving functions of the body—which is why we live in a state of high death anxiety. We can almost taste death in our own living body: it seems *designed for death*. Death doesn't have to do much to claim it—hence our standing anxiety.

hope for immortality: it thus strikes me as *unfair* that *I* should be condemned to die. There is no necessity in my death, viewed from the inside, so it is gratuitous of God or Nature to insist on it. Given my inner nature, I *could* have been made immortal, so it seems mean of the Creative Powers to render me mortal. By contrast, I have no such thoughts about complex biological entities, or even inanimate entities like mountains and planets: here death and destruction just seem part of the ontological deal. We find it hard to reconcile ourselves to the death we know (externally) to be inevitable, because the self that dies does not itself proclaim such inevitability. I know I *will* die, as a matter of brute fact, but why *should* I die? The end of the self seems purely de facto, not de jure. Death seems brute and opaque, not intelligible and transparent. Consequently, we rebel at the fact of death—and try to pin the blame on somebody (God, Fate, Nature). Just consider how different our attitudes would be if the mind transparently contained its own means of destruction. If we could sense in ourselves, or observe in others, psychological facts that inevitably and intelligibly lead to death, and knew that these were inseparable from psychological reality itself, then surely we would regard our death with much greater equanimity.[5] Suppose that (*per impossibile*) too much *thinking* about smoking and *wanting* to smoke could lead to death (without any actual smoking), so that if you did it more than twenty times a day for forty years, your mind would eventually dwindle away to nothing, as a matter of psychological law. You find your-

---

5. I don't mean that we wouldn't still regret and abhor death, since it is the end of the self; I mean that we would find it easier to accept intellectually—it wouldn't seem so adventitious, so lacking in sense and logic. The self would seem *set up* to die, instead of having death imposed on it from outside. Death would seem like a natural process and only to be expected, not like a gratuitous cosmic blow. In the first instance, we strike ourselves as transcending nature, the stuff of immortality, but then we are driven to accept that we are subsumed by nature, frighteningly so. This produces resentment, anger, confusion, incredulity, paralysis, and misery.

self obsessively having these thoughts and wishes about smoking, and as a result your mental capacities start to diminish and disappear—memory, problem solving, perceptual acuity, and so on. The more you think the unhealthy thoughts, the more decrepit your mind becomes, and evidently so from the inside. Your therapist is unable to cure you of your bad psychological smoking habit. After a final period of rapid mental deterioration, you slip quietly away into oblivion, still with an imaginary cigarette between your lips (you just can't kick the mental habit). (All this could happen if you were a disembodied mind, so that your death has nothing to do with bodily disease.) If such things could occur, then the mind could die of its own accord, of its own internal resources—and then we could see how the mind might be mortally vulnerable from the *inside*. Death would be seen to be inevitable given the laws of psychology, not just the laws of biology; it would then have a basis from within the mind. We wouldn't have the disturbing thought: "Why should *I* die just because of what my *body* suffers?" We would see that we can die because of what *we are*, namely, psychological beings. If we *never* died of biological diseases, but only of mental diseases, then we might view our death very differently, because we would apprehend death as issuing from the inherent nature of the mind, not as something fortuitously imposed from outside. We might start to see death as inevitable and necessary, given what we are—selves that are vulnerable to terminal *psychological* catastrophe. But that is not our situation, so we persist in seeing our death as contingent and adventitious—while also as inevitable from an external standpoint.[6]

6. Death is not the only thing about the mind that seems surprising from the inside but predictable from the outside. There are many psychological disruptions that result from damage to the brain that are not predictable from the inside: all those strange dissociations of perception, memory, emotion, and language that result when the wiring of the brain is damaged. Some men even mistake their wives for hats. Bits of the mind are lost when correlated parts of the brain cease to function.

It is sometimes said that animals are not aware that they will die. I think this is doubtful, at least for certain primates: they witness the death of others in their position, say by intraspecific violence, and it is a small step to the thought that they might be next. But it is surely hard to deny that animals do not *think* of death as we do—in particular, they don't think of their death as contingent in the complex manner I have just been exploring. Such modal thoughts do not occupy their sturdily practical minds; possible-worlds metaphysics isn't their thing. It is only when a subject starts to think of death in terms of biological inevitability combined with psychological contingency that the distinctively human conception of death takes hold. It is the troubling thought, *I must die, but I need not*—with all its inner metaphysical complexity—that characterizes the human attitude toward death (combined, of course, with a simple dread of death and dying). This fractured thought produces the sense of resentment, and the difficulty of reconciliation, that attend our attitude toward our death. Death strikes us as peculiarly tragic, and inherently paradoxical, because of its odd status as a (perceived) contingent necessity—contingent from the inside, necessary from the outside. Like all tragedy, it combines the accidental with the unavoidable. We just happen to live in an unfortunate world, we feel, in which minds depend on bodies; but given that we do live in such a world, things work out as they must. Animals are spared such wrenching modal reflections: death, for them, is just a simple fact (in so far as they think about it at all).

The concept of death that enters our thoughts when we contemplate the disgusting object is, then, this rather sophisticated concept (not available to animals or the young child). It is

---

But none of this seems in the cards when we consider the mind in its own right. The existence-conditions of the mind are not deducible from the mind itself. So we find it surprising when the mind turns out to have one or another type of vulnerability vis-à-vis the body—death being the most shocking example.

a conception that represents death as *gratuitous*—as not dictated by the inner nature of the thing that dies, namely the conscious self. Thus, the rotting corpse makes us think specifically of the death of a conscious being, problematically dependent upon an organic body, where this death strikes us as contingent and adventitious—a tragedy that need not have occurred, a cosmic screw-up. Such a death strikes us as absurd (in the metaphysical sense) because nothing about the conscious self as such entails it. Resentment naturally follows—and a sense of bafflement. Our disgust reaction conjures up this whole complex of thoughts and feelings. We apprehend the world as unintelligible, absurd, and contrary to reason—as well as terrifying and unpredictable. In the attitude of disgust, we take the measure of the disjunction between how the world actually works and how we would like it to be. We rebel at the sheer perversity of it all. This is why I say that disgust is a *philosophical* emotion.[7]

7. Disgust is therefore a *critique* of the world and a rebellion against it. It has an evaluative dimension: things *ought* not to be this way. Things should make sense: they should hang together intelligibly, instead of dissolving into puzzles and paradoxes—not to speak of ordeals and annihilations. Reality is not as we would like it to be as rational beings—well ordered and transparent, a place of clarity and distinctness. Instead, it is maddeningly opaque and blurred. It can't even keep life and death separate! In dead bodies and feces, we see the world's absurdity concretely enacted, and our reason rebels. Nature grinds blindly on, oblivious to our sense of order and propriety. At the center, it presents to us the great paradox of the embodied self, that incongruous duality—the ignoble hero. In experiencing the emotion of disgust, we condemn nature as much for its perversity as for its cruelty. Disgust is a kind of principled protest at the world as we find it.

10

Culture and Disgust

IN THE FIRST PART of this book, I analyzed disgust, seeking its essential character as an emotion with intentional content. In the second part, I argued that disgust is crucial to the human condition and indicated other psychological formations that flow from it, particularly repression. With these materials to hand, I want now to investigate a number of (loosely speaking) cultural phenomena in which disgust is implicated. The aim is to apply the general theory to specific areas in order to test the theory's explanatory power. The range will be quite wide; I intend only to suggest lines of enquiry rather than offer a complete treatment. Accordingly, I shall be brief and (I fear) dogmatic. These topics spill over into other areas of intellectual inquiry, requiring different kinds of expertise; I shall treat them only as a philosopher with a theoretical axe to grind. The tone will also be lighter here, but the aim is to stir some serious thoughts about familiar phenomena to which the subject of disgust appears relevant. I thus offer only a rough template, not a full-scale investigation. Jejune as some of my remarks may appear, they should be taken in the spirit in which they are intended—as mere signposts and hints. But it seems desirable to set the theoretical framework here advocated in a real-world context. What follows is then an exercise in applied philosophy.

(1) Clothes. Why do we wear clothes? Many reasons: for protection against the elements, to signify status, to attract mates, to make artworks of our bodies. But there is another reason: as a neutralizer of disgust. The naked body, with its orifices and body hair, its blemishes and discolorations, is a potential source of disgust, so we take steps to conceal and cover it. Perfume and make-up can serve the same anti-disgust function. We take especial care to obscure the regions that are the most potent loci of disgust—the genitals and anus. The Chagga, it is reported, wear an anal plug at (nearly!) all times, in order to promote the illusion that they do not defecate, so sparing the sensitivities of their tribe mates; but the plug also enables them to conceal the anus itself, acting as an item of clothing.[1] In humans, unlike many other animals, the anus is not visible in a normal standing position, because the buttocks collude to cover it (one wonders if this is a fortunate piece of sexual selection on the part of evolution). But it is still susceptible to exposure in other postures, so some form of reliable concealment is necessary. The cleft between the buttocks suggests the anus irresistibly, so it too needs covering. Even in hot weather, on a beach, say, the proprieties are maintained—not (only) because of the sexual arousal that might otherwise be caused, but because of the cascades of disgust that might be released if full nakedness were the norm. Clothes aid the natural repression that disgust occasions, by enabling us to avoid confronting what we know very well. The illusion of the non-existence of the anus can be sustained, if only within a kind of self-deceptive make-believe. Fashions may change, but the disgust zones must not be allowed to assert their reality. As "signifiers," clothes say: "there is nothing disgusting underneath us, I assure you." Animals and children have no use for clothes for that very reason—the body does not

---

1. I became acquainted with the anally fastidious Chagga in Becker, p. 32. Nothing is said about how they manage to sit down.

disgust them. The more easily you are disgusted by the human body, the more you will insist on full coverage and billowing folds. Clothing is a form of denial (I do not say that all denial is bad). It is not a mere accident that fashion has never promoted a line of clothes that depict on their visible surface the very bodily features they are designed to conceal—an anus on the seat of the pants, say. Nor has fashion ever favored apertures that plainly reveal the lower orifices. Clothes act (inter alia) as a mask for the disgusting body—a disguise, a lie.[2]

(2) Fetishism of the Inorganic. Certain consumer items are especially coveted and sought, to the point where fetishism seems like a reasonable description. Cars, motorcycles, planes, boats, houses, jewelry, and surfboards: people invest such inanimate objects with enormous symbolic value. They are notably non-disgusting, more so than (say) exotic pets and trophy wives. Are they perhaps part of our project of repression, along with clothes and guarded silences? Can they be acting as distractions from the disgust that threatens us from the organic world? The hypothesis seems fairly plausible. Being close to these things, even loving them, provokes no ambivalence—pure physical beauty *sans* the disgusting underside. And notice that our affection for these items is mainly aesthetic not practical—we like the look, feel, and smell of them, not just what they can do for us practically. We focus our attention on such gleaming beauties, making them the center of our lives, so that we can blot out, or gain relief from, the pervasive disgust that threatens to engulf us. Imagine if you could purchase and own nothing but organic

2. Of course, clothes also work to reveal and display the body in certain ways, especially in respect of shape and proportion—but these attributes are not disgust-elicitors. Jeans have proved interesting over the last few decades, because of their propensity to highlight the groin area: a bulge for men, a smooth indentation for women. The genitals are given prominence, but they are idealized—being mere undulations of fabric, pieces of abstract geometry. They are suggested, not described. The backside tells the same tactful story.

entities, and quite disgusting ones at that: then you would have no recourse outside the sphere of the disgusting in your acquisitive drive. Modern technology, exploiting the inanimate world, provides a safe and soothing alternative: things of value and beauty that are completely disgust-free. The nifty red sports car is less a version of the phallus than an alternative to it—a flight from its mode of being. Just so, jewelry is not an extension or celebration of the body, but a rejection of it. The attraction conferred by jewelry is not a biological attraction at all, like smooth skin or long eyelashes; it is a negation of the biological (ditto piercings). In seeming to be continuous with the fleshly body, jewelry denies that the body must be a center of disgust. For one thing, it draws the eye from the skin itself to the shiny bauble that adorns it—away from the soft mole to the hard gem. The more we can be seen to merge with such inorganic things—cars and houses too—the more we can put distance between ourselves and the disgustingly organic. Modern consumerism thus has roots in the human condition as a strenuous repressive flight from disgust. We surround ourselves with the anti-disgusting, the better to repress our consciousness of the disgusting. Hard shiny metal negates soft pulpy tissue—polished not dull and dirty, durable not prone to rot and disease. We seek escape from the ooze and flab of flesh in the glitter and hardness of diamonds. And diamonds, unlike organisms, are forever.[3]

And not just fetishism of the material but also fetishism of the immaterial: certain kinds of worship of the supernatural can be seen as a flight from the organic. Angels and gods, fairies and spirits—all come to us as disgust-free beings. They provide an alternative to the all-too-organic animals we encounter every day, human and other. In imagination, at least, we can escape the disgusting in the personal realm: we can contemplate humanlike

---

3. Is this why women tend to love jewelry so—because of a relatively high level of bodily self-disgust? Just asking.

forms in which the disgusting has been wholly expunged. We could embrace these rarified beings without bracing for revulsion. They have no smell, no nasty orifices, and no bloody interior.[4] The tendency to sublime selected human individuals—kings and queens, supermodels, movie stars—has the same dynamic: we transform them in imagination into pristine beings, devoid of disgusting undersides. This enables us to admire and love a human being that excites no ambivalence in us. And they attract a particularly powerful form of worship and adoration precisely because they short-circuit our natural ambivalence.[5] We *need* people and things we can love wholeheartedly, without finding them in the least bit off-putting. Otherwise, love is conflicted and qualified. Cars can do the trick, up to a point, but so can supernatural beings. Here the inanimate and the immaterial join hands, both standing apart from the messily organic. I would even include *ideas* in this category: we can worship intellectual productions without the ambivalence that attends our devotion to human individuals (or animals). A writer's books transcend the disgusting as she never can (but what if they are *about* the disgusting?); similarly for painters, architects, and musicians. Scientific theories also can be idolized, as the living scientist can never unreservedly be. As a species we have a strong need to find things to value, to worship even, and disgust always places an obstacle in our way; so we search for things that lie outside the circle of disgust. Such devotion has seemed to many observers like displacement (hence the charge of fetishism)—and if the present hypothesis is right, it is. We would *like* to be devoted

4. In the case of humans, we may strive to be odorless but we settle for a sweet smell, knowing that we cannot escape our organic being. As Montaigne noted, we would prefer to smell of nothing—no smell is the best smell: see Miller, p. 75.

5. What is a celebrity but a demigod in whom disgustingness has been banished? They are so shiny, smooth, airbrushed, and impeccable—the flashing white teeth, the bright eyes, the lustrous coiffure. They are like hunks of polished marble. They are also a complete lie.

wholeheartedly to other people (and animals), but disgust puts a damper on that worthy aim—so we resort to nonorganic entities. We redirect our thwarted love to beings, real and imagined, which pose no risk of disgusting us. Hence the quasi-erotic attachment generated by certain artifacts and divinities.[6]

(3) Nudism. A select band of heroic souls, proudly calling themselves "nudists," have set up colonies in which clothes are dispensed with. They have always been in the minority and are generally viewed with suspicion by the clothed majority. What are they up to, these nudists? They are doing battle with the forces of disgust, of course. Instead of caving in to our sense of the disgusting body, they are challenging it. They subscribe to the doctrine that the human body would not disgust us (so much?) if only we saw it in its natural state more frequently. In fact, they see in "civilized" disgust reactions to the human body a thinly disguised life-denying straightjacket of misplaced Puritanism. They hold, precisely, that the body is *not* inherently disgusting, even in its "private parts." At any rate, I can imagine a principled nudist arguing in this kind of way. If she did so argue, she would confront the following objection: what should we say about "extreme nudism," in which all bodily functions are openly performed? Nobody, surely, would maintain that people should be granted total anal freedom to defecate whenever and wherever they like—*that* would be disgusting. So there have to be limits placed on how much of the natural body other people can be expected to tolerate—which is to say that disgustingness is part of the essence of the human body. Nudism is a kind of heroic attempt to gainsay the disgusting body, but it is only credible within strict limits. Justified in the way I have sketched, liberationist nudism is a noble failure, though a per-

6. Notice the tendency to caress and even kiss certain artifacts: cars, trophies, fine silks. Sometimes these are stand-ins for a divine entity, as with crucifixes. Bikinied girls on car hoods or astride motorcycles also attest to the erotic meaning of certain artifacts.

fectly intelligible one. The nudist (as I have interpreted her) sees clearly the repressive function of clothes and wishes to undo such repression, but there is only so far that project can go before the high wall of disgust becomes insurmountable. Feces never lose their power to repel, even if bare hairy buttocks can come to seem innocuous. Nudism can be at best a compromise position, not a radical one. In effect, we as a society have become *more* inclined to moderate nudism over the years, as inhibitions about the body have loosened, but we will never, I think, go the whole hog (or Monty). The anus, in particular, will always stand between us and complete sartorial abandon: the politics of the body can never be perfectly liberal.[7]

(4) Society. We possess the following two species characteristics: we are a social species, and we are a disgust-prone species. The combination poses an obvious problem. If we had one characteristic alone, then there would be no problem, but taken together the two characteristics are in tension. We ardently seek the company of our fellow human beings but we are repulsed by their presence. Gregariousness pulls us together, but disgust pushes us apart. How might this problem be resolved? Clothes are a good start, especially about the loins. But the most essential requirement is to establish a clear distinction between the public and the private: in the private area, the disgusting can be safely unleashed, while the public area must be kept stainless and pure. The concept of the "privy" is thus born—the private place of excretion and its ancillaries. Without the privy, society would be well-nigh impossible for us—even if the place in question consists of nothing more than a designated field outside the village. We will also need a means of removing dirt from the body, and

---

7. For the record, I am quite in favor of moderate nudism myself; I sense hypocrisy in our recent liberation of the body combined with a reluctance to go further. I was once on a beautiful island in the south of France where nudism was accepted and widely practiced: it struck me as entirely natural and pleasant. But I don't accept the ideology of the body as only conventionally disgusting.

a secluded place to do it in. And eventually there will have to be a private place for copulation and associated deeds. The public/private distinction arises, originally, from the necessity for disgust-management. Some places are open to general perceptual access, while others are closed to such access (here doors and screens prove their worth). We succeed in living in social groups by shielding each other from our organic nature: crapping in the parlor, for instance, is strictly prohibited. But with this partition of spaces there also arises a need for certain behavioral innovations: we must behave discreetly, tactfully, and often secretly. We must watch our words, adjust our clothing, and not draw unnecessary attention to what we have just been privately proceeding with—so as not to remind people of what they know quite well. We must, in other words, become *actors*, managing the impression we make on others, calibrating our interpersonal impact.[8] We must develop a social self—a *role*—that exists at one remove from our private self. Thus a split in our identity is formed, as we put distance between the self we present socially and the self that must have its private hour. We begin to act a part, to put on a show; and the further that theatrical role departs from the universal fact of organic exigency, the more effective it becomes in reducing the chances of eliciting disgust. We must intentionally create an impression in others, more or less illusory, of non-disgustingness in ourselves. Now social *competition* arises: who can best act the role of non-disgusting self? The person who can best convey an impression of organic purity will win out in the anti-disgust stakes: the cleanest, least smelly, best manicured, most discreet, most smartly dressed person will have the competitive edge. That requires money and time, and an occupation

---

8. I am thinking here of the work of Erving Goffman on the self as a theatrical construct: see *The Presentation of Self in Everyday Life*. The beginning of the theatrical self lies in the need to conceal our disgusting underbelly from our fellows. We try to act the part of a god, in effect. As the saying goes: we act like butter wouldn't melt in our mouths—or its residue seep from our anuses.

that doesn't involve dirt and sweat. We go white-collar: white as snow, no grime, odorless, and stiffly starched. It also requires self-discipline: no belching or breaking wind or picking the nose (at least in company). A linguistic gift for euphemism helps, for metaphor and circumlocution. Certain virtues are then valued and cultivated, all stemming from the necessity to negotiate the disgusting in our biological bodies. The association between poverty and filth is strong, and the motivation to avoid poverty in order to ward off filth is correspondingly strong.[9] Hard work, self-control, and personal cleanliness: does any of this sound familiar? It all arises from the need to forestall disgust in a social and aesthetic species. So also does the human habit of acting a part, putting on a front, adopting a persona: this is just an aspect of the repression I discussed earlier. But such a show is inherently fragile, because the body is not always subject to our will, however strenuously we apply it: the burp will escape, the fart erupt, the urine stain. Then the whole façade comes tumbling down: the lurking organism has asserted itself, to our intense chagrin.[10] Society is thereby threatened, resting as it does on a kind of lie. We *are* disgusting—no matter how much we try to act like gods, no matter how we try to disguise our bodies. Society is founded on a contract that we are incapable of fully living up to: for we cannot altogether conceal our organic identity, though we undertake sincerely to do so. It is all a kind of vain pretense,

9. Miller's chapters 9 and 10 are fine discussions of disgust and social hierarchy. George Orwell, for all his egalitarian principles, evidently had trouble with the dirtiness and smell of the working class. The lower you are socially, the more dirty you are perceived to be (and sometimes are). The highest caste is the most spotless. The aristocracy is born clean.

10. Personifying the anus comes naturally because, as has often been remarked, the digestive process seems to have a will of its own. It works to its own schedule—and we dare not cross it. The bowels will move whether you like or not. And the fart is like a separate voice, blurting out its inarticulate message. The talking anus is a standard comic trope. The idea of a split in our being is thus easily seen as a duality of wills, and these wills can be at cross-purposes.

necessary but ultimately futile. Many good things spring from the pretense, no doubt, but it is precarious and fundamentally deceptive. Human beings are deceivers par excellence, and the basic deception concerns our very nature as excreting, secreting, and decaying creatures. What is worse, the attempted deception can never really succeed, because the truth is common knowledge: it is ultimately pointless to pretend that one is above the biological law and not a creature of nature. All we can really do is try to keep this knowledge at bay and not rub each other's nose in it. The whole shaky edifice arises from the need to combine the two aspects of our nature: our longing to be together, and our revulsion at what we are. Our minds want to join with others, but our bodies stand in the way. We are caught between these two opposing forces. Other social animals do not face the same difficulty, simply because they don't disgust each other. Solitariness would seem to be our natural condition when contemplating our propensity for disgust—the most centrifugal psychic force within us—but our need for other people pushes in the opposite direction. Much of the characteristic structure of human society results from trying to resolve this conundrum. Society depends, in a word, upon repression, which is always an unstable project, and never a happy one.[11]

(5) Sex. This is a form of human contact that tests our tolerance for the potentially disgust-inducing. At its heart lie contrary impulses: we have a strong drive toward it, but it can also set off our disgust alarm. Pleasure, power, love, and the biological imperative to reproduce—all push us toward sex. But at the same time, we must reconcile ourselves to those tumors, wounds, fluids, unnerving proximities, and patches of questionable hair that would otherwise deter us. Put it this

---

11. Here is a blueprint for sociology: explain how societies form and operate to deal with disgust. What are the strategies and pitfalls, the costs and benefits, the correlates and consequences? How is disgust woven into social structure? And how does economics figure in—how are dirt and money connected?

way: nobody would want to go through with it unless he or she had a strong reason to—sexual desire being that strong reason. The gynecologist has his reasons, of course, but he is a special case (everyone has to earn a living, even lavatory attendants); similarly with the prostitute. The essence of the sexual experience is ambivalence—attraction and repulsion. Or better: attraction triumphing over repulsion. Sexual pleasure is surely, in part, tied to this peculiar dynamic: it is a kind of achievement, like climbing a mountain, or eating an oyster or a snail (it gets easier the more often you do it)—something is being surmounted. Having sex with someone you find physically repulsive is, for most people, a highly disagreeable prospect, but all sex involves close proximity to things normally found off-putting. As has often been remarked, the closeness of anus and vagina, and the dual function of the genitals as sexual and urinary, are already challenges to our disgust-oriented sensibilities. We manage to overcome them, such is the power of sexual desire, but there is definitely something there that needs to be overcome. Some people see this as a piece of mischief on the Creator's part or a cruel oversight by our selfish genes. What it really tells us is that our animal bodies were not created to conform to our squeamish human minds, coming down to us from a time when disgust had no place on the planet. It is just an unfortunate accident that beings with these traditional bodies *also* have a psychological problem with excretion. There is an uncomfortable mismatch between human anatomy and human psychology. Animals have no such qualms: they just get right on with it. Sex, for us, is a kind of tortured maneuvering to get what we desire while avoiding the reefs of potential disgust that lie in our path.[12] The proof of this, if proof were needed, is that

12. I have heard it said that in sex we seek skin and tolerate orifices. That is a little too simple, perhaps, but it contains an essential truth, namely that we walk a delicate line between what we desire and what we desire to avoid—these two things being dangerously close together.

when we have got what we want and desire has ebbed, we proceed with all alacrity to *clean up the mess*. And who can deny the mood-destroying effect of an errant *flatus* just at the moment of erotic fervor? Sex is fraught with such gaseous and liquid dangers (watch those moistly aromatic armpits!). Not for no reason is sex sometimes referred as "the nasty" and declared "dirty." Much of seduction and courtship is concerned with deactivating the normal inter-personal disgust reflex, with clothes and perfume, conversation and music, and meticulous personal grooming: this is all a testament to the necessity to circumvent a reaction that comes all too naturally to us (just think of sex before the advances in personal hygiene we nowadays take for granted). As a phenomenologist might say, the objective intentional correlate of sexual consciousness always carries with it a secondary *noema* of disgust.[13]

One further point: sex is associated with reproduction. Two further disgust objects are thus brought obliquely into play: birth and death. Birth enters because sexual intercourse can lead to pregnancy and hence birth—and birth is a gross business. Death hovers because the cycle of life and death is invoked by an act that produces progeny: the begetting of children is just the flip side of the dying of the aged, conceptually speaking. When we think of the birth of new life we think inevitably of the death of old life—one terminus suggests the other. One generation

13. We must not forget, however, that disgusting objects can in their own right excite attraction as well as repulsion—so that things can be felt as attractive *in virtue* of their disgusting character. No doubt sexual pleasure can incorporate this kind of attraction, as well the usual kind. Freudian oral and anal pleasure has a similar structure, since it too may involve the ambivalence of the disgusting. Interestingly, the so-called higher pleasures, such as music and poetry, do not include any disgust component: is this what makes them higher? There is a dynamic of conflict in the so-called lower pleasures that does not seem to exist for the higher pleasures. Stop for a moment and think of the pleasure you get from a mouthful of masticated food: it is a disgusting pulp, yet felt as extremely pleasurable. To what extent does the pleasure derive from the disgustingness?

arises to take the place of another, which goes the way of all living things. To consciously engage in an act that creates new life is implicitly to acknowledge that old life will wither and die, and hence to accept the reality of death and decay. To beget a child is also, poignantly, to initiate the process of dying, since anything living will eventually die. The basic laws of finite organic life are implicit in the sexual act. The psychology of sex is therefore saturated with potential disgust objects: not just the ones that are most proximate, but also the potential and future ones that come with the territory. Sexual feelings are thus complex and multilayered, with disgust at their center and at their periphery. Surprisingly, it still gets done.

(6) Phases of Life. Disgust reactions develop and mutate over the course of a normal human life; they are not static. The infant, as we have noted, feels no disgust, being quite undaunted by feces and mucus. At some point in the early years, a disgust reaction begins to develop, whether as a result of parental teaching or as part of an unfolding innate program is hard to say. Often certain types of food trigger the reaction most strongly in this early phase: the texture, taste, or smell of particular foods elicits a pronounced antipathy, with which there is no reasoning (I felt this way about tapioca pudding—it was the slithery quality). During adolescence, the range of disgust objects centered on the self expands alarmingly, and the adolescent must learn to cope with the new range: body hair, pimples, acne, greasy skin, menstrual blood, semen, sweat. At the same time, the necessity to manage these objects becomes more pressing, as sexual relations and interpersonal associations burgeon. Greater self-consciousness and self-monitoring are required, as well as an ability to see yourself as others see you. The next life stage is mating, pair bonding, and family life: living together with another person in close proximity and (often) raising children. Here a new slate of challenges is presented. First, there is the challenge of living intimately with

another adult day in and day out at close quarters: the risk of mutual disgust increases, but tolerance also grows (within limits). Second, children introduce an extra layer of disgust stimuli, particularly with respect to their excretory activities. Now disgust-management takes on a special urgency, and children must be educated in the theory and practice of disgust. Disgust becomes a daily focus of family life: the sodden and filthy diaper, the runny nose, the dribbled food, and the begrimed skin. Parental maturity calls for suppression of natural revulsion and a deft deployment of repression. As the years sweep by, yet another phase supervenes: disgust as it applies to the aged. Bodily decline, disease, and incontinence come to stay—the disgust objects of the elderly. A reeducation in the manifold ways of disgust becomes necessary. The body invents new methods to offend and repel—geriatric disgust. At each life stage, a specific set of age-related bodily traits calls for a new set of attitudes and behaviors. Fresh challenges arise, the emotions endure novel convulsions, and repression takes on new forms. The work of disgust-control, it seems, is never done: it must be reinvented as one stage leads to the next. Repression must adapt to new realities. There is thus a developmental psychology of disgust—as there is of intelligence and sexual activity. Freud was interested in the latter, Piaget in the former: where is the developmental psychologist to investigate the changing patterns of human disgust?[14] Perhaps only in advanced senility does disgust finally leave us, marking a return to the innocence of our pre-disgust infancy.

14. Paul Rozin has the strongest claim, but he does not have the fame of the other two: is that because of a general repression with respect to the disgusting domain? Also, his work has not been primarily developmental. If I were a developmental psychologist, I would investigate the *interactions* between emotion, desire, intellect, imagination, and language in the developing child; then I could begin to articulate a general theory of the human mind as it grows and changes. Dare I say that there is a kind of *holism* at work here, in addition to the usual modularity?

(7) Love. Love clearly comes in different forms: romantic, paternal, maternal, fraternal, filial, and so on. It can also be directed toward a leader or a god or a revered ancestor. Love typically involves a high evaluation of its object and a wish to be on intimate terms with the beloved. Yet love is also directed toward an object that is, as a matter of fact, inherently repulsive. How does love cope with that fact? Not by blindness or outright denial, but by a kind of bracketing. The beloved is acknowledged to possess certain repulsive characteristics (how could that be seriously disputed?), but they are relegated to a secondary status. They are not the *essence* of the beloved, but mere contingent accompaniments. The psychological target of the love—its "intentional object"—is really an idealized and fragmentary being, not the whole organism. We may seek to identify this purified object with the inner self or soul, but more often it is granted corporeal status but with the disgusting bits blocked out. The imagination is what makes this possible, because it can achieve partiality, omitting features it prefers to leave unspecified. You can imagine the beloved's face without the blemish you know she actually possesses, and you can erase from your mental image all hints of secretion and excretion. We edit and trim, foregrounding the traits we find lovable, eliding others. We perform the psychological equivalent of the sculptor's work in idealizing the human form (see below), excluding and occluding. Thus we do not love (*de dicto*) the complete human being, strictly speaking, but only a partial simulacrum. We always love "under a description," and that description excludes the traits that we find repulsive. The greatest challenge to love occurs when the disgusting traits cannot be ignored or bracketed—when the beloved is (say) incontinent by our side or visibly oozing pus. Then we must strive to make love overpower revulsion—not eliminate it, since that cannot be done, but exert greater force than it does. This is a far more difficult achievement than the standard trick of simply eliding the disgusting

traits from one's intentional object. Fortunately, we generally have the latter psychological mechanism to make love (especially romantic love) a feasible project—one that requires no great heroism or resolve or strength of character. Love is possible, in the teeth of the disgusting, because the mind has the ability to be selective in its attributions. To put it differently: love thrives on repression, enabled by the selectivity of imagination. And don't we love more purely in imagination than we ever can when perceptually presented with the loved object?[15] In the simplest case, we just refuse to *attend* to what we find off-putting, dwelling rather on the attractive traits of the beloved. Attention is inherently selective, so it provides the perfect faculty to render the project of love possible. Without such selective repression, human love would not be what it now is. And yet, we must never forget that love is a *troubled* project, precisely because repression is inherently unstable and unreliable. We love *despite*....[16]

(8) Art. Winfried Menninghaus' *Disgust: Theory and History of a Strong Sensation* is a lengthy disquisition on the role of disgust in art, which I strongly recommend to interested parties. Here I shall limit myself to a few brief remarks, referring to his magisterial work for a fuller treatment. There are basically two points at which the disgusting may enter a (representational) work of art: as subject and as medium. That is, a painting may

15. I am reminded of the plaintive opening line of a popular song from my childhood: "I dream of Jeannie with the light brown hair." The singer's love seems at its strongest when he *dreams* of his beloved, not when he sees her standing solidly before him. In dreams, i.e., imagination, he can select the light brown hair, ignoring the less lovely mole on the chin. As Shakespeare well knew, romantic love is an achievement of the imagination, more than of reason (I would add perception): see *A Midsummer Night's Dream*. And isn't imaginatively anticipated sex the best kind?

16. Animal love is not like that, because their love is not qualified by the specter of disgust lurking in the background. They can love more wholeheartedly. Is this why we value the love of our pets so much?

take as its subject a gross object, say a heap of excrement, yet be composed in oils; or it may itself be *made* of a gross material, such as excrement, yet not be *of* anything gross. Likewise, a sculpture might be of a human figure and yet be constituted by excrement; or it might be constituted by bronze and be of excrement. The question of whether the gross and disgusting has a place in art therefore divides into these two sub-questions, and might be answered differently in the two cases. Menninghaus has a detailed and illuminating discussion of Greek sculpture, in which he points out the many techniques of disguise and elision that these artists employed to negotiate the orifices of the body: these orifices were not deemed aesthetically acceptable and so had to be somehow expunged or modified. In this ancient art form, the disgusting (including even the interior of the mouth) could not be permitted even as a subject of art, because it compromised the beauty of the human figure. Later art softened (or hardened) on the question, but it is a rare painting or sculpture—in fact, I don't know of any—that candidly depicts the orifices and excretions of the human body.[17] Has there ever been a realistic still life of an excremental mound? If so, it could only be in modern *avant-garde* art. The reason, presumably, is that a disgusting subject matter runs the risk of making the work of art itself disgusting—and that art works must not be. For the actively disgusting in a work of art would cause the spectator to turn away, or to want to bury or destroy the work. Still, it does seem at least conceivable that a work of art might depict a genuinely gross subject and yet manage to hold our

17. I refer here mainly to art before the twentieth century: in that century many traditional aesthetic precepts were intentionally disregarded. Modern art is far more willing than traditional art to flout taboos about the body. Even still, impressionist or cubist pictures of women defecating are few and far between. You have to get to the present day before art becomes willing to traffic in the disgusting, and even here only in a glancing and ironic manner. The anus has still not found its Picasso or Matisse. There is just no market for it.

entranced gaze: there are many paintings of bloody scenes, for example, that do not provoke the effect that actual blood would.[18] However, when it comes to the *medium* of representation, I think our attitudes are far more absolute: on no account can a work of art be openly *composed* of a disgusting material. I say "openly" because it is of course possible to make a sculpture of excrement and disguise that fact somehow; what is not possible is to make a sculpture out of excrement where the material is frankly and palpably excremental—looking, smelling, and so on. And the reason is the same as before: no one would want to look at it or even be near it—and that defeats the purpose of art. Art must attract the senses; it cannot repel them. To make a painting out of daubs of phlegm and excrement, appearing as such, even of an attractive face, can never work as an art object—it would be just too contrary to the purpose of art. This is why there has never been, and probably never will be, a shit art or snot art or menstrual blood art.[19] Such a thing might work as *avant-garde* irony or as a conceptual exercise, but no normal person would wish to view it. The gross is too much the antithesis of the beautiful for it to succeed as a material of art. Even

18. The work of Francis Bacon might be cited as reveling in the gore of the human body (and there was the earlier enthusiasm for the grotesque, as with Bosch), but really it is not so clear that the disgust value of the original is preserved in such works, despite the clear representational content. Beauty of the original can indeed be transmitted through pictorial representation, but I don't know of a painting that preserves the disgust value of its original; there is always some transformation or etiolation at work. It is much the same with film.

19. Perhaps I should say that there will never be such an art *with general appeal*. Of course, an artist is free to *make* such things, and may attract a cult following. I don't think the work of Damien Hirst, for example, falls into this category, despite his use of bifurcated animal bodies, because there is too much framing and aesthetic distance. These are not actual rotting corpses, stinking and deliquescing. They are suspended moments—and they edgily test the viewer's tolerance for the grotesque. A portrait actually composed of fresh blood, snot, and shit is quite another proposition—or vomit action painting. Nor is it easy to imagine a musical genre of fart noises.

artists of the grotesque never go so far as to include actual cadaverous material *in* their works. People don't want to go to an art gallery in order literally to vomit.

The classical artistic canon reveals instead a flight from the disgusting. The human body is unvaryingly depicted in its more attractive aspect, as pure form, not as a vile sack of internal organs. I suspect that this is precisely because art (classical art anyway) is an attempt to transcend the disgustingness that surrounds us in ordinary life. Art is intended to draw our attention away from our gross nature, to provide an alternative to that disturbing vision. Art provides a spectacle for the senses that is absent the disgusting, thus supplying us with an object of aesthetic evaluation that does not simultaneously revolt us. If that is its fundamental motivation, then there is no point in incorporating the disgusting *in* art. Art is one part of our systematic attempt at repression of the disgusting—distracting us from it and the heavy mental burden it imposes. Attention is finite, so directing it toward beautiful objects that carry no hint of the gross prevents us from dwelling unhealthily on the noxious objects and processes that confront us in our very nature. Art is a way of not thinking about the body as it *actually* is, but only as we *wish* it to be—purged of the gross and unsettling. In classical art, accordingly, the human form is free of the duality that defines our actual human identity: it depicts us as unified beings, with no revolting aspect (the bodily interior is rigorously denied). We have extension and form, color and mass, but there is no hint of what heaves and bubbles beneath the skin or lurks in the lower regions (except in a highly stylized form). This is not so much sexual prudishness as a principled aesthetic decision: the disgusting cannot find a place in objects of artistic beauty. Classical art *opposes* the human body, as it actually exists, depicting instead an artificial idealized body—the body of a god, in effect, not a biological entity. Remembering that such art might originally be found, not in art galleries, but where people live and gather, its function as a *substitute* for the full human reality becomes clearer. It provides an image of ourselves that is more to our liking, facilitating the repression we crave. A classical nude is never suppurating and carbuncled, or even dirty and sweaty, but always an idealized volume of smooth and scrubbed epidermal heaven. Even the mouth is never allowed to reveal its salivary interior, the snakelike tongue, and the plunging esophagus. Such bodies do not do anything so squalid as *digest*.[20]

(9) Etiquette. We are admonished to have good table manners and punished for bad ones. You must not eat with your mouth open, dribble food down your chin, or spit it out. You are told not to "wolf" down your food, or eat like a "pig." You must not "shovel" food into your mouth or cram it too full. On no account may you burp, expectorate, or break wind at the table. The elegant use of a napkin is *de rigueur*, as is the proper deployment of utensils (no licking the plate or eating from the fingers). The purpose of these rules is plain: to minimize the opportunities for disgust on the part of your fellow diners. Eating, unlike defecation, is performed in public, but it is still part of the digestive process: mashing the food in the mouth, mixing in the saliva, and swallowing—these are digestive events. The end result of this digestive process is not a matter of remote conjecture but haunts the proceedings (first the dining table,

---

20. But two points should be made about this artistic tradition. First, such art is fundamentally not *truthful*—it does not depict the human body as it really is. Second, it cannot ultimately defeat the forces of disgust, because the orifices must always be represented in *some* form, however muted; even the most idealized figure must have a mouth, a nose, ears, and a cleft between the buttocks. The body's secretions and interior cannot be totally expunged from the viewer's aesthetic consciousness. The very act of intentionally disguising the body only reminds the viewer of the repellent truth. But if we choose to let the disgusting into art, in the interests of truth and honesty, we run the risk of alienating the viewer and depriving art of its function. The dilemma is sharp: falsehood and failure or disgust and turning away. Maybe art, as traditionally conceived, is just not possible: it combines contradictory intentions.

then the toilet). It is definitely forbidden to speak openly of shit while dining with others; and no one wants to know you've been having diarrhea lately. Dining etiquette is thus a device of repression: it keeps the underlying process as hidden as possible, so that it can be publicly performed. We know quite well what is going on inside those munching mouths, behind those pursed lips, but we don't want to be reminded of it by an untimely gape—that mass of organic pulp on the brink of descent into the bilious hell of the stomach. We must control as best we can the manifestations of the peristaltic process; we must airbrush the unseemly reality of digestion. Nor can we allow someone to sit at table in a dirty or disheveled state, embodying the gross and contaminated. Table manners are a manual for disgust-management, and quite necessary.[21]

Nose etiquette belongs in the same category. The nostrils are a potent source of revulsion, with their noisome contents only millimeters from the visible face. Nothing must be permitted to escape these narrow chambers into the domain of public perception, and inserting a finger is strictly forbidden. Children are strongly cautioned against "picking their nose," that is, cleaning the nose's interior with their fingers in public (in private all is forgiven). If the nose is spontaneously disgorging its contents, as with a "runny nose," then the proper recourse is to use a tissue or handkerchief, not the back of your hand or your sleeve. This is common knowledge, as we come to know how to walk and talk. The mucus is apparently touchable by the body when it exists inside the nostrils, but the hands may not

---

21. Of course, rules of etiquette can be taken to ludicrous extremes: never speaking while eating, rigid rules for the use of knife and fork, compulsory formal dress, constant dabbing with the starched napkin. One can be too prissy, too proper. A society in the grip of such rules might be suspected of abject fear of the body, a total unwillingness to accept reality. We have become notably more relaxed about table manners, as Victorian dread of the body has receded. Still, some proprieties must be observed.

make contact with it. Of course, the height of horror is to re-cycle the mucus by re-ingesting it—even though it springs ini-tially from the throat. Any civilized person must learn rigorous nose etiquette and acquire the skills of nose control. Social life depends on it. Etiquette here is not merely a matter of being conventionally finicky, though from a clinically objective perspective it may seem so, but an essential protection against the more nauseatingly viscous aspects of our being. The nose is highly conspicuous and continually active, so it must be regu-lated conscientiously; its proximity to the mouth is particularly perilous. Of special concern is its state during communal dining: it must be as clean as a whistle and its contents never discussed. The nose can ignite nausea all too easily. The whole business is precarious and fraught, and repression is an indispensable element. The rules of etiquette, as they pertain to the nose, are stratagems for not knowing.[22]

It is much the same story with etiquette as it bears on such matters as armpit sweat, foot odor, and gaseous releases. It is deemed good manners to use deodorant, change your socks, and contain your flatulence. These all relate to smell, but the same holds for visual disgust, as with unkempt nails, dirty clothes, and bristling nose hair. The point is to counter the natural forces of the disgusting body, to render it palatable. Society requires voluntary manners in order to counter involuntary disgust. Nature cannot be allowed to go its own way—our minds cannot tolerate what our bodies take for granted. We have cultural rules

---

22. Freud, characteristically, thought the nose a phallic symbol, with mucus the analogue of semen. Once again, he gets things the wrong way round: mucus is found *more* disgusting than semen. Also, why cannot both organs be co-equal disgust elicitors? The nose and penis are only vaguely morphologically similar anyway. Sneezing and ejaculating bear only the most passing resemblance to each other. And what are females doing with a penis on their face? This whole phallic symbol business is obviously vastly overblown and unconstrained by any reasonable standards of evidence.

of etiquette because biological evolution failed to harmonize the sensitivities of the refined human mind with the blunt realities of our creaturely body. Etiquette cloaks and tames the ancient organic body for the sake of the delicate modern mind. Animals have no need of it, because for them there is no friction between body and mind.

(10) Technology. We can view technology as the expansion of the human into the inorganic world. For most animals, their species identity does not extend much beyond the bounds of their own body: the odd nest or burrow is all we see of their instrumental impact on the world beyond. But humans have changed the environment significantly: we have machines, buildings, dams, and so on. I have already discussed the human fetishism of the sleekly inorganic, but I now want to make a more specific point about how we build extensions of ourselves in inorganic materials. Let us focus on electronic devices, because they illustrate the point best. The great thing about these devices is that they completely lack the offensiveness of the organic: televisions, computers, phones, cameras, music systems, and the like. We hold them, cradle them, play with them, gaze at them—and they never disgust us. Yet they are our intellectual products, extensions of us, like external brains (they manipulate information). We have an inordinate fondness for such devices, for interacting with them, seeing and touching them.[23] Then the hypothesis is this: we love technology, not merely for the instrumental functions it performs, but also for its material being, its mode of existence. Technology reflects us, but it is not *of* us; it is human but also "mechanical." Electricity itself, which drives these devices, is a thoroughly inorganic

---

23. The cell phone is the current favorite: held in the palm, manipulated by the fingers, cradled next to the ear, constantly gazed at—people do love their cell phones. They transmit the human voice without the danger of bodily revulsion. They are hard, shiny, bright, and odorless. In them, we find personal intimacy without the chance of disgust.

phenomenon: when it courses through a device, the process is nothing like food passing through a digestive system. Electricity is pure and clean (unlike oil, which is organic), and hence disgust-free. An electric shock may be painful, but it is never nauseating. And the parts of an electronic device are metallic and glassy, not fleshy. It would be different if these devices could only be made from organic materials, such as blood vessels, neurons, earwax, toenails, and body hair; then, I surmise, our affection for them would be markedly different. The meaning of technology for us, as an affective configuration, is that of the anti-disgusting (at least in part)—yet these things are curiously animated and "alive." You turn on the TV: it springs to life, as if from a deep sleep; it starts to talk and project pictures of people; it glows and shimmers—yet it never oozes or smells. The phone is pressed to your ear, a voice emanates from it: but it never has the clamminess of a frog or the aroma of feet. It provides intimacy without the risk of disgust. It gives us what even our pets cannot. In technology, we have pushed human reality beyond the organic, and we like what we see: the hardness, the gleam, and the dryness. These clever devices are our friends without the icky aspects of flesh. One can only speculate about what will happen to human society when friendly robots are manufactured for mass consumption (with or without an inner consciousness)—conversation and companionship, maybe even sex, without the risk of organic eruption. People are already more enamored of their mobile phones than they are of their neighbors. Our love affair with technology may be only just beginning. This is not a mere extension of technologies already long in place, like furniture and buildings, which also dodge disgust (discussed in [2]); it is the advent of the machine as human surrogate—devices that mimic people. These are devices that form part of modern human society, as members not adjuncts. The computer has insinuated itself into the human psyche far more deeply than the car.

(11) Neurosis. My thesis has been that the emotion of disgust is central to human life, showing itself in a variety of psychological and cultural formations. Specifically, we suffer from "auto-disgust," which leads to distress and repression. Might it also lead to neurosis, in somewhat the way sexual emotions are held to lead to neurosis in Freudian thinking? Evidence for that hypothesis can be found in the areas of dreams, obsessive-compulsive disorder, and fetishism. Who has not dreamt of bizarre bouts of public defecation, where one finds oneself atop the toilet bowl in a public setting, with other people wandering by, chatting, and looking askance? The sense is of doing something one really ought not to be doing but not being able to avoid doing it. Then there are dreams of being soiled by feces and being unable to wash them off. I don't think this has much to do with so-called anal pleasure, as Freud conjectured, but it has everything to do with anxiety about being exposed as a shameless shitter. Social embarrassment is the dominant emotion of such dreams, as the private and public domains disturbingly intersect. The waking fear of being walked in on while defecating is a familiar experience; in dreams that fear is lived out. In sexual dreams, too, the disgustingness of the body is a common theme, with the sexual organs sometimes assuming strange shapes and exuding odd substances. Anxious awareness of the organic body is standard dream fodder.[24]

In obsessive-compulsive disorder, we frequently find such behaviors as repeated hand washing, excessive fear of "germs," and not wanting to touch certain things. Some apparently quite normal people have a "phobia" about shaking another person's hand. Extreme bodily cleanliness is a common symptom of

24. I would like to see this subject systematically investigated; my remarks are merely impressionistic. The developmental psychology of disgust dreams would be particularly interesting: are disgust dreams coeval with waking disgust reactions, and how are the contents related? There is also the question of cultural diversity or universality of dream content. And: how are disgust dreams related to the kind of insanity that involves disturbance to normal disgust responses?

such compulsions. In this, we see an exaggerated response to something we all feel to some extent: disgust at dirt, fear of contamination, anxiety about body odors and secretions. The body is a great accumulator of muck and grunge, both extraneous and homegrown, and inside it is a sarcophagus of filth. Some people find this more intolerable than others; those who can't stand it for another second are called "neurotics." From one point of view, however, they are quite sane and the rest of us are in deep denial: for there is plenty to jib at in the human body's aptitude for the gross and soiled. Perhaps the filth neurotics among us are just more deficient than most at the trick of repression—which is to say, they are more devoted to the truth.[25] They know how dirty and disgusting reality is, in exquisite detail, while most of us shield our eyes from the facts. In any case, it is not surprising that disgust can overwhelm and dominate the psyche, causing pathologies of different kinds.

Some types of fetishism seem to reflect uneasiness at the grossness of the human body. Take shoe fetishism. The foot is one of the body's most suspect parts: it is a club-like extremity, with none of the dexterity and expressiveness of the hand; it is prone to smell bad unless washed frequently; it is close to the dirty ground; it is sometimes home to fungi and warts; it is often deformed (ingrown toenails, bunions, hammer toe). We regard the human foot with mixed emotions and seldom extol its beauty; some feet, honestly, can be downright repulsive.[26] There are those,

25. Recall the earlier comment that it can be insane not to be insane, in view of the true human condition (see note 8 in chapter 8, "Repression and Disgust").

26. Becker is very sensitive about the human foot, writing: "The foot is the absolute and unmitigated testimonial to our degraded animality, to the incongruity between our proud, rich, lively, infinitely transcendent, free inner spirit and our earth-bound body" (p. 237). He also sees the shoe as the negation of the foot, with an attached fetish. The practice of foot binding is of a piece with revulsion at the natural human foot. We long to flee the foot. If it weren't so useful, we might be tempted to lop it off (so, at least, Becker intimates). I am not so foot phobic myself, though I do think foot modesty is generally indicated.

correlatively, who take a particular shine to shoes, either as regular consumers (the Imelda Marcos syndrome) or as sexual "perverts." When the shoe is eroticized in this way, it is easy to detect a kind of displacement at work: the foot is found disgusting, but the shoe can cover it, negating its abhorrent power. The shoe is like the foot but not like it: the shape is similar, and it is worn *on* the foot, but it is not *of* the foot. It is not moldy natural flesh but a designed artifact, often shiny, variously colored. The shoe is an idealized foot, or a mimetic counter to the foot's natural grossness. Considered as works of art, shoes are like classical sculptures—the human body rendered clean, shapely, and pure (and unreal). The shoe makes the foot aesthetically acceptable, despite its innate lack of charm (consider Chinese foot binding, pedicures, the fastidious application of nail polish). Some shoes seek utterly to transform the foot, as with extreme high heels. Shoe fetishists are thus the exact opposite of foot fetishists, though both are sensitive to the disgusting: one seeks to transcend the despised foot, while the other seeks intimacy with it (compare anal fetishism). In the same general category we find leather fetishists. Leather is like skin (in fact, it is skin) but it has had many of the dubious features of skin removed: the hair, the creaturely warmth, the fleshiness, the bumps and lumps, the discolorations. Leather is transformed skin—or *re*formed skin. To wear it next to the skin is to don a second skin, covering the first. It can also be worked and detailed according to aesthetic fancy. If you find ordinary human skin a bit on the repulsive side—and it cannot be denied that it frequently is—then leather can fill a niche in your psyche: it is skin that you can touch, stroke, and smell without feeling apprehensive. Leather gives us a revised version of skin we can live with. Shoes are usually made of leather, of course, so shoes give us foot skin that acts as a substitute for the questionable skin of the real foot. Sandals are an interesting case: here natural living skin peeps from behind leather, and the result is often an aesthetic disaster in the making. The foot, unlike the hand, is a source of uneasy negotiation and bodily anxiety. Foot neurosis is our common lot.[27]

(12) Humor and Swearing. Here I must tread lightly, as this whole book may be regarded as an invitation to mirth, as well as containing a fair amount of offensive language. Also: the connection between disgust, humor, and swearing is close to the surface, so my comments are bound to seem banal (as opposed to wildly speculative). Banal or not, the connection is clear: much humor concerns disgusting things, and swearing is mired in disgust. Dead bodies, excrement, bad smells, repulsive sex—these are all the stuff of jokes. Not all jokes, obviously: some concern other taboo subjects, like racial stereotypes. It would be interesting if disgust humor constituted the core, from which the other types branch out; but I see no convincing argument for that, neat as it would be. Nevertheless, humor is characteristically concerned with the taboo and discomforting—even the terrifying and sickening—and disgust fits that bill perfectly. Humor signifies unease, a field for repression; and disgust is up to its neck in unease and repression. Instead of being miserably revolted at ourselves, in despair over our given nature, we mock ourselves; we convert pain into a kind of wincing pleasure. I could give many examples of jokes that illustrate the point, but one stands out in my mind for its utter filth: "How do you know your sister has her period? Because your dad's cock tastes funny."[28] In this vicious little joke, several objects of disgust are juggled nastily together: menstrual

---

27. I am painfully aware that I am skating over a complex and controversial field in these brief remarks. My excuse is that I am trying to gain a synoptic view of the terrain, with an emphasis on more abstract themes, and focusing exclusively on the disgust perspective. The clinical detail of the psychological phenomena being discussed I leave to others more qualified.

28. I came across this appalling joke in Martin Amis's *London Fields*. It is a joke I find it impossible actually to tell, because it takes bad taste to a new level; but it does illustrate the point perfectly. Nice things may always be nicer than nasty things, as the elder Amis noted, but nasty things are often funnier than nice things, as the younger Amis has demonstrated.

blood, incestuous sex, and unpleasant tastes. One's response is hardly even laughter, more a kind of reluctant grimace, as the "joke" sinks in. Shit is always good for a laugh, of course, though I don't know any funny lines about earwax. In jokes, the disgusting object is alluded to but placed in an incongruous context that endows it with comic value; we can then laugh at what would otherwise merely repel. Jokes, then, are also a means of repression: they enable us to neutralize our feelings of disgust, because of their amusement value. Laughter takes the place of vomiting. And these two reactions are physiologically not dissimilar: both take the form of explosively and noisily expelling something from the mouth, with a resulting sense of release and relief.

Swearing is even more clearly disgust-related. Nearly all the words that are used in imprecatory speech acts signify objects of disgust: "shit," "piss," "asshole," "bloody," "bugger," "cunt," "prick," "douche bag," "motherfucker." The unadorned "fuck" might be thought an exception, because it signifies an act not in itself considered disgusting: but surely its power as a swear word depends upon its disgusting connotations (we don't say "make love off!"). And it is frequently used in conjunction with other clearly disgust-related words, for example "fucking asshole." Perhaps the most concise such combination is the pithy, "fuck that shit," taken to mean, roughly, "ignore that nonsense." The idea of fucking shit, literally, is powerfully disgusting, no question. In swearing, we wish to make our strong negative feelings evident, and invocations of the disgusting *as* disgusting perform that office perfectly. If humans felt no disgust, it is doubtful that the practice of swearing would exist at all—at least not in anything like the form it exists today. It would be greatly etiolated and underpowered. Terms signifying disgust are the perfect vehicle for vehement denunciation. Swearing is the one area in which we let our repressive guard down and wallow in the disgusting—and, of course, it is an act traditionally much frowned upon. In swearing, the valve is opened and the repressed material comes spewing forth: we thus reestablish contact with what we have shunted aside (repression always seems to need a break from itself). To be sure, such words can become formulaic and wanting in punch, especially if used repetitively; they retain their power only when they are used selectively and aptly. In swearing, we dip our toe in the disgusting, so to speak, only to withdraw it quickly (most effective swearing is brief and to the point).

I have not mentioned curses that include reference to animals. Chief among the words used here are: "rat," "pig," "snake," "worm," and "slug." Not surprisingly, these all refer to disgusting animals: we compare the individual so cursed to the animal that evokes the appropriate disgust reaction in us. We may describe someone negatively as a "snake," but we never call someone a "tiger" if we mean to derogate him—because tigers are not disgusting (as a species). Animal curses work by assigning the cursed individual to a species that is disgusting as a species, thus convicting him or her of disgustingness through and through. This is presumably why it is worse to be called a "rat" than an "asshole": the rat is nasty *tout court*, while the asshole is merely a nasty part of something larger.

Saying "you make me sick" to someone is surely one of the harshest condemnations available. Although it contains no lexical swear word, it directly relates the target individual to the realm of the disgusting: the person in question provokes the very emotional and visceral response that a paradigmatic disgust object provokes—namely vomiting—with no need to get specific about which one exactly. Such insults trade on the negative charge carried by the generality of disgust objects. To be nauseating is to be one with the whole category of the disgusting.[29]

---

29. It is interesting that the other main class of imprecations has to do with God, who lies at the opposite extreme to disgusting matters: "goddamn"; "god awful"; "By God!"; "God save us!"; "Jesus Christ!"; "Jesus wept"; and so on. Yet in so "taking the Lord's name in vain," don't we drag God down to a baser level? The obsolete "God's blood!" does so quite manifestly, by mixing the divine and the organic. Then too we have the contemporary expletive "Jesus fucking

(13) Movement. Movement as such can never be disgusting: so I am prepared categorically to assert. The claim might seem doubtful: is not the descent of a turd disgusting, or the arc of a flying phlegm ball? But it is because of *what* is descending or flying that we find these things disgusting, not because of the trajectory itself. There is no path in space such that moving through *it* is ipso facto disgusting—as it might be, a figure-eight shape as opposed to a circle. If we substitute for a disgusting moving object a non-disgusting one that moves in just the same way, then no residue of disgust remains. Mere movement through space is never a disgusting attribute of an object. But can movement do something more positive—can it somehow negate disgust? When an object *is* intrinsically disgusting, can its movement work to nullify or mitigate that disgust? Can the effect of movement on a perceiver be such as to cancel or reduce the disgust value of what moves? I think there are two main areas in which that can indeed happen: sport and dance.[30] In sport, the body radically transcends the narrow confines of the biological: skilled movement, directed toward a non-biological goal, becomes the body's dominant theme. The idea of a *game* takes center stage, with conventional rules and goals, and winning and losing. In tennis, say, the players must propel a ball over a net with a racquet according to an elaborate set of rules in order to gain points. The skilled and speedy action, directed toward conventionally determined ends, distracts us from the body as an object of disgust; all that is forgotten in the athletic

---

Christ!" Given that God is taken to exist on a vastly superior plane, invoking him in this crude way is implicitly to demote him in the great chain of being. Bertrand Russell tells us that he once exclaimed, "Great God in boots, the ontological argument is sound!": but God does not wear boots, and he has no smelly feet to put in them anyway. So the realm of the disgusting is not so far away from this form of swearing as it might appear.

30. I suppose we should also include marching in formation and synchronized swimming, if these are not forms of dance or sport; or simply running for joy, or skipping, or bouncing.

moment. Movement takes over from organic process, as if the body has been designed for a higher purpose. The body is now more kinetic than organic, aesthetic not biologically functional.[31] The foot, in particular, undergoes a remarkable transformation: from being a clumsy and unsightly device for balancing on, with its many disgust features, it becomes a supple instrument of power and control (this is true of soccer especially). In running, jumping, and pivoting, the foot sheds its disgusting aspects and operates as an instrument of speed and agility. From being dirty, smelly, and misshapen, it is transformed into something fleet, graceful, and purposive. The foot at rest is one thing; the foot in action is quite another. The athlete is a kind of magician, producing a nimble rabbit from a dull and seamy hat: he or she takes the gross body and performs a metamorphosis on it before our very eyes—by creating pure directed movement. No sport incorporates the disgusting aspects of the body into its execution; the focus is elsewhere. There are those awful eating contests, but they are the exception that proves the rule: not really a sport at all, grotesque to watch, and of merely minority interest—they invoke the disgusting only to exclude themselves from the category of the athletic. And you can be morally certain that crapping contests will never catch on. Real sports accentuate the potential for coordinated movement in the human body, while bracketing the disgust elements most evident in stasis (the still corpse, the seated defecator). We rely on sport to further our repressive project by highlighting non-disgusting

31. I will permit myself to say, portentously, that these activities constitute an aesthetic totality within which the body has a structural place, and as such the salient thematic of the athletic body is movement. The overall *Gestalt* takes the body as a part of a structured whole, whose meaning transcends the individual nature of the elements. The aesthetic unity foregrounds pure movement and eclipses biological categories. Less pompously: we don't notice the body as an organic entity because our attention is focused on the activity of which it is part. Sweat, say, is interpreted in the context of a purposive activity; it is not merely a gratuitous secretion.

aspects of the body—musculature and movement—so there is no future in a "sport" that flaunts the disgusting aspects. Sport is all about goal-directed skilled movement, and movement is never disgusting considered per se. What athletic movement does, especially at a high level, is render the inherent disgusting-ness of the body invisible and irrelevant by highlighting the unities defined by the movements themselves—for example, hitting a beautiful backhand down the line in tennis. This is why it is strangely jarring when a tennis player leaves the court to take a "bathroom break": we have been in the enchanted realm of the pure moving human form and now we are reminded of its base biological character. That, we think, must be another kind of creature altogether—a creature of urine and excrement, not a creature of graceful, thrilling, purposive motion. From the inside, too, playing the game oneself, the body is experienced as a source of speed, power, and beauty, not as a dismal receptacle of organic functions: it becomes, subjectively, another kind of being altogether.[32] Athletic dress aids this transformation, as does the equipment characteristic of a sport (there is nothing gross about a tennis racquet). Even the arena of activity seals sport off from the normal run of biological life. In sport it seems that the body is turned from one kind of material into another—by a kind of disgust-negating alchemy. No longer laden and squelchy, the body is now light and steely, a source of pure kinetic energy, like the body of a god (it helps if you are a good player). Indeed, sports stars are often regarded as virtual gods—with no anus in sight. Put differently: in the stance of play we forget the sludge and slime of the animal body, because pure coordinated movement takes center stage.

32. The joy of engaging in sport, and the desire to repeat the experience, must have a lot to do with this felt transformation—becoming another kind of being for the duration. Here we may feel godlike, by dint of leaving the organic body behind, to be replaced by the athletic body. The gods and heroes of myth generally possess abnormal powers of movement, especially flight.

If this is true of sport, then it is even more obviously true of dance. The foot, again, tells the essential story: in dance the foot becomes aesthetically central, an instrument of grace and agility, the focus of our entranced attention. Classical ballet illustrates the point perfectly, with the foot attaining to feats not encountered in daily life, particularly in the use of *pointe*. The foot is celebrated and adored in ballet, not regarded with suspicion and distaste. Again, costume contributes, and lighting, not to mention choreography and music. The lowly foot has a lot to overcome if it is to act as the main fulcrum of a sublime aesthetic experience (it helps to have a beautiful ballerina attached to it). In tap dance, the foot is likewise prominent, perhaps even more so, but now it is typically shod in shiny leather and operates as a percussion instrument. It moves with amazing rapidity and precision, beating out its sharp rhythms. The grimy and lumpish foot has been banished—to be replaced by a flashing instrument of rhythm and grace.[33] This is why the actual foot of a professional dancer is often such a shock to behold: that such a beaten, calloused, and disfigured thing could be a vehicle of such beauty! But it is not just the foot: the whole body of the dancer is a renunciation of the body as locus of disgust. The dancer must be slim, smooth, unblemished, stylishly dressed—with nothing to remind the viewer of what he or she is really like underneath. Quivering jelly-like flesh is not acceptable, nor is ringing flatulence. The essence of dance is illusion—tricking the eye into seeing nothing but the pure movement of an

---

33. Fred Astaire is the obvious reference—the man with the most elegant feet in the world (look at how he walks!). Interestingly, Astaire was not known for his handsome face: all the aesthetic appreciation was concentrated on his lower extremities. His feet *were* his handsome face. Fred—the inverted man. And in the case of dance as it occurs in movies, we have another anti-disgust dimension: film itself is a device of disgust cancellation, or refraction. The transformation of solid human bodies into two-dimensional patches of light already projects those bodies out of the zone of disgust. The whole topic of disgust and film deserves extended treatment. I allude to some of this in *The Power of Movies*.

idealized being: the ballerina as ethereal goddess—not a congeries of dank organs and distressing secretions. This illusion again furthers our lifelong project of repression, of distancing ourselves from the soggy and putrid reality of organic life. Skilled movement, aided by the resources of art, is the magic that transforms the dancer's body from the gross to the sublime. And this is possible because movement itself, even of inherently disgusting bodies, lies outside the realm of the disgusting (rather like Cartesian extension). We might say that the skilled dancer is an agent of amnesia, temporarily erasing from memory the knowledge of our gross nature. She gives us the tantalizing vision of a perfectly disgust-free existence.

(14) Religion. I have spoken of gods and angels, incorporeal spirits, contrasting their nature with ours. They signify to us a form of existence that is denied to us as organic beings. This prompts the question: how much of religion is bound up with disgust and our wish to escape from it? Religions come in many varieties, of course, but three components stand out as characteristic: (i) taboos about food and sex, (ii) rituals regarding death, and (iii) a metaphysical conception of what we are in our innermost essence. I shall comment very briefly on each of these. Food taboos typically insist that certain animals are "unclean" and must not be consumed; to eat them would be to make oneself unclean. The pig is singled out in some religious traditions; shellfish are deemed off limits in Orthodox Judaism. In some traditions, certain foods must only be eaten on certain days, or must be prepared in a certain ways. Some religions proscribe the eating of offal, that is, internal organs. The notion of the "holy" is tied to such prohibitions: we must not do what is "unholy." Religion thus steps in to regulate our eating habits, with the realm of the disgusting in the background. It is natural to see such taboos as (distorted) attempts to cope with our disgust reactions in the area of ingestion: disgust either as encouraging such taboos or as caused by the taboo itself.

The prohibition always seems correlated with a disgust reaction, not merely with a calm unemotional decision to abstain from certain foods (as with the decision not to eat carbohydrates in the interests of keeping slim). In the matter of sex, taboos surround incest, adultery, intercourse with animals, and masturbation, among other things—all areas in which disgust operates. The ideas of the unethical and the disgusting mingle here and are perhaps not clearly distinguished in the early (or even contemporary) phases of religion. Such activities are stigmatized as "abominations," as "defilements," as "offensive to God"—all disgust-laden concepts. Religion identifies something as disgusting and enacts prohibitions against practices that might traffic in it, recognizing certain natural human temptations. Satan and his minions are often depicted as revolting and bestial, again testifying to the linkage between religious conceptions and the disgusting. The good is "pure" and "clean"; evil is "filthy" and "foul." We must be "pure in heart" and not succumb to "moral corruption." The body is our "temple" and must be kept "undefiled." Our soul must remain "spotless." We must not let ourselves be "contaminated" by "rotten" doctrines. And so on and forth.[34]

---

34. Then we have the occasional oddity, where something prima facie disgusting takes on a divine status—as with the consuming of the "host" in Catholic ritual. The faithful are told, and evidently believe, that this is the "body of Christ," and they take it into their mouths and swallow it. On the face of it, this looks an awful lot like cannibalism, yet people engage in it quite happily; no aversive disgust is instigated. However, the whole business is so steeped in ritual and symbolism, and so hard to take literally, that the normal response to consuming the flesh of another person is bypassed. It is true that the body of Christ is not just normal human flesh, what with him being the Son of God and everything; but this doesn't defuse the paradox, because eating the body of God would seem to be equally cannibalistic. Is it really acceptable to convert the body of *God* into human feces? Perhaps we should put this case down to one of those quirks of human psychology with which we are all too familiar—or interpret it as just an instance of the blind obedience that is so characteristic of the religious sensibility.

Burial rites and rules for the transportation of corpses also feature in most religions. The dead and decaying body is clearly an object of universal revulsion; religion prescribes rules for handling this most potent of disgust stimuli. Fixed rules and procedures take the risk out of dealing with the dead body, minimizing the chances of an unfortunate reaction. Embalming and cosmetic procedures, sanctioned by religion, spare the grieving from the inevitable response to a putrefying corpse. Here religion performs the useful function of controlling our natural disgust reflexes, which must not be allowed to erupt at this most sensitive of times. It cares about the fate of the soul, but also about the body and its effect on the living. I would not be amazed if a historian of religion had come up with the theory that the ancient origins of religion lie in rules for the disposal of dead bodies, with an accompanying narrative—because this is such a pressing and difficult matter. The bodies of the dear departed must not be permitted to lie around festering, however much the grieving may not want to see them go; and a strong set of rules, backed with divine authority, is necessary to ensure that the proper procedures are followed. If so, disgust lies at the very root of religion—and disgust of the most primeval kind.

As for the metaphysics of man, the very idea of the soul as man's essence follows directly from the desire to find a part of us that is absent all disgust. True, we have an animal body, with its gross anatomy, but we also have a soul or mind or self that transcends such grossness. This entity can even survive the awful dissolution of the body, continuing without any disgusting encumbrance after death. Thus we arrive at the idea that the unclean body is contingent and the pure soul essential. That is a reassuring doctrine for anyone steeped in feelings of disgust at his or her own nature and anxious to identify some part of the human creature that does not evoke revulsion. And it is perfectly true that psychological traits cannot evoke (non-moral) disgust: the soul is then the entity that *has* these traits, and it can exist without the gross body. The religious metaphysic of human nature thus tracks our disgust reactions perfectly: we are literally made up of two parts, one disgusting, the other not, and it is the latter part that is of the essence. Religion, then, is caught up in the repression I have been emphasizing: it is a technique for reducing the burden of disgust our biological nature places on us (in part—no doubt it has other functions too). Its ontological picture delineates a disgust-free zone and declares that zone to be what we most fundamentally are, with the body merely an extrinsic appendage. *I* neither digest nor copulate nor die—only my *body* does these revolting things. *I* am godlike at my core, the creation of God, and destined to be with God in a heaven blissfully innocent of all disgusting elements. That organic stench that now fills my nostrils is just a temporary affliction, an emanation from outside my inner nature; my essential identity is not *biological* at all. *I* have no plumbing. That is the elevating message that religion strives to bring to us: that it is merely a passing illusion that we are disgusting biological creatures. And it is a powerful and attractive message, a marvelous intellectual conjuring trick on the part of our repressive apparatus. That it is palpably false has not deterred countless generations from embracing it.[35] Ideologies always spring from some deep human need, and the need to escape our divided and troubled nature is as deep as any.

---

35. I have not here argued that it is false—and that task would take me too far afield. But the obvious considerations have to do with the dependence of the mind on the brain, which is itself a repellent internal organ. The religious metaphysic (roughly, Cartesian dualism) underestimates the formative and constitutive role of the brain in producing conscious selves. It seems to me a very interesting hypothesis that this whole metaphysical picture has emotional roots in wanting to avoid the disgust that is proper to the body: we need to find a separate ontological category for the conscious self, so that it is not contaminated by the organic body. Thus the idea of metaphysical dualism arises originally and primitively from our aesthetic sensibilities.

(15) Civilization. To what extent was our rise from a state of nature driven by our disgust sensitivities? Imagine our distant ancestors, in field, valley, and forest, soiled and stinking, without sanitary facilities, yet social and chatty, and quite devoid of any sense of how revolting they actually are. Lacking the means for grooming available to mammals in general, they are a repellent bunch, with matted hair, parasite-infested, unruly of nose and armpit, anally messy—but not yet apprised of their true aesthetic condition. Defecation is publicly performed; childbirth is a form entertainment; and dead bodies fall and rot. No one seems to mind. Then, one fine day, out of the blue, these early humans wake up to find that rampant disgust has arisen in them (the result of a neutrino storm from space perhaps): what earlier did not perturb them at all now sends spasms of revulsion through them, invading their very souls. They now can't stand the sight, smell, and touch of each other, and are none too sanguine about themselves either. The species totters on the edge of extinction. Something must clearly be done. Marriages and families are falling apart. No one can stand to live in the same hut as anyone else. No one can keep his food down. They could deploy tongue and saliva in the manner of cats and dogs, but that seems like awfully hard work, and anyway their new-found disgust responses will not permit it. The concept of filth has invaded human consciousness, but they have no existing means for coping with it.[36]

Then some genius suggests using water as a cleaning agent, hitherto used only as a potable. That turns out to work fairly well, though not with the most stubborn stains. But they need a more plentiful water supply and must be sure to live close

---

36. I am fudging a bit with the neutrino story, since the change needs to affect the genes in order to be transmitted. The general idea is just that a genetic muta-tion occurs that is selected for and hence passed down the generations. But allow me some poetic license.

enough to water to fill their expanded needs. They now have to be more careful with their water resources and need better vessels for carrying the water (you can't always be going all the way down to the lake when you need a quick rinse). Their first defense against the assault of the disgusting was therefore plain water—which luckily they already had around for another purpose. Then after another couple of centuries a second now-forgotten genius invents soap. Eureka! By then other disgust-related innovations have been introduced: special areas for defecation and urination have been designated; shacks have been built to ensure privacy (for sex as well as excretion); laws have been enacted to punish violators; the washcloth and towel have made their appearance; primitive clothes have been adopted; the grave has been invented. Soap is a major new step forward, though, bigger even than the use of fire to warm the water for washing. There is rejoicing throughout the land. Perfume is soon added, mass production begins, and soap merchants prosper (needing accountants, banks, etc.). With all this comes a revolution in manners: people are mindful of the responses of others, taking care to eliminate all avenues of interpersonal disgust they can. Food consumption is transformed. Sexual behavior is strictly monitored. Grooming and shaving become commonly practiced. Whole occupations and industries develop to cater to these new needs. Specialized training is required. Qualifications are awarded. Within only a few short millenniums, there are people calling themselves "beauticians." There are also plumbers, clothes designers, sanitation workers, undertakers, and fitness trainers. Not only that, but art and religion have developed, along with sport and dance—all dedicated to providing relief from the filth consciousness that has come to define the human species. Science, too, has had to grow, to produce the technology that cleanliness requires—hydrodynamics being the original hot field. In fact, virtually the full panoply of civilization has materialized around the necessity to respect our sense of the disgusting—where before we were content to live in filthy squalor, as ignoble savages. We have gone from being dirty brutes to being well-scrubbed entrepreneurs, artists, and priests. The wheel played its minor role, it is true, but it was soap and water that really pushed things forward, once our disgusted self-consciousness set in. Who knows what would have happened if we had remained as other animals—disgust-free (but naturally much dirtier)? The onset of disgust gave urgency to our efforts, owing to its extreme unpleasantness. The wheel, by contrast, was a luxury item, not a moment-by-moment necessity.[37] In the later stages of civilization, as everyone knows, we introduced the modern toilet, the shower, the spa, all manner of cosmetic aids, high fashion, cremation, garbage collection, electronic devices, sports cars, ballet, tennis, to list just a few— all in the ultimate service of disgust-management (among other things). Disgust was our original biological predicament; civilization was our response to it. When you get right down to basics, muck was the engine of it all (or do you think I am exaggerating slightly?). Fortunately, we had the brains to do what was necessary—those celebrated frontal-lobe monstrosities— but the motivation was all about avoiding the filth that our aesthetic sensibilities revealed. Dirty by nature, it took disgust to force us to invent civilization as an antidote.

(16) Perfectibility of Man. The project of perfecting the mind of man has long captured the imagination of millenarian thinkers. Can we be made perfectly good, perfectly happy, and perfectly knowledgeable? That is an excellent question, but not

---

37. Ask yourself how you would feel if some modern catastrophe reduced humans to the state of filthiness I describe in the text, with our disgust sensibilities still firmly in place. You would surely feel a strong urgency about getting the anti-disgust infrastructure up and running again as soon as possible—hot water, soap, toilet facilities, and so on. You would feel the pressure within days, if not hours. Getting wheels turning again would not seem like such a priority. Our sense of well-being is heavily bound up with fending off self-directed disgust.

the question I am interested in here, which is: can we perfect the *body* of man? The answer, I think, is No. We have improved the body of man, by means of medicine, diet, exercise, and methods of personal hygiene. No doubt we will improve it further (I look forward to exfoliating waterless showers and quicker shaving). But the project of ridding the body of all disgust elements is utopian in the bad sense: for that would be to rob it of its very biological identity. Part of us no doubt yearns for such sweeping reforms, but we don't think it is really possible—or even desirable, all things considered. The only conceivable method would be to replace the organic body with the body of a clanking robot, run by some sort of battery, or maybe a new type of plastic with a nuclear power source. That seems both undesirable and probably impossible. Undesirable, because flesh has attractions that metal cannot duplicate (sex between robots may not be disgusting, but it sounds pretty grim, and far too simple[38]). Nor is it clear that our minds could be supported by anything other than organic material. Even if we put the organic brain into a robot body, we would still have a disgusting body part far too close to home. In any case, such a project is so far from scientific possibility that we may as well discount it. So we are stuck with flesh and blood, feces and mucus, earwax and viscera. We may develop better ways of managing our messy biological nature, but there is no reasonable prospect of eliminating it; and with that nature comes the aversive emotion of disgust. Our imperfect human condition—

38. I say "far too simple" because of the complex layers of ambivalence that characterize our sexual feelings and the special character of erotic pleasure. Sex with no undercurrent of potential disgust, as between metal robots, would be dull and one-dimensional; all the interest and challenge would be taken out of it. The surmounting of disgust by love and urgent desire would no longer exist. Sex would become boring, relatively speaking, because merely the sensation of orgasm preceded by the necessary friction. The whole complex human psychology of sex, in all its gory glory, would be missing. So I don't recommend having the operation.

the incongruous combination of a transcendent mind and an organic body—is our permanent condition. We can therefore never be fully reconciled to ourselves. But there is one good thing to be said for our predicament: we shall never be guilty of the immodesty that declares itself godlike. We shall never be able to worship ourselves as a god (unlike, presumably, God Himself). We are just too disgusting for that, and painfully aware of the fact. A healthy misanthropy will always characterize our species. Total species narcissism will always be beyond us.[39]

I conclude from the above that the emotion of disgust plays a vital role in many cultural formations, powering and shaping them. It is not just a matter of individual psychology; disgust finds expression in many domains of collective human life. Nor is it an insignificant quirk of human psychology, of marginal relevance. The theory of disgust sheds light on many cultural phenomena, unifying them, explaining their roots. To a considerable extent, disgust makes us what we are.

---

39. The same might not be true of intelligent species elsewhere in the universe, depending on the nature of their minds and bodies. There may be species of advanced beings that are not at all disgusted at their own nature and who nurture the self-image of the heroic godlike figure. These are the ones to be afraid of, since there is no natural cap on their self-worship. Their hubris and narcissism will likely rage unchecked. It may be tragic for us that we consciously have an incongruous nature, with the weight of the disgusting to drag us down, but the humility it generates is one of our better characteristics. We must always be muttering apologies for ourselves, and that is not necessarily such a bad thing.

BIBLIOGRAPHY

Becker, Ernest. *The Denial of Death*. New York: The Free Press, 1973.

Bersani, Leo. "Is the Rectum a Grave?" *October* 43 (1987): 197–222.

Darwin, Charles. *The Expression of the Emotions in Man and Animals*. Chicago: University of Chicago Press, 1965. Originally published, 1892.

Fodor, Jerry. *The Modularity of Mind: An Essay in Faculty Psychology*. Cambridge, Mass.: MIT Press, 1983.

George, Rose. *The Big Necessity: The Unmentionable World of Waste and Why It Matters*. New York: Henry Holt, 2008.

Goffman, Erving. *The Presentation of Self in Everyday Life*. New York: Doubleday, 1959.

Griffiths, Paul. *What Emotions Really Are: The Problem of Psychological Categories*. Chicago: University of Chicago Press, 1997.

Kolnai, Aurel. *On Disgust*. Edited by Barry Smith and Carolyn Korsmeyer. Chicago and La Salle, Ill.: Open Court, 2004. Originally published in German in 1929.

McGinn, Colin. *The Power of Movies: How Screen and Mind Interact*. New York: Pantheon Books, 2005.

McGinn, Colin. *Truth by Analysis: Games, Names, and Philosophy*. New York: Oxford University Press, 2012.

Menninghaus, Winfried. *Disgust: Theory and History of a Strong Sensation*. Translated by Howard Eiland and Joel Golb. Albany: State University of New York Press, 2003.

Miller, William Ian. *The Anatomy of Disgust*. Cambridge, Mass.: Harvard University Press, 1997.

Nussbaum, Martha. *Hiding from Humanity: Disgust, Shame, and the Law*. Princeton, N.J.: Princeton University Press, 2004.

Rozin, Paul, Jonathan Haidt, and Charles McCauley. "Disgust." In *Handbook of Emotions*, edited by Michael Lewis and Jeannette M. Haviland, 575–594. New York: Guildford, 1993.

Solomon, Robert C. "Emotions and Choice." In *Mind and Cognition: An Anthology*, edited by. William G. Lycan and Jesse J. Prinz, 827–838. 3rd ed. Oxford: Basil Blackwell, 2008.

Suits, Bernard. *The Grasshopper: Games, Life and Utopia*. Broadview Press, 2005. Introduction by Thomas Hurka. Originally published, 1978.

INDEX

acquisitiveness, 159n20

adaptations of traits, 126n1

aesthetic emotions, 6, 8–9, 9n9

aesthetic experience, 9n9

affective perceiving, 60n19

age

  as phase of life, 196

  signs of, 20–21, 21n9,
    108–9, 109n13

Age of Innocence, 159

Amis, Kingsley, 168n9

Amis, Martin, 210n28

anal plug, 184

The Anatomy of Disgust
    (Miller), 4n2, 79–80

angels, 152

animals, 27–29. *See also
    specific animals*

  absence of death anxiety
    in, 85–86, 180

absence of disgust

  from, 55, 58, 69, 72, 85,
    124, 129, 139, 153

absence of dual nature
  in, 139, 153–54

absence of emotions
  for, 58n15

attraction-repulsion
  dynamic and, 48

bifurcated, 200n19

clothes and, 184

consciousness in, 86, 154

curses, 212

death-in-life theory
  and, 112–16

desires of, 124, 129–31,
  130n5, 166, 171

dirt and, 32, 117–18, 118n20

disgusting and
  nutritional, 68

animals (*continued*)
  human body compared
    to, 73–79, 77n11, 79n12,
    136–37, 149–50
  love and, 198n16
  non-disgusting, 28
  sexual behavior of, 120,
    120n21
  soul differentiating humans
    from, 25n13, 73
animal-heritage theory, 73–79
ants, 113
anus, 26, 27, 29, 35
  anal plug, 184
  in evolution, 147, 147n14
  personifying, 191n10
appearance, sensory, 8, 10,
    10n10, 14, 14n2
appetitive repression, 162, 169
aristocrats, 152–53, 191n9
Aristotle, 136n1
art, 198–202, 199n17,
    200nn18–19, 202n20
artifacts, 188, 188n6
Astaire, Fred, 216n33
asymmetry, self-other. *See*
    self-other asymmetry
attraction-repulsion dynamic of
    disgust, 35, 46–49, 130n4
  animals and, 48
  aversive emotions and,
    49, 49n7
  death and, 47–49, 98–99,
    99n1

feces and, 47–48
psyche and, 47–48, 49n7
sex and, 47, 192–95,
    193n12, 194n13
auto-disgust, 207
aversive emotions, 3–12. *See
    also specific emotions*
  attraction-repulsion
    dynamic and, 49, 49n7
  evaluation and, 6n6
  existence and, 8–9
  perception, consciousness
    and, 10–11, 11n11
avoidance, 5, 6–7, 10–11, 86

Bacon, Francis, 200n18
bats, 16, 45–46, 46n4, 113,
    114n17
beards, 21, 66–67, 67n3,
    108n12
beauty, 8, 25, 61n19
Becker, Ernest, 4n2, 82–83,
    83n16
  The Denial of Death, 4n2,
    82–83, 83n16, 167n6
  on dual nature, 150n16
  on heroic nature of hu-
    mans, 137n2
  on repression, 167n6,
    167n8
beetles, 114, 114n17
behaviors, 34–37
being, 8

bifurcated animals, 200n19
birth
  gestation and, 100–101
  sex, death and, 194–95
blame, 38n20
blood
  death-in-life theory
    and, 103
  menstrual, 19, 112
  vampires' association
    with, 15, 15n4
bodily substances, 18–20.
    See also waste products;
    specific bodily substances
  contextual theory and,
    18, 105
  death-in-life theory
    and, 19, 19n8, 102–5,
    102n6
body, human. *See* human
    body
body of Christ, 218n34
bones, 17, 24, 87–89
brain, 25
brain-mind connection, 141,
    141n9, 220n35
breath, 104
Brockes, Barthold, 100n4
burial rites and rules, 219

cadaver. *See* rotting corpse
cancer, 106–7
cannibalism, 14, 218n34

Cartesian dualism, 175n3,
    220n35
castration, 16
Catherine of Siena
    (saint), 60n18
celebrities, 187, 187n5
cell phone, 205n23
Chagga tribe, 184, 184n1
children, 55–58. *See also*
    birth
  absence of disgust
    from, 55, 69, 139, 195
  absence of emotions
    for, 58n15
  clothes and, 184
  development of disgust
    with, 55–58, 55n12,
    85n19, 96n27
  phases of life and, 195–96
Chomsky, Noam, 56n13
civilization, 221–23,
    223n37
class of disgusting things,
    4, 4n3
cleanliness, 31, 207–8, 222
clothes, 184–85. *See also*
    nudism
  as form of dirt, 33
  genitals in, 185n2
cognitive component of
    disgust,
    56–58, 58n14
compulsion, 129
condemnation, 34

consciousness, 154n19
in animals, 86, 154
aversive emotions, perception
and, 10–11, 11n11
death-in-life theory
and, 94–96, 94n26, 99n2,
106n10
death theory and, 85
dual nature and, 139–43,
140nn7–8, 141n9,
143n10, 154, 154n19
evolution and, 154n19
explicit, 165, 165n4
feces and, 71n7
objects of, 143n10
senses and, 71n7
conscious self, 220n35
death and, 94, 173, 181
Consumers, 156–59
contact, 41–44. *See also* touch
avoidance of, 5, 6–7,
10–11, 86
with feces, 43–44
Kolnai on, 44n1
metamorphosis to disgust-
ing through, 43–44
with mouth, 42, 69
with rotting corpse, 43, 44
contamination
dirt and, 157
by touch, 45n3, 72n8
contextual theory, 18, 105,
105n9
contraception, 119

coprophagia, 114n17, 128, 129
coprophilia, 49
corpses. *See also* rotting
corpse
burial rites and rules
for, 219
sex with, 127–28, 170
creation story, 154–59,
159n20
defecation in, 157
God and, 73, 154–56, 158
Kant's, 147n14, 159n20
rotting corpse in, 158
cremation, 97
cryogenically preserved
bodies, 17, 89
crystals, Martians on feces
and, 61–62
culture, 183–225
art and, 198–202, 199n17,
200nn18–19
civilization and, 221–23,
223n37
clothes and, 184–85, 185n2
etiquette and, 202–5,
203n21
fetishism and, 185–88
humor and swearing
and, 210–12, 210n28,
212n29
love and, 197–98, 198n16
movement and, 213–17,
213n30, 214n31, 215n32,
216n33

neurosis and, 207–10
nudism and, 188–89,
    189n7
perfectibility of man
    and, 223–25
phases of life and, 195–96
religion and, 217–20
sex and, 192–95
society and, 189–92,
    192n11
technology and, 205–6
curiosity, 99n1, 159n20
curses. *See* swearing

dance, 213, 216–17, 216n33
Darwin, Charles
    The Descent of Man, 76
    *The Expression of Emotions
        in Man and Animals*,
        66–67
    on taste, 45n3, 66–69,
        67nn2–3, 69n5
Dasein, 8–10
dead bodies. *See* corpses;
    rotting corpse
death. *See also* life and death
    animal-heritage theory
        and, 77–78
    attraction-repulsion
        dynamic of, 47–49,
        98–99, 99n1
    conscious self and, 94,
        173, 181

contingency of, 173, 176,
    179–81
fear of, 83, 83n17, 93,
    98–99
in form of smoke and
    ashes, 88n21
immortality and, 173–75,
    175n3, 177–78, 177n4,
    178n5
inevitability of, 173,
    178–80
mind and, 175–79, 179n6
mortality and, 17, 83, 85,
    103, 175
as necessary, 173, 176,
    179, 180
religious rituals
    regarding, 217, 219
resentment about, 177–78,
    180–81
self and, 94, 173–78,
    178n5, 181
self-other asymmetry
    and, 99–100, 100n3
sex, birth and, 194–95
thoughts of, 173–81
death anxiety
    absence of, in animals,
        85–86, 180
    high state of, 177n4
death-in-life theory, 88–96,
    90n23
    animals and, 112–16
    blood and, 103

death-in-life theory (*continued*)
  bodily substances and, 19,
    19n8, 102–5, 102n6
  consciousness and, 94–96,
    94n26, 99n2, 106n10
  dirt and, 117–18
  disease and illness
    and, 107, 107n11
  feces and, 94–95, 101–2,
    102n6
  hair and, 107–8
  insects and, 114–15,
    114n17, 115n18
  internal organs and,
    109–10
  moral disgust and, 121–22
  plants and, 116–17
  putrefaction and decay
    and, 91–93, 91n24
  rotting corpse and, 90–95,
    94n26, 97–101
  sexual behavior and,
    118–21
  waste products and, 101–5,
    101n5, 102n6, 103n7,
    105n9
  worms and, 113, 117n19
  wounds and, 103, 106,
    109–10
death theory, 82–88
  consciousness and, 85
  digestion and, 84, 101–2
  rotting corpse and, 84, 181
  wounds and, 84–85

decay. *See* putrefaction and
    decay
defecation
  in creation story, 157
  evolution and, 147, 147n14
The Denial of Death
    (Becker), 4n2, 82–83,
    83n16, 167n6
Descartes, René, 135–36,
    136n1
The Descent of Man
    (Darwin), 76
desires
  of animals, 124, 129–31,
    130n5, 166, 171
  in evolution, 127–28
  excessive, 123–31, 126n1,
    127n2, 128n3
  id, ego, superego
    and, 130n5
  lust for excitement
    and, 128n3
  repression of, 161–62,
    161n1, 169–72,
    170n10
  sexual, 63n22, 161n1, 162,
    165–67, 170, 193
developmental
    psychology, 196,
    196n14, 207n24
development of disgust, with
    children, 55–58, 55n12,
    85n19, 96n27
deviant sex, 35–36, 119–21

digestion
    death theory and, 84, 101–2
    etiquette and, 202–3
    feces and, 74, 84
    life-process theory and, 79,
        81n14
dirt, 30–33
    animals and, 32, 117–18,
        118n20
    civilization and, 221–23,
        223n37
    clothes as form of, 33
    contamination and, 157
    death-in-life theory
        and, 117–18
    feces as, 31
    hair as, 33, 108
    on human body, 31–33
    Kolnai on, 33n17
    obsessive-compulsive
        disorder and, 207–8
    poverty and, 191
    self-other asymmetry
        and, 50
    on skin, 31–33, 118
    untidiness as dirtiness, 32
disease and illness
    death-in-life theory
        and, 107, 107n11
    human body and, 15, 15n3,
        19, 97–98, 104, 175
disembodied mind, 175,
        177n4, 179
disembowelment, 24

disgust
    absence of, 55, 58, 69, 72,
        85, 124, 129, 139, 153, 195
    cognitive component
        of, 56–58, 58n14
    as contact-sensitive, 41–44,
        44n1
    core examples of, 65
    development of, with
        children, 55–58, 55n12,
        85n19, 96n27
    elicitors of, 13–39
    English writers on, 67–68,
        68n4
    fear, hatred and, 5–12, 7n8,
        10n10, 12n12, 54, 59
    first-person and third-
        person perspectives
        on, 139n6
    function of, 123–32,
        168–69
    German writers on, 68, 68n4
    meta-philosophical
        position on, 122n23
    as philosophical
        emotion, 181, 181n7
    as sense-based
        emotion, 44–46
    studies on, 4, 4n2
    talking about, 3, 3n1,
        164–65, 165n3
    theories of, 65–96
    value, determining, 43,
        105, 146

Disgust: Theory and History of a Strong Sensation (Menninghaus), 4n2, 198–99

disgust drive, 38n21

disgustingness
knowledge of, 162–64, 169–70
as not secondary quality, 61–63, 61n20

disgust reactions
controlling, 49, 51
inverse square law for, 43
nausea as, 14, 83
types of, 45
vomiting as, 14, 37–38

disgust reflex, 60

divine beings, humans as, 136–38, 150–52

dreams, 131n6, 198n15, 207, 207n24

dualism, Cartesian, 175n3

duality of wills, 191n10

dual nature, 135–59
absence of, in animals, 139, 153–54
Becker on, 150n16
consciousness and, 139–43, 140nn7–8, 141n9, 143n10, 154, 154n19
of Jesus, 150–51
metamorphosis and, 145–47
soul and, 137–38, 138nn-3–4, 143, 150, 151n17

eating
feces, 127–28
worms, 35

ego, 130n5

electricity and electronic devices, 205–6

elicitors of disgust, 13–39
animals as, 27–29
behavior as, 34–37
bodily substances as, 18–20
dirt as, 30–33
human body as, 13–27
moral disgust, 37–39
plants as, 29–30
rotting corpse as, 13–18, 14n2, 15nn3–4

Elizabeth II (queen of England), 151

embarrassment, 63

emotions, 58n15. *See also* aversive emotions
absence of, 58n15
aesthetic, 6, 8–9, 9n9
explicit consciousness and, 165n4
negative and positive, 142
philosophical, 181, 181n7
primitive perceptual, 44–45
prudential, 5
sense-based, 44–46
tears and, 103–4

encapsulation, 59–60, 59n16, 60n19

English writers on
    disgust, 67–68, 68n4
epistemic repression, 162, 169
etiquette, 202–5
    food and, 202–4, 203n21
    nose, 203–4
evisceration, 85, 110
evolution, 74
    consciousness and, 154n19
    defecation and, 147, 147n14
    desires in, 127–28
    of human body, 144–47
    worms in, 144
excessive desires, 123–31,
    126n1, 127n2, 128n3
excess theory of function of
    disgust, 123–32, 171
    food and, 123–25, 127n2
    greed and, 126–27
    psyche and, 130–32, 131n6
    sexual behavior and,
      124–25, 128, 128n3
excrement. *See* feces
existence, aversive emotions
    and, 8–9
existential anxiety, 154
explicit consciousness, 165,
    165n4
The Expression of Emotions in
    Man and Animals
    (Darwin), 66–67
extinction, species, 121
extreme nudism, 188
eyes, 26

family life, 196–97
family resemblance
    model, 4n3
farting, 63, 152n18
fear
    of death, 83, 83n17, 93,
      98–99
    disgust, hatred and, 5–12,
      7n8, 10n10, 12n12, 54, 59
    evaluation and, 6n6
    fearsome property, 62
    as future-directed, 6
    as prudential emotion, 5
    self-protection and, 5
feces, 18, 18n7. *See also*
    defecation
    attitudes toward, 55
    attraction-repulsion
      dynamic and, 47–48
    consciousness and, 71n7
    contact with, 43–44
    death-in-life theory
      and, 94–95, 101–2,
      102n6
    digestion and, 74, 84
    as dirt, 31
    eating, 127–28
    humor and, 63
    Martians on crystals
      and, 61–62
    as non-disgusting, 9, 10n10
    sculpture of, 200
    self-other asymmetry
      and, 50–52, 52n9

feces (*continued*)
  smell of, 71n7, 72, 72n8, 102
  snake as fecal symbol, 115
  soul and, 151n17
fetishism, 49, 185–88,
    207–10, 208n26
  imagination and, 186–87
  leather, 209
  shoe, 208–9, 208n26
fetus, 100–101
film, 216n33
filth, 221, 223, 223n37.
    See also dirt
"The Filthiness of Birth"
    (Brockes), 100n4
flesh. *See* skin
fly, 114
Fodor, Jerry, 59n16
food. *See also* eating; taste
  epistemic repression
    and, 169
  etiquette and, 202–4, 203n21
  excess theory of function of
    disgust and, 123–25, 127n2
  hair in, 21n10, 69n5
  rejection of, 67, 67n2,
    68–69
  religious taboos
    about, 217–18, 218n34
foot, 41
  movement and, 214, 216,
    216n33
  neurosis, 208–10, 208n26
foul-odor theory, 69–72

freckles, 23
Free Will, 158
Freud, Sigmund, 196
  on id and superego, 130n5
  on nose as phallic
    symbol, 204n22
  on repression of sexual
    desires, 63n22, 161n1,
    162, 165–67, 170
  on sex, 38n21, 63n22, 194n13
  on sex drive and disgust
    drive, 38n21
  on snakes and penis, 115
function of disgust, 123–32,
    168–69. *See also* excess
    theory of function of
    disgust
fungus, 30, 116–17

Garden of Eden, 154, 156
genetic mutation, 221n36
genitals, 26, 47, 50. *See also*
    penis; testicles
  in clothes, 185n2
  dual function of, 193
geriatric disgust, 196
German writers on
    disgust, 68, 68n4
gestation and birth, 100–101
God
  creation story and, 73,
    154–56, 158
  swearing and, 212n29

godlike, humans as, 139,
140n8, 215, 215n32, 220
god who shits, 139, 151
Goffman, Erving, 190n8
good and evil, 218
The Grasshopper (Suits), 4n3
greed, 126–27
Griffiths, Paul, 59n16
guilt, 58n15, 131n6, 170n10

habituation effect, 51, 52n9
hair, 21–23
absence of, 22n11, 107–8,
108n12
death-in-life theory
and, 107–8
as dirt, 33, 108
in food, 21n10, 69n5
pubic, 22
hatred
as aggressive, 6
as directed to past, 6
fear, disgust and, 5–12, 7n8,
10n10, 12n12, 54, 59
as moral emotion, 5–6
hearing, 7n7, 45–46, 46n4
heart, beating, 24,
83n17, 106
heroic nature of
humans, 137–38, 137n2
Hirst, Damien, 200n19
homeless hippy with grey
bogey, 131–32

homosexuality, 35–36, 120,
120n21
human body, 13–27. *See also*
bodily substances; dual
nature; waste products;
specific body parts
animals compared to,
73–79, 77n11, 79n12,
136–37, 149–50
art and, 198–202, 199n17,
200nn18–19, 202n20
cryogenically preserved, 17, 89
dirt on, 31–33
disease and illness and, 15,
15n3, 19, 97–98, 104, 175
dissatisfaction with, 146n13
evolution of, 144–47
exterior of, 20–24, 25n13, 106–9
interior of, 24–26, 25n13
internal organs of, 24–26,
83n17, 85, 109–10
as machine, 135, 136n1
orifices of, 19, 24, 110, 199,
202n20
parts of, 14–17, 16n5, 35
punishments and ordeal
with, 25
as wormlike, 149, 150
humor, 210–12
feces and, 63
jokes, 63, 63n21, 210–11,
210n28
repression and, 63n22
hygiene, 76

id, 49n7, 130n5
ideas, worship of, 187
identity, 52n10
  acknowledging facts of
    bodily, 73
imagination, 130–31
  fetishism and, 186–87
  language and, 172,
    172n11
  love and, 197–98
  sensory, 44n2
immortality, 173–75, 175n3,
  177–78, 177n4, 178n5
incontinence, 103
infants. *See* children
innate metaphysics, 58n14
inorganic materials. *See*
  fetishism; organic and
  inorganic materials;
  technology
insanity, 49, 132, 167, 167n8,
  177, 208n25
insects, 13n1, 46n4, 82n15
  death-in-life theory
    and, 114–15, 114n17,
    115n18
intellectual disgust, 37–38, 46
intelligent design, 145n11,
  148n15
internal organs, 24–26,
  83n17, 85, 109–10
interspecies sex, 35
intestines, 24, 29n15, 110
  worms' similarity
    to, 29n15, 75

intimacy
  with technology, 205n23, 206
  touch and, 42, 70n6
inverse square law for disgust
  reactions, 43

Jesus, 150–51, 212n29
jewelry, 186, 186n3
jokes, 63, 63n21, 210–11,
  210n28
judgment, 60

Kant, Immanuel, 58n14, 152
  on aesthetic experience, 9n9
  creation story of, 147n14,
    159n20
kidneys, 26
kissing, 47
knowledge
  of disgustingness, 162–64,
    169–70
  repression of, 162–67,
    163n2, 165n4, 167n8,
    169–70, 170n10
Kolnai, Aurel, 4n2
  on class of disgusting
    things, 4n3
  on contact, 44n1
  on *Dasein* and *Sosein*, 8
  on dirt, 33n17
  On Disgust, 4n2, 5, 91–93
  on disgust as aversive
    emotion, 5

on hearing, 7n7
on macabre allure, 46n5
on skeleton, 87n20
on smell, 45n3, 70n6

language, imagination
    and, 172, 172n11
leather fetishism, 209
lepers, 15
life
    concept of, 81–82
    fecundity of, 82n15
    phases of, 195–96
    profligate, 13n1
life and death. *See also*
    death-in-life theory
    concepts of, 81–82
    Miller on, 82
life-process theory, 79–82,
    81n14
life soup, 80
lions, 10, 28
literary disgust, 37
London Fields
    (Amis), 210n28
love, 197–98, 198n16
Lucky Jim (Amis), 168n10
lust for excitement, 128n3

macabre allure, 46n5
madness, 128
maggots, 14
makeup, 31, 32–33, 184

Nussbaum, Martha, 168n9
Martians, 61–62
masturbation, 36
Matrix, 148–49
memory
    images, of disgusting
        things, 44n2
    species, 159
Menninghaus, Winfried, 4n2,
    21n9, 100n4, 198–99
menstrual blood, 19, 112
metamorphosis
    to disgusting, through
        contact, 43–44
    dual nature and, 145–47
meta-philosophical position
    on disgust, 122n23
metaphysics, innate, 58n14
metaphysics of man, 217,
    219–20, 220n35
Miller, William Ian, 45n3,
    60n18
    *The Anatomy of
        Disgust*, 4n2, 79–80
    on life and death, 82
mind
    brain-mind
        connection, 141, 141n9,
        220n35
    concept of, 55n12, 56,
        96n27
    death and, 175–79, 179n6
    disembodied, 175, 177n4,
        179
    as non-disgusting, 81

mind-body connection,
55n12, 135, 141, 141n9,
151n17. *See also* dual
nature
The Modularity of Mind
(Fodor), 59n16
Monroe, Marilyn, 152
moral disgust, 34, 37–39
death-in-life theory
and, 121–22
physical disgust compared
to, 38, 38n20, 46
vices exciting, 37
morbid fascination, 47–49
mortality
death and, 17, 83, 85,
103, 175
of subjective self, 174n1
motivated ignorance, 162,
164, 167
mouth
attitude toward, 26, 47
contact with, 42, 69
distance from, 41
movement, 213–17, 213n30,
214n31, 215n32, 216n33
mucus, 30n16, 62
etiquette and, 203–4
inside compared to outside
body, 103
semen and, 204n22
tree sap's similarity
to, 30n16
murder, 121–22

nakedness, 156, 184
narcissism, 50, 73, 225,
225n39
natural selection, 67, 145n11
nausea, 14, 83
navel, 110
necrophilia, 14, 49, 128, 129
neuroscience, 141n9
neurosis, 207–10
Nietzsche, Friedrich, 166
normative response-depen-
dent concept, 63n21
nose
etiquette, 203–4
as phallic symbol, 204n22
nudism, 188–89, 189n7
nurses, 51, 60

obesity, 107n11
obsession, 129, 168
obsessive-compulsive
disorder, 207–8
On Disgust (Kolnai), 4n2, 5,
91–93
organic and inorganic
materials,
53–54, 54n11, 88–89,
136n1
organs
internal, 24–26, 83n17, 85,
109–10
sexual, 110–11, 155–56
orgasm, 111n14

orifices of human body, 19, 24, 110, 199, 202n20
Orwell, George, 191n9

pain, 7n8
paintings, 198–99
parasites, 29
Pascal, Blaise, 167n8
penis, 27, 109–11, 111n14
nose and, 204n22
snakes and, 115
perception
affective perceiving, 60n19
aversive emotions, consciousness and, 10–11, 11n11
primitive perceptual emotion, 44–45
perfectibility of man, 223–25
perfume, 184, 222
phallic symbol
nose as, 204n22
snake as, 115
phases of life, 195–96
philosophical emotions, 181, 181n7
physical disgust, moral disgust compared to, 38, 38n20, 46
Piaget, Jean, 196
piercings, 23
pimples, 20
plants, 29–30

death-in-life theory and, 116–17
non-disgusting, 17–18
poisonous, 30
sap oozing from tree, 30n16
poisonous plants, 30
poverty, dirt and, 191
primitive perceptual emotion, 44–45
prince and frog, 153
private and public areas, 189–90
privy, 144, 189
profligate life, 13n1
prudential emotion, 5
psyche, 38, 59
attraction-repulsion dynamic and, 47–48, 49n7
excess theory of function of disgust and, 130–32, 131n6
repression of desires and, 171
sex and, 38n21
pubic hair, 22
public and private areas, 189–90
putrefaction and decay
death-in-life theory and, 91–93, 91n24
death theory and, 87
as elicitors of disgust, 13–15
life-process theory and, 79–80

rabbit, 155–56

rats, 18, 30, 113, 113n16, 212

rectum, 101, 101n5

religion, 217–20

  metaphysics of man
    and, 217, 219–20, 220n35

  rituals regarding death and,
    217, 219

  on taboos about food and
    sex, 217–18, 218n34

repression, 161–72

  appetitive, 162, 169

  art and, 201

  Becker on, 167n6, 167n8

  of desires, 161–62, 161n1,
    169–72, 170n10

  epistemic, 162, 169

  humor and, 63n22

  of knowledge, 162–67,
    163n2, 165n4, 167n8,
    169–70, 170n10

  love and, 197–98

  phases of life and, 196

  releasing, 168

  selfishness and, 167n7

  of sexual desires, 63n22,
    161n1, 162, 165–67, 170

  unconscious, 161n1,
    162–63, 170

reproduction, 79, 81n14,
    194–95

repulsion. *See* attraction-
    repulsion dynamic of
    disgust

robots, 54, 114, 135, 150, 206

  sex and, 224, 224n38

Rosenkranz, Karl, 91, 91n24

rotting corpse, 13–18,
    15nn3–4, 79

  contact with, 43, 44

  in creation story, 158

  death-in-life theory
    and, 90–95, 94n26,
    97–101

  death theory and, 84, 181

  sensory appearance of, 14,
    14n2

Rozin, Paul, 59n17, 67n2,
    79n12, 196n14

Russell, Bertrand, 213n29

Sartre, Jean-Paul, 142

satiety, 123–24, 127n2

sculptures, 199–200

seaweed, 116–17

selective revulsion, 36

self

  conscious, 94, 173, 181,
    220n35

  death and, 94, 173–78,
    178n5, 181

  feelings about, 174n2

  social, 190

  subjective, 174n1

  theatrical, 190, 190n8

self-conception, 73, 76, 78,
    140n7, 149

self-disgust, 50, 78, 106n10, 143, 186n3, 223n37
selfishness, 167n7
self-loathing, 142, 144
self-other asymmetry, 50–53, 52nn9–10
death and, 99–100, 100n3
dirt and, 50
feces and, 50–52, 52n9
identity and, 52n10
with waste products, 50–53, 52nn9–10
self-protection, 5
semen, 19, 27, 103, 111
mucus and, 204n22
senses, 44–46, 71n7. *See also* *specific senses*
sensory appearance, 8, 10, 10n10
of rotting corpse, 14, 14n2
sensory imagination, 44n2
sex drive, 38n21
sexual behavior, 34–37, 192–95. *See also* necrophilia
anatomical side of, 112, 112n15
of animals, 120, 120n21
attraction-repulsion dynamic of, 47, 192–95, 193n12, 194n13
birth, death and, 194–95
death-in-life theory and, 118–21
deviant, 35–36, 119–21
excess theory of function of

disgust and, 124–25, 128, 128n3
Freud on, 38n21, 63n22, 194n13
homosexuality, 35–36, 120, 120n21
interspecies sex, 35
procreative and non-procreative, 118–21, 121n22
psyche and, 38n21
religious taboos about, 217–18
robots and, 224, 224n38
sex with corpses, 127–28, 170
sexual desires, 63n22, 161n1, 162, 165–67, 170, 193
sexual dreams, 207
sexual organs, 110–11, 155–56. *See also* genitals
sexual pleasure, 193, 194n13
Shakespeare, William, 198n15
shame, 58n15, 63n21
shit. *See* feces
shoe fetishism, 208–9, 208n26
skeletons, 17, 87–91, 87n20, 89n22. *See also* bones
skin, 20–21, 26
dirt on, 31–33, 118
non-disgusting aspects of, 23–24
purpose of, 25, 27, 27n14
signs of age and, 20–21, 21n9, 108–9, 109n13

slime, 116, 116n19
smell, 42
  absence of, 187, 187n4
  etiquette and, 204
  of feces, 71n7, 72, 72n8,
    102
  foul-odor theory and,
    69–72
  Kolnai on, 45n3, 70n6
  as tactile sense, 42, 70n6,
    72, 72n8
smoke and ashes, death in
    form of, 88n21
smoking, 178–79
snakes and reptiles, 115–16,
    212
soap, 222, 223
so-being, 8
social hierarchy, 191n9
social self, 190
society, 189–92, 192n11
sociology, 192n11
Sosein, 8–10, 59n17
soul
  differentiating humans
    from animals, 25n13, 73
  dual nature and, 137–38,
    138nn3–4, 143, 150,
    151n17
  feces and, 151n17
  as within or inner, 25n13
  metaphysics of man
    and, 219–20

South Park (cartoon), 102
species extinction, 121
species memory, 159
spiritual side of
    human nature, 138,
    150, 165
sports, 213–16, 214n31,
    215n32
studies on disgust, 4, 4n2
subjective self, 174n1
sublimation, 162
suicide, 106, 177
Suits, Bernard, 4n3
superego, 49n7, 130n5
supernatural beings, worship
    of, 186–87
swearing, 210–12, 212n29
sweat, 19–20, 19n8, 32, 104,
    214n31
Swift, Jonathan, 132, 142, 146
Swift's syndrome, 144

tactile sense, 42, 70n6, 72,
    72n8. *See also* touch
talking about disgust, 3, 3n1,
    164–65, 165n3
taste, 42, 45n3
  Darwin on, 45n3, 66–69,
    67nn2–3, 69n5
  taste-toxicity theory,
    66–69, 123
tattoos, 23

tears, 19–20, 19n8, 103–4
  emotions and, 103–4
technology, 205–6
testicles, 109, 110–11
theatrical self, 190, 190n8
theories of disgust, 65–96.
    See also death-in-life
    theory; death theory
  animal-heritage, 73–79
  contextual, 18, 105,
    105n9
  foul-odor, 69–72
  life-process, 79–82, 81n14
  taste-toxicity, 66–69, 123
throat, 26
toilet facilities, 18, 18n7,
    223n37
toilet training, 55, 56
touch, 41–44. *See also*
    contact
  contamination by, 45n3,
    72n8
  as first sense to
    evolve, 66n1
  intimacy and, 42, 70n6
traits, adaptations of, 126n1
turd. *See* feces

ugly old woman, 21, 21n9
unconscious
    repression, 161n1,
    162–63, 170

universal disgust
    grammar, 56
untidiness as dirtiness, 32
untouchables, 42, 153
urine, 18, 18n6, 111

vagina, 25, 26, 111–12
vampires, 15–16, 15n4, 48
vices exciting moral
    disgust, 37
Vile Bodies (Waugh),
    145n12
vomit, 18
vomiting, 14, 37–38
vultures, 113

warts, 106
waste products, 18, 101–5
  death-in-life theory
    and, 101–5, 101n5,
    102n6, 103n7,
    105n9
  self-other asymmetry
    with, 50–53, 52nn9–10
water, 221–23
Waugh, Evelyn, 145n12
What Emotions Really Are:
    The Problem of
    Psychological Categories
    (Griffiths), 59n16
Wittgenstein, Ludwig, 4n3

worms, 28–29
  death-in-life theory
    and, 113, 117n19
  eating, 35
  in evolution, 144
  human body as
    wormlike, 149, 150
  intestines' similarity
    to, 29n15, 75

wounds
  death-in-life theory
    and, 103, 106, 109–10
  death theory and, 84–85, 103
writing, shoddy or sloppy,
    37, 121

zombies, 15–16